… **The Modest Commitment to Cities**

The Modest Commitment to Cities

Morton J. Schussheim
University of Pennsylvania

Lexington Books
D.C. Heath and Company
Lexington, Massachusetts
Toronto   London

Library of Congress Cataloging in Publication Data

Schussheim, Morton J
  The modest commitment to cities.

  1. Housing—United States. 2. Urban renewal—United States. 3. Cities and towns—Planning—United States. I. Title.
HD7293.S36   309.2'62'0973   73-18185
ISBN 0-669-91272-7

Copyright © 1974 by Morton J. Schussheim

All rights reserved. No part of this book may be reproduced in any form without permission in writing from the publisher, except by a reviewer who may quote brief passages in a review.

Published simultaneously in Canada.

Printed in the United States of America.

International Standard Book Number: 0-669-91272-7

Library of Congress Catalog Card Number: 73-18185

I propose we launch a national effort to make the American city a better and more stimulating place to live.

Lyndon B. Johnson
January 4, 1965

Contents

	List of Tables	xi
	Preface	xiii
	Acknowledgments	xv
Chapter 1	**The Larger View**	1
	Beyond Shelter	2
	Where Housing Fits	3
	Ideology and Institutional Change	5
	Decision Making	7
	The Democratic Process	8
Chapter 2	**The Housing Problem**	11
	Views of the Housing Problem	13
	Shortage of Money	14
	Cost Trends and the Technocratic Response	15
	The Private Income Approach	16
	Black Power	18
	Your Housing Problem and Mine	20
Chapter 3	**American Values and Community Development**	23
	Individualism and Private Rights in Land	25
	The Premium on New Things and Moving On	26
	View of the City	28
	Law and Order and Safety	30
	The Social Scale	31
	Attitudes toward the Poor	34
	On Government	38
	In Retrospect	42
Chapter 4	**National Goals and Housing**	45
	Why Goals Thinking Became More Explicit	45
	Enter PPBS	46
	Metagoals and Subordinate Goals	47
	Full Employment and Stable Growth of the Economy	48
	Environmental Quality	53
	Equality of Opportunity	55
	Redistribution of Income	58

	The Housing Goal	61
	Concluding Thoughts	63
Chapter 5	**Government Housing Programs**	65
	Housing Programs for Moderate and Low Income Families	68
	Production Levels and Goals	78
	A Word on Housing Finance	79
Chapter 6	**Some Alternatives in Housing Policy**	81
	In an Ideal World	81
	In the Real World	82
	Why Government Assumes Responsibility	86
	Who Should Get Subsidies?	88
	How Much Should Families Pay for Housing?	89
	How Much of a Subsidy?	90
	New or Existing Housing?	91
	How About Housing Allowances?	93
	Are There Less Expensive Alternatives?	95
	Can the Older Houses be Maintained or Rehabilitated?	98
	Weighing the Pros and Cons	105
Chapter 7	**The Older City and Urban Renewal**	107
	The People Problem	109
	The Fiscal Bind	110
	Urban Renewal	112
	Some Lessons from Urban Renewal	120
Chapter 8	**Model Cities**	123
	Conceptual Roots	124
	From Proposal to Legislative Enactment	125
	Conflicts and Pitfalls in Program Design	126
	Choosing the Model Cities	127
	Performance under Model Cities	128
	Some Accomplishments	129
	Model Cities: An Interim Judgment	130
Chapter 9	**Revenue Sharing**	133
	Growth of Federal Aid	134

	General Revenue Sharing	135
	Special Revenue Sharing	137
	Community Development Grants	139
	Prospects for the Older Cities	141
Chapter 10	**New Development**	**145**
	The Demand for Space	146
	Structure of American Government	147
	Public Services in Suburban Areas	148
	Exclusionary Land Use Practices	150
	Costs of Development and Occupancy Expenses	152
	Trends in Housing Costs	157
	Structure of the House Building Industry	158
	The Emerging Pattern of Development	160
	Racial Segregation	162
	Segregation of the Elderly	163
	New Development: Pluses and Minuses	163
Chapter 11	**Shaping Urban Growth**	**167**
	Where Are We Heading?	168
	What Kind of Urban Development Do We Want?	170
	What Are the Objectives?	170
	The Urban Development Process	174
	Who Wants to Be Coordinated?	175
	Federal Support for Planning	176
	Linking Physical and Social Planning	179
	Guiding Growth	180
Chapter 12	**Role of the States in Urban Development**	**183**
	Organizing Themselves	183
	Financing Housing	184
	Land Development	184
	Industrial Building Codes	185
	Equalizing School Expenditures	186
	Conditioned State Aid to Localities	186
	Protecting the Natural Environment	187
	Next Steps for the States	188
	The States Can Do More	193
Chapter 13	**The Government and Urban Change**	**195**

Notes 207

Index 223

About the Author 233

List of Tables

6-1	Family Types and Indicated Public Approaches to Housing	84
10-1	Components of Development Costs for Single-family and Row Houses	153
10-2	Annual Costs and Rent for a Row House Unit	154
10-3	Required Rent for a Row House Unit under Different Cost Assumptions	156

Preface

This book had its origins in the middle 1960s when I was a housing official in Washington. I felt then—and I still believe—that the federal government must provide not only dollars but strong leadership in community development and housing. We Americans approach urban problems with more maturity and vision as a nation than as individuals or localities. This is especially true when we are dealing with the poor, with the disadvantaged, and with the needs of future generations. And though progress is hard to measure in helping the poor, extending equal opportunity, and protecting the natural environment, for a time we seemed to be moving in the right direction. But it has not been a steady advance. Sometimes a new approach has run up against an old tradition. Sometimes old government agencies have dragged their feet. And sometimes the votes were not there in the Congress or in the country.

I have worked in city hall, in state government, and in a federal agency. In all of these places I found dedicated and competent men and women. They deserve the support and respect of the American people. The large majority of public employees are committed to doing a good job. They are also entitled to leadership and support from our elected officials whose policies they must carry out.

In writing this book, I have kept in mind the men who helped raise the standards of public administration in the United States, men like Charles Merriam, Leonard White, Louis Brownlow, Luther Gulick, John Gaus, and Karl Bosworth. I have been mindful also of the constructive approach to public affairs taken by some businessmen such as Beardsley Ruml, Chester Barnard, Marion Folsom, Paul Hoffman, and Philip Klutznick.

The Ford Foundation provided financial support for the preparation of this study. I am happy to acknowledge this help and the cooperation of Ford Foundation executives Louis Winnick and William Pendleton.

A half year of scholarly leave from the University of Pennsylvania in the fall of 1972 gave me the time to complete the work. My students and colleagues at the university contributed ideas and moral support. Professor William G. Grigsby and Dr. Louis Rosenburg were particularly resourceful friends in the academy.

I also want to thank former associates in government who helped me with materials and insight, especially Henry B. Schechter, Hilbert Fefferman, and Philip Brownstein. Paul Ylvisaker has similarly been a source of stimulation.

I am grateful to Dr. Robert C. Weaver, first Secretary of the Department of Housing and Urban Development, with whom I worked in Washington from 1961 to 1966. Many of the ideas presented in this book grew out of discussions with him and papers prepared for him when I served in the old Housing and Home Finance Agency as Assistant Administrator for Program Policy.

Fortune smiled when Charles Abrams asked me to come to New York and work for him in 1955 in the New York State Housing Rent Commission. Charlie Abrams will always be remembered as a man of high spirit as well as a leading inventor of housing and urban development programs in the United States and around the world.

Elizabeth, Rowen, Amy, and Charles—each has helped in one way or another. My full partner in this as in all other endeavors during the past two decades has been my wife Hanna L. Schussheim.

Morton J. Schussheim
Philadelphia, Pa.

Acknowledgments

Some of the materials in this book have been adapted from papers and monographs previously published by the author. Chapter 2 draws upon a piece called "Housing in Perspective" which appeared in *The Public Interest,* no. 19 (Spring 1970), pp. 18-30, copyright by National Affairs Inc., 1970. Portions of Chapter 10 are adapted from a paper prepared for a congressional committee under the title "National Goals and Local Practices: Joining Ends and Means in Housing," printed in *Papers Submitted to Subcommittee on Housing Panels,* Part 1, Committee on Banking and Currency, House of Representatives, 1971. Sections of Chapter 12 are based upon a report prepared for the Pennsylvania Department of Community Affairs on "Residential Development in Pennsylvania" by the author and James R. Westkott in 1971. The book also reflects ideas and factual materials developed by the author in a monograph entitled *Toward a New Housing Policy: The Legacy of the Sixties* published by the Committee for Economic Development in 1969.

A number of individuals and organizations have generously given permission to use material from a copyrighted source. Specific credit is herewith acknowledged for the following items:

Stokely Carmichael and Charles V. Hamilton, *Black Power,* published by Alfred A. Knopf, Inc. and Random House, Inc., copyright 1967.

Oscar Handlin, "The Social System," passage reprinted by permission of *Daedalus,* Journal of the American Academy of Arts and Sciences, Boston, Mass., Winter 1961, *The Future Metropolis.*

Otto Eckstein, "The Economics of the 1960s—A Backward Look," in *The Public Interest,* no. 19 (Spring 1970), pp. 86-97, copyright © by National Affairs Inc., 1970.

Steven V. Roberts, "Voters in Typical Suburb Puzzled over Candidates," *The New York Times,* July 30, 1972, © 1972 by The New York Times Company. Reprinted by permission.

1 The Larger View

This is a book about housing and the way we do things in America. For many American families, snug in their homes and apartments, housing is neither a serious personal problem nor a major public issue. The critical problems now facing the country, according to opinion surveys, are taxes, prices, energy, crime, and drugs; housing, if mentioned at all, is low on the list.

But housing deserves attention—and not just as brick and mortar and mortgages. It is a mirror of American values and attitudes, how we feel and how we live. The reflection is not a pretty one. We live for ourselves and at arm's length from our neighbors. The influential members of society seek privacy and exclusive living arrangements. The less affluent have smaller houses but they put up fences and hedges. Neighboring in the street and on the stoops is a lower class life style associated with Puerto Ricans and blacks and working class Italians. Yet the suburbs are filled with people whose parents or grandparents lived in tight quarters and dense city blocks. In those days we had a housing problem. Today we have a community problem—or rather, a noncommunity problem.

Three generations ago, even two, shelter was a pervasive problem in this country. Between 1901 and 1910 almost nine million men, women, and children immigrated to America. Finding a place to live was an urgent matter. For many the first night's rest in the United States was with a relative or friend from the old country; others settled for an overpriced lodging house. Then they moved into a New York tenement, a Boston three-decker, or a Baltimore row house.

In 1933 there were twelve million unemployed workers. In the cities and towns and on farms, 300,000 families lost their homes that year through foreclosure, perhaps a half million more by eviction from rental quarters. People doubled up or took in roomers to meet the payments. Men took to the road and gave up permanent shelter. Most of the families without decent housing in the thirties were sturdy yeomen. They were people out of work or working part-time or at low pay through no lack of skill or will on their part, but because the economic system had broken down. In 1937 economic conditions were only moderately improved. President Roosevelt, in his second inaugural address, stated that "one-third of a nation [is] ill-housed, ill-clad, ill-nourished."

In 1943 the United States was at war. The factories needed labor. More than five million workers moved that year, mostly from South to North, from farms and small towns to cities. The supply of housing grew tight and rents rose. Rent control was imposed in major cities from New York to San Diego. Building materials were rationed but defense housing got a priority. Two hundred forty thousand units of housing were put up that year for war workers and their families. The rooms were small and the buildings all looked alike. But they provided basic shelter at rents people could afford.

Beyond Shelter

Now, some three decades since the believable war against fascism and three generations since the great in-migration from Europe, most Americans are well-housed. Those who have adequate shelter have much more. Those who do not, lack much more—they are outside the opportunity system. As a nation we are beyond shelter.

Today, housing has at least four functions. First, it provides privacy, enabling a family to have its moments of intimacy and its quarrels in private; it permits the unmarried young woman to get away from her parents' home and the bachelor to have his entertainment pad.

Second, housing is an index of status—where you live tells a lot about who you are and where you stand in the pecking order.

For millions of homeowners, the house serves a third purpose—a way of accumulating savings, partly by the monthly payments that reduce the mortgage and partly through inflation of real estate values. Many families have had the pleasant experience of making capital gains on their homes as they traded up from a good neighborhood to a better one. Corporate executives and professionals have been particularly enriched and with high mobility have grown accustomed to this form of capital accumulation. Not everyone has gained, of course. The lower middle class and working people have not done nearly as well since their properties are more likely to be in the older and less desirable parts of the city. In fact, many have had to take losses or even abandon their properties, which has occasioned deep bitterness and accentuated racial or ethnic hostility against those who gained entry to their neighborhoods.

Finally, housing is the ticket of admission to good schools and community facilities or poor ones, to superior public services or mediocre or inferior ones. These services directly affect the quality of life linked to one's house; indirectly they have considerable influence on the future earning capacity of the children.

Public policies and pronouncements on housing frequently finesse these issues of status, of capital gains (or losses), and of the quality of local services. For the most part the focus has been on production and mortgage finance. In the years between 1961 and 1973 there was an expanded public effort to meet the housing needs of lower income families. The main thrust of this effort was to subsidize the production of new housing units.

Indeed, the conventional approach to defining the housing problem is to estimate the number of "units" required for two groups: those who now live in substandard dwellings and the net increase in households expected to be formed over the next ten or twenty years. Add a vacancy factor for turnover, allow for houses that will be destroyed or become substandard, and you get the total need for dwellings. The need can become a production goal as in 1968 when the Congress called for the construction or rehabilitation of 26 million housing units over the following ten years. Convincing the Congress to set this housing target and to enact new subsidies to increase housing production gave President Johnson and his administration a great sense of achievement. And in its first term the Nixon administration, to the surprise of some critics, affirmed the housing goal. After a cutback to help slow inflation, they began to administer the new programs with some sense of duty.

Production of subsidized housing rose to a level of more than 400,000 in 1971 and about 350,000 in 1972. Another 2 million nonsubsidized houses were produced, bringing the 1972 total to an all-time high of almost 2.4 million housing starts. In addition, almost 600,000 mobile homes were sold in 1972.[1]

But high production numbers might not do the trick, the Nixon administration warned in mid-1971:

> Given the kind of economics now prevailing in the housing market and the structure of present housing subsidy programs, it appears unlikely that the housing needs of the Nation's poorest families would be fully met, even if the numerical goal of producing 26 million new units during the 1969-78 decade is achieved.[2]

The housing problem, as this government statement indicates, is more than a production problem; it is also an income and distribution problem.

Where Housing Fits

What is attempted in the chapters to follow is to show where housing fits in the value system, how it affects and is affected by the national economy, and its relation to other goals of American society. The kinds of housing policies and programs we have are only understandable in terms of the dominant ideology and attitudes that have shaped the country. The premium on individualism and self-interest helps explain why we have been able to build many housing units and subdivisions, but few genuine communities containing a blend of income groups and races. The mythical faith in private enterprise gives credence to larger subsidies to the rich than to the poor and inducements to the producers rather than to the consumers.

The nineteenth century belief that America's natural resources were unlimited laid the foundation for present-day two-acre zoning and the lavish use of lumber, copper and other resources in the construction of houses. Late in the twentieth century a counterculture of environmental protection began to perceive home builders and affluent home buyers as threats to a shrinking natural habitat. From New Jersey to Key Biscayne, Florida, moratoria have been imposed on home building pending the availability of sewerage and water facilities.

Home builders are also worried about the emerging consumer protection movement led by Ralph Nader and increasingly recognized by federal and state governments. The home building industry is even concerned about efforts to slow national population growth and thus cut down the potential market.

In 1962, the National Association of Home Builders predicted a serious curtailment in house construction if President Kennedy's impending Executive Order on Equal Opportunity in Housing were actually issued. Kennedy did put out such an order but there was hardly a ripple in the new house market. In fact, 1963 was a banner year for housing construction, as private behavior nullified the government's announced policies. Nor was there much effect on racial patterns in housing. Even the stronger sanctions of the Civil Rights Act of 1968 have thus far had little effect in changing discriminatory practices against minorities or changing patterns of racial segregation in housing. Younger black spokesmen have all but abandoned the open housing fight and are concentrating on securing control of their own neighborhoods.

Meanwhile, on another front, former Housing Secretary George Romney launched a technological attack on housing costs under the title "Operation Breakthrough." After several years of experimentation, he and his associates came to view the cost problem more as one of breaking down institutional barriers such as local building codes and zoning ordinances, than as rationalized building technologies per se. Attempts to introduce new technology have been opposed not only by conventional builders and construction workers but by the LMI phenomenon—Last Man In. "I've got my house now, so let's close the gate before the town loses its charm."

Prior to the 1960s, home builders were a fun-loving crowd of small businessmen who worried mostly about the availability and cost of mortgage money. Now house building is challenged by a host of high social priorities, countermovements, and official sanctions. The small stick builder of twenty or thirty houses may not entirely disappear, but he is becoming less important as larger-scale building companies with specialized divisions adapt to the increasingly complex market situations and government requirements.

Concurrently, we have to look at the older cities and older neighborhoods. A new phenomenon still poorly understood is the abandonment of inner city housing—not just dilapidated structures that ought to be eliminated, but sound houses as well. The owners and managers of some older property seem to be throwing in the sponge. Even though capital costs are low in many cases, rents and values have not been high enough or steady enough to keep up with rising operating expenses, taxes, and wanton vandalism. Exploitation by landlords and realty firms was all too common in such areas in earlier decades, but there were also responsible landlords and management firms. These have been leaving the inner city areas and so far there are no competent replacements. Small shopkeepers have also been departing, as age, marginal profits, and fear take their toll. The people who remain in such neighborhoods find themselves with deteriorating housing services and fewer places to buy bread or aspirin. It is a process that feeds on itself and no one knows how to reverse it.

One approach has been to turn the former tenants into homeowners. The Federal Housing Administration prior to 1965 avoided such neighborhoods. Then, with good intentions and prodding from Washington headquarters, the local FHA offices began to insure mortgages in these risky areas. Naturally, foreclosures have been higher in neighborhoods of lower income purchasers than in the middle income suburbs and towns that the earlier FHA programs assisted. Here and there scandals were disclosed, as some FHA appraisers and underwriters looked the other way or even connived in the placing of excessive valuations on older properties: the house picked up by a realty company for $5,000, patched up for another $1,000, and sold with an FHA-insured mortgage for $11,000 or $12,000.[3] In some countries, governments fall when such scandals become known; in the United States, the cynicism of the average citizen about his government deepens, and the bilked lower income purchaser (typically a black family) gets more bitter and more alienated from his society.

Ideology and Institutional Change

How do we build humane communities? How do we begin to restore faith in our government and our institutions? These are the larger questions within which the problems of housing and urban development must be explored. Even as we set production records in home construction (as in 1971 and 1972), we must ask, what is progress? How do you evaluate results? Are we measuring all the real costs? More specifically, why is it that a nation as rich as the United States still has five million households living in substandard dwellings and another eight million or more families paying far too large a percentage of their low incomes for housing? For the community-at-large, would we be better off if we put relatively more of our resources into community services such as schools, neighborhood centers, and playgrounds and less into large private lots and sprawling ranch houses?

The American political scientist Richard Hofstadter once wrote:

> We need a new conception of the world to replace the ideology of self-help, free enterprise, competition, and beneficent cupidity upon which Americans have been nourished since the foundation of the Republic . . . [4]

The times, he went on, require social responsibility, cohesion, centralization, and planning. But the rights and responsibilities of the national community and the metropolitan community have been confronted by an enduring faith in the sanctity of private property, the value of opportunity, and the rectitude of self-interest and self-assertion.[5] Yet, these are not universally held values: among the young who have tasted the fruits of materialistic self-interest there are some who are reaching out for more communal life styles and less exploitation of the natural environment for private gain or privatized amenity. Even among the middle-aged and older people, faith in the old virtues of individualism and self-help has been undermined. Fear of ill health and limited income in old age have been contributing factors.

We see this change in the demands for new institutions and the reform of old ones. Institutions are essentially built-in ways of doing things to carry out certain social ends: government bureaus like the FHA, settlement houses in poor neighborhoods, industrial corporations that use public streams and public air—all are institutions. And they all have one thing in common: public or private, they are invariably reluctant to wither away. Each organization engenders a cadre of people dedicated to perpetuating the life of the institution. An institution can persist as long as some men and women believe in it or benefit from it.

The demand for institutional change is always the assertion of one set of values or beliefs against another. The black revolt, the crusade to save the natural environment, the campus rebellion against colonial wars—all have ideological roots in American soil. The young blacks shouting "Freedom Now" grew up in a country that attributes much of its advancement to personal freedom. Those who oppose radical change also do so in the name of time-honored attitudes: "In a democracy, the majority rules." And: "I worked for what I got, why can't they?"

Institutional change is an abstract concept. What are some concrete examples?

1. The shift of public education expenses from the localities to the federal or state governments would be a major reform. It might not entail the loss of local control over the day-to-day operations of the schools, although it would probably increase the pressure for racial and class integration in schools.

2. The assurance of minimum incomes to all families in lieu of the patchwork welfare aids we now have is an idea that has reached the stage of legislative proposals.
3. The participation of ghetto residents in setting priorities for neighborhood improvement and in the management of low-rent public housing projects is already built into several federal-aid programs for cities.
4. Metropolitan general governments seem a long way off in most areas. A small step has been the requirement since 1966 of a planning body review of proposed federal-aid projects that have areawide impact.
5. A system of flood insurance predicated upon zoning against improper construction on the flood plain was enacted by the Congress in 1968. The urgency of public measures to prevent building on flood-prone land was headlined by the deaths and property losses inflicted by Hurricane Agnes in the summer of 1972. Few states or localities are yet inclined to prevent their people from rebuilding on the bottom land.

Decision Making

Old ways die hard; new ways sometimes don't take. People need something to hang on to in times of peril and confusion. We seem to be going through a period of great social upheaval and no one can foretell the outcome. Is there a way of determining what is right? Our problem, President Johnson once said, is not to do what is right, but to know what is right. His predecessor, John F. Kennedy said: To govern is to choose. But how does one choose among several seemingly desirable but conflicting objectives?

Is there a scientific way out? Is it possible that social scientists, systems analysts, or policy planners can devise more or less precise methods for determining the right solutions? Having put a man on the moon, can't we use similar skills to build and maintain humane and efficient cities? To some extent—yes.

Since World War II there have been major strides in methods of decision making. Operations research proved useful for the analysis of certain types of military problems. In the years since 1945 these methods and related approaches of systems analysis and cost-benefit techniques have been extended to various types of corporate management questions. In the public sector, they have been used to evaluate proposed water and transportation projects. New institutes were established to apply these techniques, such as the RAND Corporation and Herman Kahn's Hudson Institute. Such institutes were seemingly helpful to the Defense Department, particularly under Secretary Robert McNamara. Impressed with these efforts and facing large budgetary choices generated by his Great Society domestic programs, President Johnson in 1965 ordered all civilian departments to install a new approach to program planning and budget making. It was called PPBS— planning-programming-budgeting-system. State and local governments were also encouraged to experiment with PPB systems.

In a sense, all analysts today are systems analysts, just as all economists from Milton Friedman to Paul Samuelson are Keynsians. The format of this book is an example, starting with a statement of problems, trying to clarify goals and objectives, and examining alternative ways of satisfying these goals. Analysts increasingly look at social questions from the viewpoint of outputs or results, see each purposive organization or "system" within its environment, and try to allow for secondary consequences or "feedback." In this study, an effort is made to see housing in relation to the larger community and competing social needs and goals and to recognize the impact of new housing construction on the natural environment.

It is fashionable these days to talk about systems approaches. There is a growing literature of neat solutions to public questions. But there are limitations to these methods that must be understood. For the most part, these newer analytic techniques are applicable only to activities that have quantifiable results (usually in dollar terms) and few spillover effects. They may help with public problems that resemble those facing the private corporation. For a private company the main criterion is what appears on the bottom line of an income and expense statement, net profits after all costs are allowed for. The same may apply to a revenue-charging water district or bridge authority. For larger social questions—whether to tax more heavily to improve schools or police protection or health care or whether to locate low-rent housing developments in middle class neighborhoods—systems analysis and program planning can sometimes help by clarifying the questions, but cannot offer definitive answers.

The Democratic Process

For the most difficult questions, those that presidents and big-city mayors are faced with, there are no neat technical solutions. When planners or engineers say: "This is simply a technical problem," elected officials and community groups have learned to be on their guard. The technical problem to the engineer may be *where* to run the crosstown expressway or to place the exposition. To the mayor and city council and civic groups it is *whether* to build the road or to have an exposition. Is it worth disrupting ten thousand inner-city families to get a transportation link or to hold a world's fair? The choice may be between stability of one part of the population and the economic advantage of another. The costs of building an inner belt roadway, in other words, include more than outlays to contractors; there are relocation costs. The costs of relocation are not only in money but in the additional psychic damage that may be inflicted on poor or minority families, people who may have been displaced before by public actions. Here the value of "economic progress" is pitted against "social stability," and the secondary costs and potential gains are large and incalculable. Such questions cannot be solved by technicians. They must be resolved by a sense of fair play and accommodation through the political process.

At the national level there are similar issues: whether to issue a fair housing order if it means losing Southern votes in the Congress for a low income housing program; whether to stimulate a slack economy by raising public expenditures or reducing taxes. After two years of grappling with such questions as Special Counsel to President Kennedy, Theodore Sorensen observed: "White House decision-making is not a science but an art. It requires, not calculation, but judgment."[6]

The democratic political process is one of give-and-take. As Pendleton Herring and other political scientists have pointed out, the democratic process requires not universal agreement about ends but common acceptance of rules for deciding public issues.[7] The rules mandate open discussion and debate, a hearing by all who want to have a say, and finally a vote. The traditional view is that the majority will have its way and the rest will go along. Those who lose may come back to argue another day and through the same process they may try to reverse or alter the decision. Once decided, however, the decision stands until changed in accordance with the rules.

But majority rule will not be secure unless there is respect for the rights and interests of minorities, racial minorities and ethnic minorities, religious minorities, sectional minorities, and minorities of poor and deprived.

The wide gaps in education and income that separate whites and blacks in the United States pose a real threat to the survival of the democratic process. The downgrading by many college-age people of certain beliefs held rigidly by older and more traditional Americans—"Give peace a chance" vs. "My country right or wrong"—also means that we can no longer take for granted the continuance of political democracy. For the democratic process seems to work where there is a broad sharing of fundamental attitudes and there are no great disparities in the education, wealth, income, and opportunities of the various segments of the population.

In housing and community development there are issues that lend themselves to technical solutions: what volume of mortgage funds will be required to produce two million housing units and how much money is likely to be placed in residential loans by financial institutions. Economists can make reasonably accurate estimates of these magnitudes. Housing market analysts in FHA can prepare fairly reliable estimates of the effective demand for housing in Philadelphia or San Francisco over the next two years.

There are other questions, however, that are too big to leave to the technicians. Is it wise to reinforce the ghetto by improving services and living conditions in segregated neighborhoods or should we also attempt to disperse the ghetto blacks among the suburban whites? Should Congress be urged to curb the growth of metropolitan areas and favor the revitalization of small towns and rural America? Should we try to eliminate private gain of "unearned increments" in land values by heavy taxation or through public land banks? Judgments on these matters involve values and social philosophy. They will be resolved and re-resolved through the political process—if at all. Hopefully, a democratic political process. Democracy: a recurrent suspicion, said E.B. White, that half of the people are right at least half of the time.

2 The Housing Problem

What is the housing problem? Clearly there is a problem. Almost every two years Congress passes some substantive legislation dealing with housing. Mayors demand funds for housing, and civic groups organize for or against housing projects. But people see the problem in different ways.

Maybe we need to start with a definition. A problem, says Webster's, is a perplexing situation. More helpful is Herbert Simon, one of the most creative social scientists on the scene: a problem exists when a gap is perceived between one's aspirations for society, the nation, a community or group and present conditions or performance. When such a gap is a cause for sufficient concern or dissatisfaction, it triggers a search for alternatives likely to reduce the causes of dissatisfaction or discontent.[1]

When it comes to public problems, some men see more than others. Judging by legislative output, President Johnson saw many problems, but President Eisenhower saw relatively few. Sometimes problems prove intractable, in which case one's aspirations may be lowered. In 1970 former Housing Secretary Romney in effect lowered the national housing target, in the view of the National Association of Home Builders, by including mobile homes with conventional housing starts in estimates of total housing production. At a humbler level, the housing problem to a group of poor blacks in Baltimore was not so much the condition of the dwellings, but the poor community services such as inadequate street cleaning and trash pickups and the lack of play areas for small children.[2]

A textbook approach is to say that housing is a potential problem for a variety of social and economic reasons:

1. Housing production is a major claimant upon national resources. In 1972 private residential construction and repairs absorbed $54 billion, almost 5 percent of the gross national product, and provided in the order of four million on-site and off-site jobs. State and local governments invested about $25 billion in public works in 1972, perhaps half of which directly served the new houses—schools, streets, and utilities.
2. The housing industry lags in productivity behind manufacturing industries, which means that new home costs tend to rise faster than prices in general.
3. Housing and related facilities are a long-term fixing factor in the physical pattern of communities. Residential development takes up about 40 percent of all the raw land that is converted each year to urban uses.

Housing lasts forty years or longer and is very expensive to replace, thus freezing in the arrangement of activities for several generations.
4. Housing is a major component in the cost of living and the standard of life available to our people. Direct payments for housing including operations take about 23 percent of the average American's income, but as much as 35 or 40 percent of the income of the very poor.
5. For many, housing is a door to participation in the labor force and the social and civic life of the community. Some people, however, are confined to neighborhoods that do not have good access to the growing job centers or the better shopping and recreational opportunities of the area.

What groups in the population are particularly affected by housing problems?

First, there are fifteen to twenty million persons (five to six million households) who occupy shelter that falls below the standards of decency in our society. Some live in places without toilets; some must share their houses with other families; some have too little space; some live in buildings or shacks that are beyond repair. With few exceptions, the occupants of these substandard dwellings are among the very poor of the nation—the city poor and the rural poor. Many are disabled or helpless people—children without fathers, women without husbands, migrant farm workers, in-migrants to cities, physically handicapped, chronically ill, and elderly persons. In many ways, these mishoused people are the misfits and castoffs of society. Not only are they outside of decent shelter, but to a large extent outside of the opportunity system.

Second, there are perhaps sixty million persons (about twenty million households) who live in obsolescent houses in aging city neighborhoods and towns. One sees them in Boston, Massachusetts and Davenport, Iowa, Tulsa, Oklahoma and all across the country. The dwellings may have plumbing and the roofs may not leak, but they are in neighborhoods that fall far below the image of the American way of life. Schools are old-fashioned, play space is scarce, and streets are cluttered with traffic and parked cars. European visitors express surprise that the United States has such extensive "gray areas" in its cities and towns. The houses in these pre-Depression districts take many forms: row houses of brick, wooden two- and three-deckers, walkup flats, and small frame houses on individual lots. But they have a common function: to provide quarters for millions of families with limited means and limited choices. Here live the semiskilled workers with take-home pay of $110 a week, the retired couple on social security and a small pension totaling $300 a month, and others in the moderate and lower income classes.

Third, there are the gathering cohorts of tomorrow, by the year 2000 adding 55 million people or more (18 to 20 million households) to the 1972 population of 210 million. These additional families will be insistent claimants for housing and all that goes with it—water, waste disposal facilities, roads, schools, and recreation areas.

In 1968, Congress set a ten-year production target of 26 million houses, with 6 million earmarked for low and moderate income families. To achieve this and related goals, the Department of Housing and Urban Development had more than seventy programs, and additional aid was available through other federal departments and agencies. By 1972 housing starts were about 2.4 million units, very close to the target. Within the totals, construction of subsidized dwellings for moderate and low-income families exceeded 300,000 units—a substantial achievement although less than in 1971. But finding good locations for low and moderate income housing was a growing difficulty. Further, the process of blight and abandonment continued to eat away houses in older city districts; and the backlogs in supporting public facilities—schools, sewers, and water lines—remained large.

Will performance in the next ten years be better? It depends on how the problem is viewed and what one seeks to accomplish. On this there is no consensus.

Views of the Housing Problem

There are at least four different schools of thought on the underlying causes of the housing problem and prescriptions for dealing with it. First, the failure to build enough housing is due to an inadequate volume of mortgage funds and recurrent cyclical fluctuations in capital available to the housing sector. In inflationary periods especially, housing cannot compete effectively against other borrowers in the money market. With ample financing, and income supplements for housing to the poor, everybody can be decently housed. This is the position of many functionaries in government, the home building industry, and allied industry groups.

Second, housing costs are too high and must be brought down. How? By modern mass production techniques. Rationalization of the entire housing delivery system is necessary, from land assemblage and house production to marketing of the finished units to proper management and maintenance of the houses after the families move in. The present participants in the provision of housing must be replaced by large-scale producers such as automobile makers or the aerospace industry. George Romney, Secretary of the Department of Housing and Urban Development in the Nixon administration from 1969 through 1972, was a leading proponent of this approach. He was aided by research and development technicians recruited from the Space Administration and from private industry, and supported in this approach by large corporations such as General Electric, Lockheed Aircraft, Boise Cascade, and Westinghouse Electric.

Third, people live in bad housing because they are poor and disadvantaged and/or the victims of racial discrimination. Public policy should stress not housing programs but job training, education, income maintenance, and the elimination of discriminatory barriers to mobility. Thus strengthened, poor families would be able to secure good housing in the private market just as other higher income consumers do. With variations on the theme, sociologist Nathan Glazer of Harvard and economist Henry Aaron of the Brookings Institution, among others, take this position.

Fourth, slums and ghettos result from the inability of disorganized and politically impotent segments of the population to control their own destiny. Many institutions systematically exclude or neglect the poor and the blacks—schools and colleges, corporations and local governments. These people must seek control of their own neighborhoods, the houses they live in, the schools, retail shops, and even industrial firms; and ultimately city hall. Good housing is secondary to neighborhood control but can be achieved when absentee landlords are gone and neighborhood people are in charge. This is a view put forward by some black activists and finds support among certain white intellectuals and reformers.

Shortage of Money

Housing experts and home builders will readily understand the first point of view. It is the outlook of the suppliers of new housing. Inside and outside of government, year by year, they have built up the policy that flows from it. At the heart of this approach are "captive funds" for housing. Institutions have been developed with the primary mission of channeling private savings into residential mortgages. The principal group in the postwar years are the savings and loan associations. This industry has grown phenomenally from mortgage holdings of $7 billion in 1946 to about $200 billion in 1972. But the net inflows of savings to the savings and loan associations go up and down with movements of the national economy and investment opportunities and yields: $11 billion in 1963, down to $3.7 billion in 1966, back to $10.7 billion in 1967, and down to $4.1 billion in 1969. Housing starts have swung up and down with these monetary gyrations.

Moreover, the funds available through private savings institutions have never been enough—certainly not for the construction of housing for moderate and low income groups. Thus, various attempts have been made to channel government-borrowed funds into housing. One method invented in the 1930s by the Roosevelt administration is the sale of tax-exempt local housing authority bonds to private investors with the federal government paying the interest and principal on these bonds over the years. This is an ingenious financial device, but community support for public housing has never been deep. From 1937 to 1971 about one million housing units were built with such financing. This compares with the production of forty million privately-owned housing units during the same period.

Since 1968 there has been a major change in response to the money problem. Through a clutch of new or refashioned government agencies, the residential mortgage market has been linked to the securities market. For example, the Federal National Mortgage Association (FNMA) was cut loose from the federal budget. FNMA sells debentures to private investors and uses the proceeds to purchase government-insured and even conventional mortgages. The Federal Home Loan Bank System (FHLBS) and an associated entity called the Federal Home Loan Mortgage Corporation (FHLMC) have also been encouraged to tap the securities market and to make the funds available for housing. These and other tie-ins with the general capital markets have had a swift and large impact on residential finance—so much so that it has been tabbed a "new system." In fact, these federal intermediaries accounted for about two-fifths of the increase in total residential mortgages in both 1969 and 1970. In 1971, however, when private savings increased, the federal group's share declined to 9 percent.

Cost Trends and the Technocratic Response

The nub of the housing problem, according to the second school, is the backwardness of the home building industry and the consequent rises in production costs. Between 1965 and 1972 residential construction costs increased at an average annual rate of 6.5 percent, according to the widely used Boeckh index. This is a higher rate of increase than in consumer prices (4.5 percent) or wholesale prices (3 percent). Costs of improved sites for new one family homes rose even more sharply than building costs—7 to 8 percent a year. The median price of new one family homes sold in the last quarter of each year was $20,000 in 1965 and $28,000 in 1972. Certainly the moderate and lower income households were no closer to the new home market in 1972 than in the previous five or ten years; even the median income family with $11,000 would have a tough time affording a new house in many areas of the country.

Why have house production costs been rising so inexorably? For one thing, house building is a highly local and fragmented activity. Nationally there are 50,000 or more firms assembling finished housing on specific sites and another 200,000 special trade subcontractors. The typical house builder must take as given the wage rates negotiated by trade unions, the cost of lumber and other materials, the interest charges on land and construction loans, and the building and land development regulations of local governments. The smaller house builder (under 100 units a year) usually relies upon a dozen or more subcontractors from excavators and masons to plumbers and electricians. To these elements of cost he adds an overhead and profit fee of 10 to 15 percent and sometimes makes money on the land. In short, neither the home builder nor anyone else has effective control over development costs or quality of work.

Faced with such a piecemeal business structure and cost trends, it was entirely in character for an industrialist-turned-statesman like George Romney to seek a technological answer. What Romney and his advisors hoped to do was to attract large-scale corporations into the housing industry, with the ultimate objective of mass producing tens of thousands of houses a year at perhaps 25 percent or more below the prevailing unit costs.

Suppose a cost reduction of 25 percent were effected. What would that mean in terms of monthly housing expenses? A house in the Northeast selling in 1972 for $30,000 could presumably be marketed for $22,500. (Whether the producer would pass on the full savings to the home buyer would depend upon the strength of demand and the alternatives available in the existing housing supply to the consumer. In this example, we simply assume he would.) For a homeowner who paid 20 percent down, the monthly housing expense on a $30,000 house in the Northeast came to about $335. For a $22,500 house with 20 percent down, monthly costs would be $275. Mortgage payments would be proportionately lower and property taxes somewhat lower, but the expenses of heat and other utilities, maintenance and insurance would remain almost the same. After federal income taxes, with deductions for interest and local property taxes, the net saving to the home buyer would be about $45 a month. So the 25 percent cut in development costs reduces to a saving on monthly housing expenses for the family of roughly 13 percent. Almost the same savings could be achieved if mortgage interest rates were to come down from 7.5 or 8 percent to the 5.5 percent rate of the early 1960s.

Putting it another way, a family would need an income of $15,000 to $16,000 to handle all of the expenses associated with a new house purchased at $30,000. It takes $12,000 to $13,000 to manage a $22,500 house. So a 25 percent price cut could bring a substantial number of additional families into the new house market. In 1972 7.9 million families, or 14.6 percent of all American families, had incomes between $12,000 and $15,000. But a one-shot cut in development costs and prices even of this magnitude cannot bring new homes within the range of moderate and low income families —the one-third with incomes below $8,000. They would benefit indirectly, however, if prices and rents on existing housing were to come down as a result of lower prices on new houses.

The Private Income Approach

To a third school, the problem of poor living conditions is much larger than housing and must therefore be attacked on a wider front. Nathan Glazer, for one, has taken the income approach. Testifying before the Douglas Commission in July 1967, Glazer said:

> As I view the experience of the American city with slum dwellers, I have seen that the normal pattern of emergence from the slum has had little to do with housing. It has to do with the state of the economy, the development of new job skills, the rise in educational level. At that point, the slum dweller either moves from the slum, or in some cases has enough money to improve his quarters and stay there. I have therefore thought of how one aids and improves and adapts this process for present slum dwellers. And if we are to do that, our main efforts must be in job creation, job training, education and the like.[3]

Glazer went on to recommend that, so far as the present poor neighborhoods are concerned, the main physical improvements should not be to the dwellings but to public facilities such as streets and playgrounds, and the removal of fire hazards. He would oppose expensive rehabilitation of existing housing or the extensive rebuilding of such areas with public housing. Ultimately, he hopes to see most of the present slum dwellers in an income position to opt for owning single family houses in better neighborhoods.

Glazer's perception is of a housing problem gradually dissolving in the social chemistry of rising income and social mobility. It is the American dream extended to the last remnants of our disinherited. It is an incomplete formulation, however, for it focuses primarily upon the demand side and seems to assume that decent homes and neighborhoods can be supplied automatically in the private market. This has never been true—even for the wealthy. For the present poor and minorities, strenuous local and federal governmental efforts to enforce housing codes and open occupancy laws would be necessary—two areas in which governments so far have not been notably successful. Good living environments also require large direct investments by government, as well as deliberate public policies to channel resources into the production and maintenance of the housing stock. The housing supply is immobile, long-lived, and unresponsive to short run changes in demand. In the face of a large spurt in demand, prices and rents of housing are likely to run up. Under such conditions, private market forces cannot be expected to yield satisfactory results for society in the housing sector. In a word, enlarging economic opportunities for the poor and providing fair income shares for those who cannot work is a policy much to be welcomed, but it will not do away with the need for public policies and programs that attend to the supply of decent homes and neighborhoods.

A housing-oriented demand approach has been offered by Henry Aaron. Under his housing assistance plan, cash payments would be made to some fourteen million households at the lowest end of the income range. The cost would be $5 to $6 billion a year. Initially the households could use the money as they wished, but after a market adjustment period the income supplements would have to be used for housing. He would require this only if code enforcement and open occupancy programs are working well. Otherwise, much of the money would be siphoned off by landlords and builders operating under monopolistic supply conditions.[4]

The Aaron plan is predicated upon an effective filter-down process in housing over the long run. That is, households with the means to acquire new housing would exercise their options, there would be an accelerated turnover of good existing housing, and the chain of transactions would make available to the income-supplemented poor an ample supply of good housing suitable to their family requirements and within their budgets. Note that an alternative to a housing assistance payment would be a general income maintenance program. But if that were pegged to a decent housing budget for the same number of households it would cost much more, perhaps four or five times as much, because all items in the budget—not just housing—would have to be adjusted upwards.

Some seasoned observers of American housing markets and policies are skeptical about the filter-down process working well for the poor. There are just too many real and artificially created restrictions upon certain types of families in local housing markets. If housing allowance schemes such as Aaron's are to be tried, they would argue for concurrent public efforts to expand the housing supply generally and to augment specific types and locations of housing where shortages persist. With Aaron, they would press aggressively to curb racial discrimination in housing, along with efforts to maintain standards of existing houses by vigorous code enforcement, and to lower the real unit costs of producing new housing.

Black Power

Where Glazer and Aaron would turn the slum family into an effective spending unit in a market economy, black power advocates seek to build group unity. Eschewing integration as an immediate goal, they seek control of ghetto schools and other neighborhood institutions by organized black groups. With regard to housing, Stokely Carmichael and Charles Hamilton have written:

The tenements of the ghetto represent another target of high priority. Tenants in buildings should form cohesive organizations— unions—to act in their common interest vis-à-vis the absentee slumlord. Obviously, rents should be withheld if they owner does not provide adequate services and decent facilities. But more importantly, the black community should set as a prime goal the policy of having the owner's rights forfeited if he does not make repairs: forfeited and turned over to the black organization, which would not only manage the property but own it outright. The absentee slumlord is perpetuating a socially detrimental condition, and he should not be allowed to hide behind the rubric of property rights.[5]

The message of Carmichael and Hamilton, like that of other black activists, is that this community must try to free itself from its white exploiters and control its own destiny. The neighborhoods are old, the buildings lacking in modern amenities, but for the masses of blacks they are likely to be the only ones available in this country. So take them over and use them as a bastion from which to build black institutions and black pride. In this view, bad housing and poor community facilities are but one symptom, although perhaps the most obvious one, of the web of racism that envelops all major institutions in America. The appeal of black power is not to the economic self-interest of each Negro but to the emotional needs for social bonds among all the brothers and sisters.

For white Americans trained to think in economic terms, such an outlook may be hard to grasp. Does it make sense to try to gain ownership and control of played out real estate? If real estate values continue to decline in such areas, if banks refuse to make mortgage loans, and insurance companies redline these districts against property insurance, it is a bad economic deal. But the argument of black power activists is not economic—it is political, ideological, and psychological. Moreover, in the black experience, according to the psychiatrists Grier and Cobbs, there has been less obsession with individual property: it could be taken away by the courts, by the state, by the white citizenry—and often was.[6]

Still, the economics are fearsome. Carmichael and Hamilton believe that absentee landlords should be put under economic pressure to surrender their properties. Indeed, the process, operating mainly through market forces rather than organized political action, is already under way. In Philadelphia, Baltimore, New York, and elsewhere, there is evidence of a large and still growing number of vacant and boarded-up residential buildings and partially occupied blocks. In New York in the late 1960s, as many as 35,000 units a year were being lost through abandonment. In Philadelphia, despite a relatively active local effort to rehabilitate older housing, there was no apparent reduction in the 20,000 vacant and abandoned units between 1965 and 1970. A 1972 survey of selected neighborhoods placed the Philadelphia level at 35,000 units. These abandoned units represent about 5 percent of the central city's housing inventory, but as much as 15 to 20 percent of the houses available to the inner city poor. And they impair the livability of all neighborhoods in which they are located.

Many absentee and occupant owners want to get out of the older neighborhoods; few investors are interested in taking their place. Such properties may sell at only two to three times the gross annual rent roll, compared to five to seven times in more desirable neighborhoods. As white families have left the city in large numbers and middle class black families moved to better sections, they have vacated entire districts to lower income blacks, other minority families, and a sprinkling of elderly whites. Thus there is a slackened demand for inferior houses and neighborhoods.

Such houses are allowed to run down. Here and there structures are removed, while others are left standing but abandoned by their owners. The decision to abandon a house occurs when the owner sees little or no prospect of covering his operating costs and local property taxes out of the expected rentals. Even if the owner has no mortgage payments to make and is willing to forego any return on equity, there is no sense in keeping the property in use if the rents that available tenants are willing and able to pay are too low to cover water bills, heat, maintenance work, and real estate taxes.

The concept of black power extends far beyond housing and real estate. It would set up a state within a state with different values and different institutions from those of the white society. The relationships among its members would seemingly be based more on kinship and face-to-face accountability than the impersonal contractual requirements and social controls of corporate and metropolitan society. So far as housing goes, black power advocates seek to fill a vacuum created by the failure of private markets and local governmental policies.

Can black community spirit and new cohesive organizations be rooted in the hardrock economics of the ghetto? Will the arbitrary use of power by the people downtown be replaced by the arbitrary use of power by neighborhood people who assert it in the name of group unity? And if the older sections are turned over to the residents, is it part of the deal that they be precluded from participating in the newer growth sectors of the metropolitan economy? That might be a political victory for some but an economic defeat for many.

But for the near future, black power advocates have made a judgment: it is unrealistic and unwise for the masses of blacks to try to infiltrate the white social institutions and housing enclaves; there is more to be gained from building togetherness, even if it costs blacks some economic progress and must be fostered in the obsolescent blocks and houses from which the affluent have fled. And who is to say that they are wrong?

Your Housing Problem and Mine

The housing problem appears differently to different groups of people. To the home building industry, there is a supply problem, one which turns on the availability of mortgage funds, lumber, and skilled craftsmen. It is a mass production challenge to the technologists and industrialists. Maldistribution of income and the imperfection of housing markets lie at the core of the difficulty, in the view of some academicians. And it is but one manifestation of the exploitation of poor and powerless minorities, say the black ideologists. Alfred Marshall, the father of neoclassical economics, probably would have described it as both a supply and demand problem, but one that could be improved by reducing imperfections within the private market system. How he would have reacted to the black power thesis is anybody's guess.

There are still the very poor, families with incomes below $4,000 and individuals living alone with less than $2,000 a year. Virtually all of them are house-poor in the sense of their living in structures that are well below the physical standards that the community deems acceptable or because they pay too much out of their meager incomes and must therefore skimp on food, clothing, and health care. But few of them are regarded as deserving much better. They are not the sturdy yeomen of the thirties who doubled up or lost their homes through no fault of their own, but because the economic system had collapsed. The stereotype is the unwed mother with five children who breeds in any hovel simply to get a larger welfare check. The main exception to this popular image of the mishoused is the elderly white. It is no accident that community opposition to public housing softens when the project is designated for senior citizens. Americans are sometimes a magnanimous people, and through our Congress we have set a goal of six million "units" of subsidized housing to be prepared for lower income people between 1968 and 1978. Presumably the poor families will be decently housed in these units or in those vacated by better-off households. But it cannot stop there. The majority of these poor people need much more than shelter: health maintenance centers, day care facilities, vocational training, personal therapy, and a little love.

Then there are the working class and lower middle class people. They are the ones for whom most of the subsidized houses were built in 1971 and 1972 at an unprecedented rate approaching one half million units a year. (This was before these programs were suspended by the Nixon administration at the start of 1973.) But the bulk of them cannot be helped this way in the near future. What they need is better community services and, for those who are homeowners, protection of the equities (really monthly savings) in their property. These are the same people, however, who tend to vote against local bond issues for community improvements and who oppose local tax increases. Perhaps they are not far off base in thinking that the bonds or tax money will be used to improve the downtown district or some other group's neighborhood rather than their own. For these people generally live in middle-aged city neighborhoods or small towns that have been passed over by federal and local programs. We still lack effective approaches to neighborhood conservation and orderly transition of housing from one income class or racial group to another, let alone a stable interchange among different income and racial groups. This is a real problem for a substantial number of such families, one which has been understudied and underappreciated by public officials.

For the well-to-do and the rich, there is that elusive and possibly undefinable problem: the quality of life. Two out of five families had incomes in 1971 of $12,000 or more, one out of four had over $15,000. Housing is an important part of their personal life styles, and unlike the orthodox view, prosperous families do not treat it as an "inferior good," like hamburger or beans, to be consumed less when income goes up. Such people want more space both inside and around the house, and more bathrooms and appliances. But they also want more recreational areas, cleaner air and water, better schools and universities—in a word, better public goods. They want better protection against crime, but some also recognize that crime reduction may entail better living and working opportunities for the poor and minorities. Hence the conflict between private goods and public services, between less and more taxes.

Good public amenities and less reason for crime and disorder will not come cheaply. They will cost money and perhaps the compromise of some cherished attitudes and values. Having proved ourselves winners in the competition based on individual self-interest, it is now time to address a bigger challenge: the building of more humane communities.

"No problem can be adequately formulated," wrote C. Wright Mills, "unless the values involved and the apparent threat to them are stated. These values and their imperilment constitute the terms of the problem itself."[7] A look at some of the values and beliefs that underlie or seem to threaten the way we do things in housing and real estate is the theme of the next chapter.

3
American Values and Community Development

What is a good city? How should the public interest be determined? What are the obligations of the man of property to the poor? How can individual liberty be preserved when the times cry for stability and order?

Americans are not like the ancient Greeks. They do not spend much time in discussing abstract questions. But put them in concrete terms—do the nearby residents have the right to block construction of a low-income project?—and most people will have feelings and opinions about what is right or wrong. The feelings stem from values—the basic beliefs that underlie what men seek for themselves and their society. Values serve to justify the institutions and practices of the society and provide rules of conduct that govern expected behavior. Some traditional values to Americans are a belief in individual striving, a desire for economic progress, and a faith in majority rule. These are not universal values; there are cultures that care little about them. Even in the United States there are countervalues within each man and in the community as a whole.[1]

When values change rapidly or new ideas rise to challenge the old ones, deep cleavages divide the community. That is happening today. The sharpest conflict in American society stems from the claims of blacks for more respect, better jobs, and more of a say in the community. The right to equal opportunity extends to all, blacks as well as whites. Does it also justify preferential treatment in college admissions and civil service jobs to make up for shortchanging of blacks in earlier times? Is segregation in neighborhoods or college dormitories acceptable if it is self-segregation? And on the other hand, are equal opportunity and equal protection of the laws violated when entry to a suburb is possible only by affluent families?

There are other serious splits among Americans: on welfare, for example. "I think the needy should get it," says a woman clerk who probably speaks for many people, "but I don't think the undeserving should. This encourages people not to work." And on taxes: "I'm willing to pay my share," says a factory foreman, "but when that becomes more than what others pay who have more than me, then it's unfair. It's too easy for big corporations to write off things."[2]

On the natural environment and who shall have access to it, there is rising controversy. In New York state, conservationists and property owners organized against a proposed expressway alongside the Hudson River. In New Jersey, shore communities which tried to keep out nonresidents by charging higher fees than to residents were overruled by the courts. In Alaska, the oil companies have been authorized by the federal government to open the North Slope with a four-foot pipeline 789 miles long, although no one knows how serious the damage may be to the earth's mantle and America's last great wilderness. The Secretary of the Interior, sworn to preserve the nation's natural resources, issued the permit in the name of national security and economic necessity.

These issues bring "good" values into collision with other "good" values. Clearly, values that are good for one purpose are not necessarily good for another; attitudes that serve one group may harm another. The focus of many of these value-conflicts is now centered on community development and housing. What kinds of housing should the poor live in and where? Should they be concentrated block on block in projects or assisted to live among those who pay their own way? If middle class neighborhoods reject the poor, is sanitary shelter for low income families a more important goal than open occupancy?

What price symphony, art museums, ballet, and other cultural enterprises? Preserving cultural life has been a major justification for central city reconstruction with federal urban renewal money. Should cultural enterprises be subsidized by the many for the enjoyment of the few or as a legacy to future generations? Describing his city as quite similar to other urban centers in the 1950s, a civic official of Kansas City, Missouri, wrote: "There was an art gallery housed in a palatial building, visited mainly by school children and tourists. A symphony orchestra played to a limited audience and struggled to meet its budget."[3]

Should the development of the next twenty million houses be left to the decisions of private builders and local zoning officials or be governed by regional plans enforced by federal and metropolitan agencies?

These questions touch raw nerve ends in county commissioners, city councilmen, and Congressmen because they arouse the deepest feelings of the people in their neighborhoods and districts. A federal program of rent supplements for the poor passed in 1965 has been financially starved by appropriations committees of the Congress because it threatened to disperse some poor families among self-supporting households. A proposal for publicly initiated new towns was slow to emerge from the Congress in the face of opposition from big city mayors, small scale builders and outlying communities. In New York state, the Urban Development Corporation, a public agency, was established in 1968 to initiate new communities and large developments. In 1973 the state legislature voted to restrict the power of the UDC to override local zoning and building controls when some Westchester County communities objected to the corporation's proposed developments in their towns. For years civil rights advocates worked to get the Congress to pass a federal law against discrimination in housing. Finally, it was included in the Civil Rights Act of 1968, but administrative funds have been inadequate and tangible results have yet to appear.

The reform groups and Washington officials who propounded these programs undoubtedly believed that they had hard facts and right reason on their side. But were they bucking ingrained attitudes and values of too many Americans? Let us look at some traditional American values that bear on contemporary urban problems.

Individualism and Private Rights in Land

The commitment to individual rights in property has deep roots in America. John Locke (1690) saw in the North American experience evidence for his thesis that a man working the soil has an inherent right to property that precedes the state's. The role of government is to protect these private rights and to regulate affairs so that no one is deprived of life, liberty, or estate. Writing just after the Revolution of 1688 by the growing English middle class against the Crown and the landed aristocracy, Locke handed down a theory that the common good is secured when private rights are protected. Individual interest is primary, the social interest vague and uncertain.[4]

Locke's views were reaffirmed as self-evident by the founding fathers of the United States. Thomas Jefferson, author of the Declaration of Independence, took as a central premise the close connection between individual liberty and the private ownership of property. All individuals have a God-given right to life, liberty, and the pursuit of happiness or wealth; even governments can be overthrown if they persist in violating these moral laws.

The burst of economic expansion in the nineteenth century seemed to validate the primacy of private rights in property. The supply of land in the country was vast relative to the number of people. The challenge was to induce a filling up of this land mass and to gain access to the latent resources of food, fiber, and minerals. American national policy was shaped to these ends. Handsome bargains in land were offered to settlers. By a law of 1862, homesteaders could get 160 acres of land free providing they lived on the homestead for five years. Very liberal donations of the public domain were made to private railroad companies. Grants to railroads, either directly or through the states, totaled at least 129 million acres.[5]

Laws, institutions, and practices facilitated this privatization process. In the rural areas the surveyors sectored the land into one-mile squares and quarter squares of 160 acres. In the cities the layout was typically rectangular and private individuals were enabled to acquire the successive grids at low prices. Streets and avenues were kept in public ownership, but public land reserves were rarely set aside for future community needs or planned development. The commons of Boston and early Eastern settlements were not replicated in the hinterland cities. A twentieth century Kansas Citian could note with pride and a bit of surprise that in the 1890s "an imaginative city architect named Kessler secured the adoption of a comprehensive plan for boulevards and parkways which provided the backbone of Kansas City's trafficway system."[6] For the most part, only the burial grounds and natural obstacles interrupted the block by block extensions.

In brief, most nineteenth century American cities were laid out in response to market demand. Town building was essentially a matter of private initiative with little concern for a common social existence. There was no Peter the Great to ordain a majestic ensemble as in St. Petersburg, no Baron Haussmann empowered to create great boulevards as in Paris, no L'Enfant to lay out circles and radial parkways as in Washington, and no public conscience to stop the speculative building of houses without central heating or toilets for rent to the swelling working class. America became the country where one could discern in most cities a pattern determined mainly by economic considerations, unrestrained by any historical image of proper town layout, by sites or monuments important for religious or esthetic reasons, or by considerations of comfort or amenity. City growth in the United States was largely dictated by the play of individual economic interest rather than by special human-historical factors. And the dominant view undoubtedly was that this was natural and right. To this day, support remains strong for the presumption that the property owner benefits society when he pursues his individual self-interest.

Still, the private owner's freedom to use his land has never been totally unrestricted in American cities. He has been permitted exclusive rights to its use but not an absolute right. For each man has the power to hurt his neighbor, to cause damage to adjoining properties, or to diminish another's market or use value. Thus the community has exercised social controls, at first largely informal but increasingly codified and specific as the potential for conflict and damage increased with size and complexity of relationships in cities. But even as social controls are extended, it is not uncommon to see them invoked in the name of protecting private property values rather than community well-being or social needs.

The Premium on New Things and Moving On

"At the end of three or four years we'll move. That's the way to live in New York . . . Then you always get the last thing; we'll always have a new house; you get all the latest improvements . . ." Thus wrote Henry James through one of his fictional characters in 1881.[7] He was not the first to record the American penchant for new things. Tocqueville had seen the same thing in the 1830s: "In the United States a man builds a house in which to spend his old age, and he sells it before the roof is on."[8]

A nation as rich in resources as America in the nineteenth century felt it could afford to be wasteful. When you used up one piece of ground or exhausted one coal vein, you could move on to the next. Americans were under no strong pressure to conserve raw materials and land. They were risk-takers and adventurers, many of them, and a rootless lot. The English social observer Dennis Brogan noted that the western trek in the United States was made by men to whom "movement became a virtue, stability a rather contemptible attitude of mind."[9]

Technological progress reinforced this attitude. In transportation, the steam-powered railroad displaced the canals soon after they were built. In agriculture, the self-raking reaper was in use for only twenty years when it was supplanted by the harvester; and both released hand labor for work off the farm. Steam power gave way before electric power in the factories. Horse-drawn carriages and trolleys in cities were replaced by electric-driven vehicles and later gasoline engines.

From capital goods innovation American technology moved on to consumer goods. The essence of a sustained market for consumer items is that they not last too long. American manufacturers learned to build obsolescence into their products—from clothes to washing machines to automobiles.

With housing, however, the urge to dispose and get a new one cannot be satisfied for everybody—at any rate not within a short period of time. In any one year only two or three, at most four, percent of all families get into a new house. The others must occupy space in existing buildings. It is the well-to-do who set the pace, who give up the older houses and acquire the new ones. The properties they vacate are not wiped out; most remain standing and are sold or rented to families with less income. But the movement does not stop there: for each new house taken up, a chain of four or five turnovers in the existing inventory usually takes place.

Until late in the nineteenth century the wealthy could not move too far. The town houses and luxury dwellings of New York's Washington Square, Park and Fifth Avenue were little more than two miles from the heart of the tenement district of the Lower East Side. Even in smaller cities the outward moves were relatively short because of the need to have access to the shops and work places in the center of town. But the pace of neighborhood obsolescence quickened in the twentieth century. Advances in transportation opened up to urban development large areas far removed from the old city core. Institutional inventions such as the long-term mortgage effectuated the outward movement. It thus became possible for some members of society to get not only new houses but new schools, new community facilities, new recreational opportunities—a physical environment markedly superior to that available to most of the inhabitants of the older sections of the city.

And the trek goes on. Contemporary Americans are still moving frequently—one out of five each year, less often for homeowners but more frequently for renters. In one moderately priced suburban development, Levittown, New Jersey (now Willingboro) opened in the late fifties, Herbert Gans was able to classify the homebuyers as Settlers, Transients, and Mobiles. At the time of arrival, many said they intended to settle permanently—44 percent; but 20 percent knew they would be transferred again by their employers, large national corporations and the armed forces; 24 percent were undecided and 12 percent thought they would like to move again, if possible to a more expensive house. Most of the Mobiles and Transients had gone to college and had higher incomes than the Settlers. They were prepared to respond more to the push or pull of economic opportunity than to any propensity to put down roots in one community for the rest of their lives.[10]

View of the City

A country that romanticized the woodsman, sang "Home on the Range," and subsidized the farmer could scarcely honor its cities. The big Eastern cities especially aroused feelings in other regions ranging from scorn to hate. Even today Congress is likely to kill a piece of legislation if it believes that New York City will be a major beneficiary.

Americans came by this view as a child learns from its mother. Jefferson, a Virginia landholder, feared cities inhabited by unpropertied proletarians. He doubted that such men, with little education or stake in the economic order, could be counted on to preserve the democratic process. Andrew Jackson had different reasons for disliking the citified type. He had little use for the bankers of Philadelphia or the socially pretentious of Nashville. His sympathy lay with the mechanic, the farmer, and the self-made businessman; his anger was directed at powerful monopolies and aristocratic establishments headquartered in the large cities. The centerpiece and symbol of the enemy was the federally-chartered, privately-run Bank of the United States located in Philadelphia, which Jackson eventually destroyed. Later, Kansas and Iowa farmers, who received ten cents a dozen for corn and paid 10 percent interest, also came to hate the Philadelphia and New York bankers. Another pre-Civil War viewpoint was that the cities were sinful and crime-infested. To Herman Melville, New York was Babylon. Other American writers such as Hawthorne and Poe, coming from Puritan or rural backgrounds, feared the potential for crime and evil in the cities.[11]

If the ordinary residents of big cities did not entirely share the views of country folk, they had reasons of their own for disliking their communities, particularly in the years after 1860. The post-Civil War city was built on the social philosophy that, according to Parrington, motivated the entire country: preemption, exploitation, and progress.[12] Preemption meant turning the idle public land and resources over to private hands, to be made productive through exploitation. Economic progress was a euphemism for the accumulation of private wealth.

The city was a factory, a warehouse, a railroad station, a marketplace. It was a means for producing goods and amassing private fortunes. One way of acquiring wealth was to hold land: population growth and public improvements were bound to yield the private owner a handsome unearned increment. The city of this era cared little for the health and well-being of its working population. Boys and girls were recruited into the factories at age ten or twelve; in 1880, 20 percent of the ten-fifteen-year-olds were in the labor force. Men laid rail and worked on docks and in meatpacking plants for one to two dollars a day. Street cleaning, sanitation, and other municipal services were rudimentary for taxes had to be held low. Low wages and low taxes permitted the social income to be plowed back into private capital. Wealth begot wealth at compound interest. Dignity and respect could be bought only by the carriage class; if there was self-respect for the working man, it came from within and in spite of his mean surroundings.

There is something else in the American subconscious that makes big cities suspect. It is a feeling that the city reduces the individual to an atom. In the country, a boy can go his own way, sense nature, be free of artificial restraints. So said Henry Adams, who never came to terms with the teeming life of Boston or New York in the late nineteenth century.[13] Perhaps this descendant of presidents did not speak for country boys with less income and less time to reflect. Still, in a dense settlement all must march to the same beat. Eating and sleeping, traveling to and from work, the use of leisure time—all become standardized.

The people of the city could be manipulated by corrupt politicians; they were a captive market for street railway companies, water companies, and other public utilities run for private gain. In a later day, their metropolitan movements by auto would be charted by highway engineers, each man one of a million, assigned to one travel path or another. Woe to the man who stepped out of his car on the Long Island Expressway or Santa Monica Freeway to help a fellow motorist in trouble. The law of probability ordained that he too would become a casualty to the relentless stream of steel.

Where in the big city is there room for free will? In which apartment building or tract house can a man or woman preserve a sense of identity? In a day of mass communication how does a citizen make up his own mind?

Yet people have continued to come to cities from farms and small towns for ten decades. They have had to adapt to an urban discipline, just as

English country people of an earlier century in giving up their cottage trades yielded to the rigid routine of the factory system. The city has jobs, schools, shops, a greater concentration of income opportunities than can be found anywhere else. The price has been an uneasy conformance to the rules of urban communities necessary to their continued existence.

Law and Order and Safety

Order, stability, and safety in their communities have always been prime concerns of the dominant citizens. The founding fathers lived to see the unpropertied masses of Paris turn into a city mob howling for the heads of the old regime. Hofstadter writes:

> Dread of the propertyless masses of the towns was all but universal. George Washington, Gouverneur Morris, John Dickinson, and James Madison spoke of their anxieties about the urban working class that might arise some time in the future—'men without property and principle,' as Dickinson described them—and even the democratic Jefferson shared this prejudice.[14]

But no American cities reached substantial size before 1820 and no massive insurrections in the cities occurred before this time. The merchants and planters who signed the Constitution remained safe on their estates.

The industrial cities of the later decades began to justify earlier fears. In Philadelphia, Irish immigrants rioted against the blacks in the 1840s and 1850s and took their jobs on the wharves and in the construction trades. In 1863, several hundred people were killed or wounded in New York City and many buildings were burned in riots that started as a protest of working class people against conscription into the Grand Army of the Republic. The grievances of workers erupted time and again in the last quarter of the nineteenth century, as in the Haymarket affair and the Pullman strike in Illinois. The good people had little patience for the laboring class. Teddy Roosevelt wanted a go at the mobs with rifle-slinging cowboys or State-Guards.

The low wages, the uncertainty of work, the clogging of cities with untrained rural hands, and the squalid living conditions made the cities a seedbed for crime. Muggers and ruffians prowled certain quarters of the city. Handlin records that "extensive regions of the city were abandoned to their own devices. There the nominal officials had no power, the nominal law did not run. Violence was endemic and the only social controls were such as were supported by the sanctions of local associations, locally led. The established citizenry desired only to protect itself from contagion."[15]

Then as now, the men of property and righteous ways were quicker to see illegal behavior than legitimate grievances. To protect themselves they set up a local police force and armed them with clubs and guns. If the local authorities would not enforce a law, the propertied might turn to the state government. In Massachusetts a State Constabulary was organized in 1865, its special duties being to prevent crime in Boston, Chelsea, Charlestown, and other large places by the suppression of liquor shops, gambling places, and houses of ill-fame.

Other urban institutions were created during this post-Civil War period. Public schools were built and staffed and attendance made mandatory.[16] Settlement houses were planted in the immigrant and working class districts. As children we were taught that such social undertakings were motivated by the desire to teach democracy to the newcomers and to open up opportunities for all. No doubt many teachers and social workers and taxpayers thought in these terms. But they were also the means for keeping people off the streets and inculcating the working class young with respect for property and the virtue of hard work.

The quest for safety has also been a factor in the selection of residential neighborhoods. To be removed from the criminal elements, the shiftless, and the foreigners has been a prime consideration in the choice of a home by many upper and middle class families. Toward the end of the nineteenth century, suburban communities began to form in the vicinity of outlying train stations along lines that converged upon the central business districts of the large cities. In the Philadelphia area, such suburbs were deliberately chosen by executives of the Pennsylvania Railroad and others in the same income and social class. These fortunates not only acquired social status and more space but also separation from the din, dirt, and crime of the city.

Safety is an overriding concern in the contemporary city. In-town apartments increasingly rely upon lighting, fencing, and electronic scanning devices to protect the residents. New towns within commuting range of central cities such as Reston, Virginia and Columbia, Maryland are reportedly becoming more marketable because of their presumed freedom from crime. And established suburbs appear to be trying to create a *cordon sanitaire* to shield themselves from the central city populace.

The Social Scale

A culture that values individual striving and physical mobility has a special kind of status order. Some people are assured of a high place by birth into a wealthy and socially prominent family—the "Capital Society" as two social scientists call them—but they constitute only 1 or 2 percent of the population. There are people at the bottom—"slumdwellers and other disreputables"—some of whom are second or third generations of urban poor. Richard P. Coleman and Bernice L. Neugarten, whose terms and findings are used here, classified 6.7 percent of the Kansas City status structure in the mid-1950s as "slumdwellers and disreputables," 4.1 percent of whites and 25.4 percent of Negroes.[17] Most persons fall in between and are grouped by sociologists into a working class, lower middle class, and upper middle class. The majority of Americans probably perceive themselves as middle class, but are somewhat anxious about where they fit in the pecking order. The increasing proportion of American youth who are going on to college, now about 50 percent and expected to rise as a proportion of the group over the next two decades, reflects the desire to get a good position in the work force and to "get ahead."

Americans tend to sort each other by occupation, income, education, and place of residence. High-paid business executives who also participate in civic functions (but not politics) are in the top group. So are university presidents, distinguished scientists, and high-income doctors and lawyers. In descending order come other professionals, semiexecutives, and businessmen; school teachers and ministers; white-collar workers in business and government; assembly-line workers, barbers, and beauticians; street repair men, garbage collectors, and day workers. "What does your father do?" is one of the first questions exchanged by American school children. "What church do you go to?" and "where did your grandparents come from?" are less interesting questions for children and adults today.

There is one question that does not have to be asked—it can be answered by a glance. The Negro is different. He is pegged at the bottom of the social scale. More accurately, Negroes are off the social scale of the larger society; they are a separate caste. "Across the color-caste line," write Coleman and Neugarten of Kansas City in the middle 1950s, "there was no socially meaningful equality since no group of whites truly accepted any group of Negroes as worthy of the same intimate interaction or the same respect accorded a white member of the same social class. Thus, any perception of equivalence of social classes across the caste line was not a demonstrable reality."[18] This statement would not hold for some Negroes in some Eastern and Western cities in the 1970s. In government circles and academic communities there are whites and blacks who socialize as peers and respect each other on the basis of personal achievement. But in the madding crowd, every new encounter, even for a notable black person, raises the question of whether he will be recognized and treated with respect.

Residential location is an important factor in the perception of social rank in American communities. Certainly it is one of the quickest indicators. For the quality of the neighborhood and house can be rated by the average resident. Most people can point out the Gold Coast or estate districts, the country club suburbs, the older quality neighborhoods, the homes of the solid middle-middle class; the well-kept lower middle class areas occupied by homeowners; the decent working class neighborhoods; and the slums and single room occupancy districts. There is a rough correlation between neighborhood quality and income and occupational levels. Planners and social reformers have frequently called for balanced neighborhoods containing a range of incomes and social groups within the same area. But people in fact group themselves in neighborhoods of similar income and social class.

Neighborhoods are ranked and house properties valued by the race of residents and to a lesser degree today by the ethnic makeup. In the 1930s a rating scale appeared in a study of land values in Chicago, a city with a large first and second generation ethnic population. The ranking was said to register the effect of race and nationality upon land values—the most favorable first and the most adverse last. The rank order, prepared by Homer Hoyt and published by the University of Chicago Press, was as follows:[19]

1. English, Germans, Scotch, Irish, Scandinavians
2. North Italians
3. Bohemians or Czechoslovakians
4. Poles
5. Lithuanians
6. Greeks
7. Russian Jews of the lower class
8. South Italians
9. Negroes
10. Mexicans.

Hoyt then made an interesting qualification: "Except in the case of Negroes and Mexicans, however, these racial and national barriers disappear when the individuals in the foreign nationality groups rise in the economic scale or conform to American standards of living."

Such rating scales would look different today—if they could be constructed at all for metropolitan areas along nationality lines. There are still the preserves of the social elite, most of whom are of British or North European descent. But the affluent suburbs are not impenetrable by the children or grandchildren of Greek, Jewish, or Sicilian immigrants, although such people may prefer warmer neighborhoods. Real estate brokers and mortgage lenders are not oblivious of ethnic background, but they look mainly at the jobs and incomes of white home buyers.

Race, on the other hand, is even more important than it was a generation or two ago in the ranking of neighborhoods and valuation of property. Blacks are more numerous in the cities and they are just as visible. When it comes to housing, the larger community is unwilling to distinguish black middle class families from working and welfare class blacks. Although federal laws now forbid discrimination in housing, practices tend to follow the folkways. Blacks are still treated as a separate caste in the sale or rental of housing.

Attitudes toward the Poor

Three things stand out as one reviews the attitudes toward the poor in America.

1. The poor are not a monolithic group and there are a number of reasons for being poor, most of them beyond the control or choice of the individual.
2. The impoverished elements have never had much political power or influence. Only the elderly—our "senior citizens"—seem to have some political clout as a group.
3. Localism burns fiercely when it comes to assuming financial responsibility for poor people. Local jurisdictions, since colonial days, have tried to avoid the burden of the poor and to the extent possible to pass the problems on to their neighbors. Historically, big cities like New York, Philadelphia, and Boston have carried a disproportionate share of the load.

Who are the poor? They are not a typical cross section of the households of America: there is a disproportionate number of large families—too many mouths to feed. There are relatively more old folks; there are the mentally deficient and physically handicapped; there are people trapped in chronic unemployment, miners, farm hands and such, whose skills are no longer necessary. And there are people who have never developed steady work habits.

The political impotence of the poor is legendary. Men of property wrote the Constitution, but many of them had a sense of *noblesse oblige* and were not unmindful of their duties to the poor. In the nineteenth century, however, the factory system and the anonymity of the large city separated the owners and businessmen from the workers as people. It was every man for himself, and the number of rich increased even as pauperization grew rapidly—sevenfold between 1830 and 1850 for the whole country. The affluent successfully fought off the political efforts of the poor and working class. In this the wealthy were aided and abetted by the federal courts, by compromised presidents and legislators, and by local officials whose sympathies or pocketbooks were usually with the upper class. Nor did it help matters that the majority of children picked up as penniless vagrants and many of the destitute adults were foreign born. In the 1850s they were mostly Irish.

Localism in the treatment of the poor preceded the republic. After every war or social upheaval, refugees, tramps, and beggars took to the road from King Philip's War in 1675 on. In Massachusetts, the townspeople wanted no responsibility for sheltering or supporting these unrooted people. Very early, a distinction was drawn between the settled poor, for whom the locality had to provide support, and those without settlement rights. The towns were permitted to have residence requirements, which frequently were conditioned on the ownership or rental of expensive property. These rights of settlement were made more and more stringent with the passage of time. One of the main tasks of the constable was to warn unsettled poor out of town and to take them to the town line.

Early American attitudes toward the poor were shaped by English experience, religious beliefs, and political philosophy. In medieval times the English poor were cared for by the monasteries and private people; charity was considered a religious duty. In the 1500s, the enclosures of farm land for sheep grazing along with business fluctuations associated with the new woolen industry created a large class of urban poor. London assumed public responsibility for the poor in 1547 by imposing a special tax to care for the indigent. Some other industrial towns followed suit, and all parishes or local jurisdictions were required by an act of Parliament in 1601 to levy a poor rate. But poor people sought out the parishes with the best stock and largest commons, and the local officers were authorized to remove those without long residence in the community.

Similar practices were installed in Massachusetts. In 1639 the General Court ordered the towns to care for their own poor inhabitants. Disputes arose as to which of the residents were lawfully settled within the town. By an act of 1659 the right of legal settlement belonged to any resident of more than three months who had not been given notice to leave by the local officials. These settled unfortunates the town must relieve; the unsettled poor were to be maintained by the town at the expense of the county.[20] In 1701 the required term of residence for poor relief was lengthened to one year. In 1766 the burden of proof was placed upon the newcomer: the immigrant was required to petition the selectmen for admission and his application had to be approved by vote of the inhabitants assembled in town meeting.

Such meanness required a rationale. The New Englanders found it in their Calvinism: man is born in sin but can achieve salvation through a life of righteousness and holiness. Each man must fight the corruption within himself; self-help and hard work are thus high virtues. Among the small-town New Englanders, such ideas hardened into distrust of those who were different: even Quakers were apprehended and sent out. The helpless poor within the town were to be taken care of; indeed, this was a religious duty. But the able-bodied beggars from outside deserved no sympathy; their indolence was a form of depravity latent in the nature of man. In fairness, it should be added that the rural town of this period had a restricted economic base, little capital equipment to raise the productivity of labor, and no large economic surplus to share with those who did not work. The period from 1790 to 1820 was mainly characterized by disruption of business and hard times.

Industrialization between 1820 and 1840 swelled the ranks of the state poor—those without local settlement rights—and concentrated them in urban centers such as Boston. It also introduced a new object of public aid—the involuntarily unemployed urban worker. Gradually, public attitudes and policy began to differentiate among the different classes of poor.

In the third quarter of the nineteenth century, new knowledge, increased social income, and the spread of humanitarian sentiment brought changes in the treatment of the poor. It had been established that the idiot could be trained and improved in mind; new methods for teaching articulation to deaf-mutes had been devised; and techniques for instructing the blind were available.[21] Overtly, the same philosophy of self-help prevailed. Nevertheless, the generous private bequests and more liberal public grants and aid revealed a softening in public attitudes toward the dependent members of society. Facilities for the treatment of the physically handicapped and mental patients were expanded and improved; institutionalization of the dependent poor in the infamous almshouses had been discredited and was gradually replaced by the giving of relief in the home. After 1887 normal dependent children had to be boarded at public expense in private homes.

During the present century a series of selective improvements have been made in the treatment of the poor. In this process, the impact of federal legislation can scarcely be overestimated. Under federal laws enacted since 1930, millions of Americans have been kept out of dire poverty in their old age or, if permanently disabled, through the social security system. Employees have contributed to the social security fund along with employers, and they receive payments with dignity as a matter of right. But those who cannot work are not covered by social security. A separate set of aids has been established for several categories of poor: aid to dependent children, aid to the blind, and old age assistance. We have a two-track system, one for the working population and another for the welfare population. Even health care for the elderly has been set up on this split basis: Medicare for social security recipients who can pay a portion of the costs; and Medicaid for the indigents. Alvin Schorr sees this process as resulting in a duplex society: a mainstream of respectable people and a permanent underclass of poor. The latter must deal continually with a battery of caretakers, custodians, and checkers whom the majority will never need to see, and their lot will remain miserable and without respect.[22]

During the early 1960s social critics such as Michael Harrington brought to the attention of the country this "Other America," people who were outside the opportunity system and likely to remain permanently poor. Their numbers were estimated to be thirty-five million, one-fifth of the population. The national administration determined to tackle this challenge head-on. President Johnson called for a way against poverty and secured passage of the Economic Opportunity Act in 1964. How did the administration sell the program to the country and the Congress? Sargent Shriver, designated to head the program when enacted, appealed to the pocketbook mentality. The intent, he said, was to turn taxeaters into taxpayers. The poor, in other words, were to become self-supporting members of society rather than wards of the state.

This required, among other things, a change in the psychology of the poor. They were to be encouraged to stand up for their rights and to become more assertive in the political process. Thus, one component of the antipoverty war was the community action program. Federal monies were initially channeled directly to private groups in the poverty neighborhoods. These groups were to build community spirit and self-esteem through a variety of activities ranging from cleaning up vacant lots to registering residents to vote. Within months the community action groups were challenging, or appearing to challenge, the mayors and elected officials, welfare and public housing officials, and established social agencies. In some places they took up the fight against urban renewal projects or highway building programs in their areas. And they seemed to be building political machines outside of the jurisdiction of city hall. For sympathetic federal officials in Washington a classic dilemma that has plagued domestic and foreign policy was being raised: Could federal support be given to those who proposed to reform or upset the established authorities? Could the United States government subsidize local insurrectionists?

The mayors and local establishment people, suspicious from the start of programs that by-passed them, now went to the mat in the congressional arena with the proponents of independent community action. They won. From 1967 on, community action programs had to go through or be approved by the local elected officials. The poor and their emergent leaders simply lacked the political power to win a frontal battle with the elected officers of the majority.

The war on poverty proved to be short-lived and short of funds. Appropriations under the Economic Opportunity Act ranged between one and two billion dollars a year from 1965 to 1971. During the same period, the budget of the Defense Department, which had charge of real wars, ranged between $50 billion and $80 billion a year. The Nixon budget for fiscal year 1974 provided no funds for the Office of Economic Opportunity and ended federal funding for community action agencies.

Reviewing this recent experience, we see that older attitudes and practices continue to haunt the contemporary policy maker. The poor continue to be stigmatized. There is a tendency to lump them all together and to fail to distinguish the causes of poverty. Their ranks are presumed to be swelled by those who can but refuse to work, despite estimates by social analysts that nine out of ten are too young, too old, or otherwise unable to work. We continue to operate housing, health, and welfare programs that set the poor apart and identifiable. The poor have neither the numbers nor the know-how to participate effectively in the political process. States and localities continue to encourage their superfluous poor to migrate to the big cities and urbanized states. In 1970, welfare payments to four-person families under Aid to Families with Dependent Children averaged $70 a month in Mississippi compared with $336 in New York. America is changing, sings the bard, but it has not broken its legacy of earlier generations in demeaning the poor.

On Government

Earlier Americans liked their governments lean, with limited powers, and close to home. With Locke, the men of 1776 believed that the purpose of government is to preserve order, protect life and property, and to fill in the niches such as charity when the church or the family fall short. With Montesquieu, men like Jefferson sensed that power tends to be abused; governmental powers were therefore separated among a bicameral legislature, an executive branch, and an independent judiciary. At the local level, public services were kept simple, sometimes performed by rotation among residents. In Massachusetts, town affairs were under the surveillance of selectmen and the community gathered in town meeting.

From 1820 on, American behavior and thought were dominated by a business ethos. It was an era of exploitation both in the burgeoning cities and on the frontier. Government was not to set priorities for the community; it was to be used to foster private efforts. It was laissez-faire, Parrington tells us, but modified to authorize the state to guarantee the economic well-being of strategic groups on whose prosperity that of the community was believed to depend. The strategic groups were Eastern financiers and industrialists and promoters of railroads and land speculators in the West.[23] A distinction was drawn between public and private outlays. A public improvement like a school or highway was a cost; a private outlay for a factory or warehouse was an investment.

In such a time, public adminstration of laws could be lax. In 1836, for example, the Massachusetts state legislature enacted a child labor law; this forbade the employment of any young person under fifteen years of age unless the child had attended school at least three months in the year preceding his employment. Enforcement, however, was left to the town officers. This adminstrative arrangement offered no assurance that the law would be universally enforced, especially in view of the considerable influence wielded by the local manufacturers. Local officials frequently looked the other way. In 1876, a state agency, the Detective Force, was charged with enforcing all statutes dealing with hours and condition of work, including child labor.

Nor could public employment be regarded with much esteem. Andrew

Jackson felt that any man could handle a public job, no special skills or talents were required: "The duties of all public officers . . . are so plain and simple that men of intelligence may readily qualify themselves for their performance."[24] Thus jobs were dispensed as booty among his supporters—"to the victor belong the spoils."

If incompetence characterized the public service before the Civil War, corruption was its mark in the Gilded Age that followed. The dominant figures of the time were private buccaneers like Jay Gould, Jim Fisk, and John D. Rockefeller. Public men had their price. Grant was plied with liquor and cigars but he also accepted a house valued at $50,000. Lesser public officials settled for smaller bribes. But corruption was expected in public service, and many behaved as they were expected to. James Bryce, the English observer of American politics, said that men sought political office as a means of gain. Men in public life accepted shares of stock without charge, assigned government contracts to firms in which they held an interest, and took cash for their votes. Hofstadter reports that between 1875 and 1885 the Central Pacific paid as much as $500,000 a year in graft.[25] From the company's standpoint, the bribe money was well spent: the construction company of the Central Pacific made a net profit of at least $54 million on construction costing about $36 million by simply puffing up the costs on the books. The proceeds went to the insiders, Leland Stanford, Charles Crocker, Mark Hopkins, and Collis Huntington.[26] (It was a device very similar to the practice of "mortgaging out" in the early 1950s, when apartment house builders secured FHA-insured mortgage loans based on inflated cost estimates, built the housing at substantially less, and pocketed the difference.)

The reaction to this public corruption and private plundering came near the turn of the century. A Civil Service Act was passed in 1883. It was aimed at the spoils system and was the beginning of a merit system in government. But if it protected the incumbents against patronage seekers, it failed in the next several decades to enlist a wave of dedicated and competent new people. Nor did it have much appeal to the working class and the farmers; their plight could not be remedied by honesty in public service. Basically, it was the upper middle class people who supported the good government movement—civil service, professional city managers, and administrative reorganizations—just as corporate executives have endorsed metropolitan government in the interest of efficiency and economy in recent times.[27]

Some reformers with a working class orientation remained suspicious of government. Henry George, proponent of a single tax on land as the means of eliminating the exploitation of workers, believed that "government should be reduced to its minimum—that it becomes more corrupt and more tyrannical and less under the control of the people, with every extension of its powers and duties."[28]

But government was called upon to do more, not less. Some of the states, particularly industrial ones, took the initiative. Massachusetts, for one, made an impressive attack on communicable disease between 1890 and 1920. An antitoxin for diptheria was manufactured in a state laboratory beginning in 1895 and distributed free of charge throughout the commonwealth. As a result, the average death rate from diptheria fell from 83.6 per 100,000 population in the years 1886-1890 to 17.1 between 1916 and 1920. Related activities brought down the death rate from scarlet fever, typhoid fever, and other diseases. On another front, a good-roads movement was launched by Massachusetts in 1893. By 1904, 548 miles of state highway had been completed and by 1930 the net length of state highways was 1,669 miles, with another 8,200 miles of city and town roads under state maintenance and repair. In other industrial states there were similar extensions of state responsibility in the areas of health, highways, education, welfare, and other sectors.

The federal government also took on more and more responsibilities in the regulation of big business, the creation of the Federal Reserve System, the start of federal grants-in-aid for highways, and other functions. In 1913 the Congress passed a modestly progressive personal income tax and a corporate income tax, the beginning of a system for redistributing income from the well-off to the poor. Such measures were the results of the Progressive movement, a moral and political revival among elements of the middle and upper classes. It was associated with a growing recognition of the mutualism in urban-industrial society in the provision of essential services and the production of social income. In 1907 the sociologist E. A. Ross wrote: "Nowadays the water main is my well, the trolley car is my carriage, the banker's safe my old stocking, the policeman's billy my fist . . ."[29] A new view was forming about the nature of man: not as inherently depraved and sinful but as a blend of good and bad and responsive to the social environment. Better institutions could produce better people. And good people could build better institutions. Respectable people began to see in public service a way of gaining prestige and making a contribution to society.

In the 1920s the big-business ethic reasserted itself, and government again became the servant of special interests and speculators. The Harding administration was marked by scandals reminiscent of the Grant period. Then came Coolidge, about whom one may remain laconic, followed by Herbert Hoover. Hoover epitomized one version of the American dream: orphaned at ten, he worked his way through college, became a millionaire and then President. He should have known about the economic difficulties that were building up in the 1920s, for he served as Secretary of Commerce in the Harding and Coolidge administrations. But he had a dogged belief in private enterprise and a hands-off policy by government. Hoover shared the view of most economists of the time that business declines are self-correcting. So he waited. Near the end of his term in late 1932 some ten million people were totally unemployed.

By temperament as well as philosophy, Franklin Roosevelt was committed to action. Eleanor Roosevelt helped explain: "What government was now trying to do was to help the people it governs over the rough spots." She saw a new concept of social justice and government taking hold: "The fundamental change is just this, that instead of each person being out for himself for what he can get for himself. . . people must think of the people around them"[30] Her words remind us of the mutualism outlook of the Progressives of an earlier era.

In the 1930s a radical change was occurring in the views and behavior of many Americans toward the central government. Homeowners are the backbone of the country and firm believers in self-help. During the thirties more than one million homeowners gratefully accepted the help of a new federal agency, the Home Owners' Loan Corporation, which refinanced their mortgages and kept them from losing their properties. Thrift is an old American virtue but many had lost their savings when the banks closed. Savers welcomed the introduction of federal insurance on savings deposited with the banks. Working people preferred government employment to hunger and idleness. The Public Works Administration provided jobs for four million people; another 350,000 young men enlisted in the Civilian Conservation Corps and many learned useful skills in construction and forestry. Farmers participated widely in federal efforts to stabilize agricultural prices. Businessmen helped design and administer the price agreements and production quotas of the National Recovery Act. Government had replaced the private market as the linchpin of the economic system; government was doing for individuals what no one could do for himself. To some Americans it was unthinkable. But so was the economic catastrophe. After 1933 the federal government's responsibility for stabilizing the economy and maintaining high employment won wider and wider acceptance.

What are the functions of modern government? In addition to assuring stable economic growth, government is required:

1. to provide protection and information—national defense, police and fire protection, storm warnings, and consumer information;
2. to correct inequalities and to redress imbalances among the population—education, job training, aid to Applachia, equal opportunity in jobs, housing, and public accommodations for minorities, and redistribution of income;
3. to cope with the problems of togetherness—traffic congestion, air pollution, and communicable disease; and
4. to gain the advantages of large concentrations—economies of scale in sewer and water works and transportation systems.

The functions of government have proliferated since World War II and so have the costs. The citizen wants better services from his government; he also wants lower taxes and larger take-home pay. Public service costs have been on the rise, not only in absolute dollars but as a proportion of national income. State and local expenditures rose from 8 percent of the gross national product in 1950 to 13 percent in 1970. State and local public services have been the fastest growing sector of the economy in terms of jobs. Princeton economist William Baumol has warned that these trends are unavoidable due to the high labor component in the provision of public services, the pressure to pay wages competitive with the more capital intensive industries, and the cumulative social costs of dense urban living.[31]

In Retrospect

What we have seen in this review of values and attitudes is the recurrence of certain concerns among the American people and the clash of basic interests and values. The demand for law and order is not unique to our times. At the writing of the Constitution, the men of property feared the city mob, and the upper classes of the nineteenth century felt threatened by the working men when they stood up for more wages and better working conditions. Today there is fear of the black and brown underclass. From their side, the disadvantaged can also appeal to American beliefs; all we want, they say, is equal opportunity, equal protection of the laws, and a piece of the action.

Since 1820 we have had a love-hate relationship with the big city, wanting what only the city can give—incredible productivity, a variety of life styles, excitement on demand, and privacy. On the other side of the civic coin, it is a sinful place; there is loneliness and alienation. And men feel themselves being conditioned into robots.

And real estate. What a splendid way to make a killing! Still true in 1973, although Turner's frontier has long been closed and Penn Central stock sold for less than five dollars a share. The new frontier is the edge of the metropolitan area: if the freeway comes as planned and population grows as projected, the chances of capital gains are good. Meanwhile, the land can be worked or leased as a farm with interest, taxes, and operating expenses deductible against your regular business income. The reformer, recalling Henry George, says the gain is an unearned increment and should be fully taxed; another calls for a public land bank or public development corporation to obtain the development rights.

Americans remain ambivalent about the nature and role of government. There is a need for economic security, which only the state can assure. Does the extension of social security and welfare aids pose a threat to other values—privacy and freedom of movement? The Republican party platform of 1972 suggested this possibility: "We will continue to defend the citizen's right to privacy in our increasingly interdependent society. We oppose computerized national data banks and all other 'big brother' schemes which endanger individual rights."

Should government insist on providing citizens with certain goods in kind—so-called merit goods—such as subsidized housing, free health care, schools? Why not give the citizen the cash and let him decide on the quality and quantity of public services he wants, just as he would in a supermarket? Does the individual know best or do the surrogates for society? If a person is charged the full price for treatment of venereal disease, he might not buy it and would imperil the health of others, so the argument goes. In the economist's terms, there are consumption externalities, that is, beneficial effects upon members of the community other than the immediate recipient. But the case is not always so clear, and the taxpayer senses that government agencies like to expand and will make larger claims of such benefits from their services than are demonstrably true.

Another conflict is between democratic participation and organized efficiency. To the German sociologist Max Weber, this was the most frightening of all.[32] On the one side are the common man, the voters, the elected legislators; on the other, organizations of experts and specialists bound together by the organization's goals, structured to speak with a single voice, asserting as the main criterion, efficiency. Any organization so structured is a bureaucracy, whether a government agency, a hospital or a trade union. The coonskin democracy of Andy Jackson is reincarnated in a small locality which is opposed to an expressway through its park. Arrayed against the community is a powerful bureaucracy, the state highway department, staffed with professionals and capable of demonstrating by computer runs that the park site is the least costly route. Or it is a citizens' group in a black district elected to represent the residents under the community action or Model Cities program. They say they know what's best for them when it comes to schools or running a health center or deciding on urban renewal. The medical director and his technicians have a budget, schedules, and programmed services. The citizens' ideas are wild and wasteful, says the medical director. Democratic participation and organizational efficiency are both rooted in the American value system. Hopefully we shall not sacrifice the citizen to the machine.

4 National Goals and Housing

America has always had social goals. To a large extent the goals were implicit in the values of the society. Population growth—every town and city wanted that. The expansion of commerce and industry was an early national objective, fostered by tariffs, land grants to settlers and private companies, and the building of roads and canals. Such objectives sprang from the notion that the main purpose of the state is to promote the well-being of the individuals who make up the community; thus, the collective good is the sum of the satisfactions of the citizens. That the nation had needs that transcend those of its parts became clear in time of crisis and threat to survival. Jackson held this when he said: The Union—it must be preserved! Theodore Roosevelt and his chief forester Gifford Pinchot refused to accept the short-run goals of timber and mining companies as consistent with the societal goal of "perpetual reproduction of the forest."[1] Laws regulating women and child labor reflected a concern for family life and sympathy with the economically exploited worker.

Why Goals Thinking Became More Explicit

The systematic examination of national goals and objectives is a very recent development. It began in the 1960s with the convergence of two streams of thought. First, there were the real problems that seem to have deepened or that people were more conscious of: crisis in black and white, poverty amidst affluence, the fouling of the streams and air, and crime in the streets. Second, there was the seemingly inexorable extension of rationalization to every sector and to every institution. The techniques of modern society, embodied in that most modern institution, the private corporation, were being applied elsewhere—to the church, in the universities, and to government. Thus, the public goals had to be displayed, stated explicitly, then quantified to become targets, priced out, then traded off one against another. Indeed, the method becomes the end, in Jacques Ellul's unhappy insight, with efficiency and effectiveness seemingly more important than other values.[2] Goals that cannot be quantified cannot be assured a fair hearing: the value of teaching the humanities, the worth of esthetic experiences, the value of quiet.

This confluence of substantive discontents and rationalized modes of thinking fed into goal-oriented public policy discussion and analysis. It all began rather innocently and benignly at the end of the second term of a noninterventionist President, Dwight D. Eisenhower, with the appointment of the President's Commission on National Goals. The Goals Commission was privately financed, stayed at arms length from officials in the government, and took a cautious view of its role. The Commission's report and the essays prepared by experts were "directed to the citizens of this country, each of whom sets his own goals . . ."[3] But the Commission did identify in a single document an array of public problems and cast them in rational terms: the need to choose among competing ends, and the notion of costs as other opportunities that have to be foregone.

Goals analysis was not particularly the style of President Kennedy. Certainly, he and his advisers were familiar with it.[4] But Kennedy came to the White House in the middle of a business recession, and his first energies were directed to improvising measures for economic recovery. Moreover, he was faced with a relatively conservative Congress and to this pragmatic leader the idea of laying out a formal set of goals and price tags probably seemed rather pedantic. Still, the Kennedy Budget Bureau did begin to ask the departments and agencies to submit their programs as five-year projections of needs and spending levels. At the Defense Department, Secretary Robert McNamara, a former auto industry executive, ordered the development and installation of a programming system as early as 1961.[5]

Enter PPBS

It was President Johnson who ordered all civilian departments and agencies to install a planning-programming-budgeting system (PPBS) in August 1965. He did this with much fanfare, much more than would normally attend an executive order of an essentially technical and administrative nature. The circumstances associated with Johnson's announcement are revealing. By that date he knew that his administrative budget for fiscal year 1966 would exceed $100 billion, a height to which all administrations feared to go. A big jump in national defense commitments, unprovided for in the budget submitted the previous January, was now in the making as a result of the July decision to pour many more men and materials into Vietnam. On the domestic front, Congress was busily enacting and funding a dozen or more social programs called for by the President himself. Johnson had responded to the public discontents as no other president since Franklin Roosevelt. Now an unforeseen step-up in the Vietnam conflict threatened his public image as a prudent fiscal manager and endangered an array of new domestic programs that he hoped would mark his administration as the advent of a Great Society. Beyond the public relations aspects, there was a real need to economize in the face of intense competition for scarce resources both among government activities and between public and private spending. So President Johnson turned to PPBS, an approach that required the explicit statement of public goals in terms of desired results or outputs.[6]

It was intended that PPBS would be fully operational by the fiscal year 1968 budget. But the departments were not able to meet this schedule. In his budget message for that year (issued in January 1967) Johnson talked about the planning-programming-budgeting system in modest and sober terms:

> This system is primarily a means of encouraging careful and explicit analysis of Federal programs. It will substantially improve our ability to decide among competing proposals for funds and to evaluate actual performance. The full effects of this effort will not be felt until next year and later, as the necessary data are gathered and analyses now in progress are completed.[7]

Thus in a matter of seventeen months PPBS had been demoted from space-age wizardry to a tedious grind by earthbound men. Patiently they tried to disentangle statutory objectives deliberately obscured by support-seeking congressional sponsors. Doggedly they dug for data that would tell not how many projects were started but how many people were helped or harmed. Tirelessly they examined alternative programs in the face of skepticism or hostility from operators of established public endeavors. This has a familiar ring to federal officials who were responsible for program development and evaluation before PPBS. Congressmen write laws that are all things to all men; the entrenched bureaus and their clientele groups will not cooperate; and reliable information on what is really happening is hard to get.

Metagoals and Subordinate Goals

One of the results of planning-programming-budgeting was to compel program administrators and clientele groups to recognize different levels of goals. The inventive spirit of the New Frontier-Great Society era, 1961-66, produced several hundred federal enactments aimed at specific problems. Many of the policy makers in the executive branch had been recruited from Capitol Hill and they did what came naturally: they fathered a new brood of categorical aid programs. Virtually every opportunity or ill was sought out and covered by a legislative proposal. Not all were enacted, but enough to cause massive traffic jams at budget and appropriations time and serious jurisdictional disputes among federal agencies.

Toward the middle of the period there began to emerge metagoals, those which transcend the missions of individual programs. The War on Poverty was such a goal. It required combinations of programs rather than single-purpose approaches; it was directed to beneficiaries who were not immediately capable of acting in their own behalf; and it depended for its execution upon agencies and institiutions that would have to be called into being. In this new context, an established program like low-rent public housing could be viewed as an element to be meshed into the larger antipoverty effort. A new proposal such as rent supplements could be weighed in terms of its potential contribution to the larger national commitment. Indeed, the rent supplement proposal as it first emerged from the White House in 1965 was aimed at lower middle or moderate income familes rather than the poorest households. During the clearance process within the executive branch, the Office of Economic Opportunity urged that rent supplements be made available primarily to low income families. OEO did not prevail at this stage—in the face of opposition from the Bureau of the Budget. But the War on Poverty had its supporters in the Congress, among them Senator Paul Douglas of Illinois. In the hearings on the housing bill, Douglas used the Housing Agency's own tables and charts to make his case: "Now you are abandoning the 3.1 million families with incomes under $3,000 a year in your rent subsidy program, concentrating your attention on the 1.2 million families in the $3,000 to $6,000 level who are certainly in much less need than the others."[8] Thus Douglas persuaded his fellow legislators to revise the proposal and give the rent supplements to the poor. What happened to the program when it reached the appropriations stage is discussed in Chapter 5.

The War on Poverty was the catch-phrase used to describe a goal recognized in the United States since the federal income tax was instituted in 1913—the redistribution of income. Other national objectives that can lay claim to the front bench are full employment and stable economic growth, environmental protection, and equality of opportunity. Housing, sewer facilities, job training, and other specific services and programs of government can be viewed as contributors to (or detractors from) these larger ends. In some cases, a particular function may serve several major purposes; for example, the construction of low-income housing in time of recession helps to stimulate the economy and also contributes to the redistribution of income. Such an activity may also generate conflict among the major goals: if the projects are located on a flood plain, or are grossly unsightly, or reinforce racially regregated living patterns. Let us look at some of the larger goals in more detail and see where housing fits.

Full Employment and Stable Growth of the Economy

Of all our national commitments (other than national defense), full employment is the strongest. Since Franklin Roosevelt's time, no administration has been able to take its eye off the levels of employment, business investment, and household spending. To Roosevelt, getting people back to work was the main goal; all others were subordinate. During most of the thirties, unemployment rates hovered around 20 percent; as late as 1940, there were more than eight million unemployed, 14.6 percent of the civilian labor force. The entry of the United States into World War II reduced unemployment to very low levels and required the imposition of price and wage controls and rationing. But the long depression had left its imprint and there was a deep concern in some government and academic circles about the likelihood of a postwar depression.

Some businessmen also shared this fear—Paul Hoffman of Studebaker, William Benton, a former advertising executive, Ralph Flanders, a Vermont toolmaker, Thomas McCabe of the Scott Paper Company, Beardsley Ruml of Macy's, Marion Folsom of Eastman Kodak, and others. Together, they formed the Committee for Economic Development (CED) in 1942 to begin laying plans for high production and employment when the war ended. It was groups such as CED that helped to create a climate of opinion receptive to a national commitment to high employment. While conservative business groups opposed a "full employment bill" introduced by Senator James Murray of Montana, CED members testified in support of the bill and offered modifications. They were prepared to see the government utilize tax and spending powers as well as monetary policies to maintain stability and employment.

Shorn of its "Full Employment" title and reference to the "right to employment," an Employment Act was passed and signed into law by President Truman in February, 1946. A Council of Economic Advisers was established under the act, and the President is required to submit to the Congress each year an economic report on progress toward our economic goals of "maximum employment, production, and purchasing power."[9]

Government-subsidized housing construction, slum clearance, and public works have been justified on a number of grounds—human welfare, health and sanitation, and saving the central city. But the case is enormously strengthened when there is slack in the economy and unemployment in the building trades. This was the situation in the 1930s. Thus, the public works and housing activities undertaken in the early New Deal were heavily oriented toward reviving the building industry and stimulating employment. Similarly, the United States Housing Act of 1937 had three purposes: to expand construction activity and so raise the level of employment; to eliminate slums; and to provide adequate shelter for low income families. In all, 193,000 housing units were constructed under that act between September 1937 and the middle of 1944, providing for less than 2 percent of the families the law was intended to serve. It also fell far short of its other objectives of slum clearance and raising the level of employment. For Congress had authorized only $800 million in capital outlays for public housing over a seven-year period, hardly the magnitude that could contribute substantially to lifting the economy out of a deep depression.

As the war drew to a close, Congress again began to consider social programs such as housing. After extensive investigations and hearings in 1944-45, the Senate Banking and Currency Committee recommended a comprehensive housing measure known as the Wagner-Ellender-Taft bill, S. 1592. This bill was passed by the Senate but died in the House Committee. For more than three years this omnibus housing legislation remained stalled; it was finally passed in modified form as the Housing Act of 1949. Among the opponents of a big housing program in 1947 and 1948 was the Board of Governors of the Federal Reserve System. In late November 1947, Marriner Eccles, Chairman of the Board of Governors, expressed opposition to provisions in the bill that would have liberalized mortgage credit terms under Federal Housing Administration programs, such as lower down payments and longer periods of amortization on small houses.[10] In April 1948, the Board again came out against these proposals on grounds that inflationary pressures were likely to increase in the months ahead. From a cyclical point of view, the housing proposals had been poorly timed. When drafted in 1945, the prevalent view was that a business recession would follow soon after the war ended. The generous subsidies and guarantees to private enterprise were intended to cushion an anticipated deflationary trend in the national economy. Instead, the period 1946-48 was characterized by strong inflationary pressures. In the building industry, skilled workers as well as materials were in short supply; both residential and nonresidential construction demand was heavy. In the view of the Federal Reserve, the already easy mortgage credit for housing was one of the major factors contributing to the inflationary situation. While the opponents of the housing legislation certainly included other interests besides the monetary authorities, it is clear that housing policy had to reckon with economic policy.

In the early fifties, Catherine Bauer Wurster criticized the urban redevelopment program, authorized under the comprehensive Housing Act of 1949, on economic as well as social grounds. Urban redevelopment was displacing poor families in the midst of an acute housing shortage and making additional claims upon the construction industry when it was already operating under bottleneck conditions, thus contributing to the upward push of building costs. Conceived during depression, urban redevelopment, she held, was a misfit in the fifties.[11] At the time she wrote the urban housing supply was indeed tight, especially in cities experiencing substantial migration from the South, Puerto Rico, and rural portions of other regions. Residential construction costs had climbed by 54 percent between 1945 and 1950.

Since the end of World War II the United States has experienced five recessions: 1948-49, 1953-54, 1957-58, 1960-61, and 1970-71. In a period of recession, the indicated governmental response is to run a budget deficit. This can be achieved by raising public spending or reducing taxes with the purpose of inducing larger private spending by business firms and households. Concurrently, the monetary authorities are likely to facilitate an increase in the availability of credit and a lowering of interest rates. These actions tend to stimulate housing starts, thus contributing to the general economic recovery. In 1959, for example, nonfarm housing starts increased by 150,000 over the previous year. The Emergency Housing Act of 1958, passed by Congress without encouragement from President Eisenhower, clearly contributed to this pick-up. The act authorized the Federal National Mortgage Association to purchase $1 billion in FHA and Veterans Administration mortgages on new construction. Resulting production was estimated by FNMA at 70,000 housing units.

President Kennedy came to the White House in the midst of recession. Immediately upon taking office, he called upon the Housing Agency, among a number of departments and agencies, to take administrative measures and develop legislative proposals that would stimulate the building industry and the general economy. His program to restore economic momentum, announced on February 2, 1961, included a lowering of the FHA mortgage rate, an increase in purchases of new mortgages by the Federal National Mortgage Association and reduced sales from the FNMA mortgage portfolio, and an acceleration of public works loans and federally-aided urban renewal projects. A key feature of Kennedy's housing package, signed into law in June as the Housing Act of 1961, was the below-market interest rate program for moderate income rental housing. Administered by FHA and FNMA, this new program was designed to permit a quick start-up through limited-return and nonprofit sponsors. Housing and related construction did in fact rise substantially in the next several years in response to the increased flow of mortgage funds at stable interest rates. The moderate income program's contribution, it should be said, was a relatively small part of total housing starts.

In the early sixties, a period of recession and underemployment of manpower and capital plant and equipment, housing was a helpful tool of economic policy. Those who wanted housing as an end in itself, for the elderly, the moderate income families, the college population, and other groups, found supporters on the White House staff and in the Council of Economic Advisers. Old foes in the Bureau of the Budget, the Department of the Treasury, and the Federal Reserve Board were temporarily neutralized. The increased housing activity was not the principal means of lowering unemployment. Far more important, of course, was the tax cut of 1964, which mitigated the excessive tax burden—fiscal drag. Otto Eckstein explains:

By July 1965, before defense contracts began to rise, unemployment was down to 4.5 percent and falling rapidly, the economy was growing at over 5 percent a year, and wholesale prices were still stable and no higher than five years earlier. The economy had shown, at least for 18 happy months, that it could prosper without war with sensible, modern economic management . . . [12]

Throughout this period 1961-65, housing perked along, comfortable in the feeling that it was a useful member of the economic team.

Then came the inflationary years and housing was cut from the squad. Some may argue that it was not the deliberate intent of the economic policy makers to harm the housing sector. But surely these sophisticated men were aware of the excessive burden placed upon this one sector by the method used to check inflation. Certainly the Secretary of Housing, the FHA Commissioner, and the National Association of Home Builders were pleading their case with the White House and the Federal Reserve Board. Indeed, the Home Builders Association was even arguing for a tax increase, for the administration in 1966 was placing virtually all the emphasis on tightening credit—monetary policy—as the means of curbing inflation. And housing, more than any other industry, is sensitive to changes in the availability and cost of credit.

Tight money forced housing starts down from a rate of about 1.5 million units a year at the beginning of 1966 to less than 900,000 on an annual basis by October and 1.2 million for the year as a whole. Meanwhile, corporations increased their borrowing, net borrowing by the Treasury increased to finance the enlarged war in Vietnam, and consumer installment credit continued to grow, although slower than in 1965. The correct economic policy, according to Eckstein, was a broad across-the-board tax increase at the start of 1966 along with a tougher monetary policy even earlier than the Federal Reserve actions. But President Johnson was reluctant to ask for a tax increase for a number of months, and Congress dallied until mid-1968 before finally passing a tax surcharge.

Out of this experience came significant institutional changes for housing. A major development of the late sixties was the linking of the mortgage market with the securities market through changes in the charter and actions of the Federal National Mortgage Association, the Home Loan Bank System, and private groups such as real estate investment trusts. What this means is that housing is no longer so dependent upon the traditional thrift institutions for its supply of capital. A study group of CED, considering various ways of financing the nation's housing needs, is sympathetic to the use of variable interest rates on housing mortgages as a way of keeping this sector competitive with others over the business cycle. The likely consequence of such an approach would be to make funds available on a steadier basis during fluctuations of the economy, but at higher rates than in the years preceding 1966. Such measures indicate the pressure upon housing to make its peace with a more compelling national objective—high employment and stable economic growth.

Environmental Quality

Environmentalism swept over America like a new evangelism in the 1960s. The word went forth that for man to live in peace with man, he must find harmony with nature. It urged clean air and clean streams and less noise and an end to the misuse of natural resources; but it was more than the sum of these parts, it was a call for a new public ethic. The ecologists have challenged some older values of American society—population growth and economic growth as intrinsically good. Not more but better is their message. Man must stop being so obsessively materialistic and so extravagant in the spending of nature's gifts.

The environmental spirit caught on with many young people and some adults as well. In April 1970, a nationwide observance called Earth Week attracted thousands of people in different parts of the country. Automobile traffic was halted as young men and women marched to demonstrate their concern for a clean environment. In one area a new automobile was lowered into a pit in a symbolic burial.

Environmental quality has many parts. To most people it conjures up images of streams and lakes clean enough to swim in; city air free of smog and soot and automobile exhaust fumes; and the removal of junked cars, beer cans, bottles, and litter in public places. From the days of Theodore Roosevelt it has also meant conservation of forests, protection of wildlife, and prevention of soil erosion. In more recent decades this concern for sound land management has turned to the urban areas. In 1962 the Outdoor Recreation Resources Review Commission, chaired by Laurance S. Rockefeller, reported to the nation that the most urgent need for open space and outdoor recreation is near metropolitan areas. They said: "Over a quarter billion acres [of land] are public designated outdoor recreation areas, [but] most of the land is where people are not. The problem is not one of total acres but of *effective* acres."[13] While the concern of this commission was mainly with recreation rather than all aspects of urban development and nondevelopment, it helped mobilize public support for new federal programs of open space, land and water conservation, urban parks and city beautification, and the notion of long-term regional and metropolitan planning. A more recently established public group, the Citizens' Advisory Committee on Environmental Quality (also chaired by Laurance S. Rockefeller), has urged the formation of "regional bodies with authority to plan and control those facets of land use that transcend local boundaries, such as transportation, pollution abatement, low-cost housing, and open space."[14] The same committee sees environmental quality as encompassing adequate housing, education, jobs, recreation, cultural opportunities, and transportation.

The nation's commitment to protect the environment is broad but diffuse. The analog to the Employment Act in this area is the National Environmental Policy Act of 1969. This act also provides for a presidential council—the Council on Environmental Quality. Enforcement of federal antipollution laws is vested in an Environmental Protection Agency. The EPA resembles the Office of Economic Opportunity of the mid-sixties in its strong sense of mission, the ability to attract vigorous administrators, and an affirmative public image. It is a modern-day product of the good government movement of the turn of the century. But it also has its problems: who are its constituents? What interest groups will rally to it in a head-on clash with the industrial corporations, the utilities, the big agribusinesses, and the thousands of special districts and authorities that clutter the metropolitan areas? And where is the body of expertise to set objective criteria and standards for environmental quality? In this respect the environmentalists labor under the same handicaps as city and metropolitan planners who seek to assert their ethos over highway engineers, sanitation experts, and airport designers. Their "specialty" is the ability to perceive the broader goals of the community at large and to determine the long-term public interest. But is that a technical skill or the assertion of a public philosophy?[15]

What are the implications of the environmental movement for housing? Its most direct impact is on the location and density of residential development. If environmentalists have their way, certain areas would be permanently off limits for building: flood plains subject to frequent flooding, lands endowed with unusual vistas and natural beauty, and areas required for intensive public recreation. There would be a higher premium on retaining wetlands, marshes, and bays as sanctuaries for birds and other wildlife. To conserve land and to hold down public costs of sewer and water facilities, there would be incentives for more compact community development. Many environmentalists advocate new towns and planned satellite communities at higher densities than characterize single family developments in suburban areas. Row housing, garden apartments, and high-rise structures would be encouraged rather than detached single family houses. There would be more community swimming pools and play areas and less need for private ones. In the interest of holding down the growing demand for electricity, the acquisition of more and more power gadgets would be discouraged. In addition, opportunities to speculate in land and reap capital gains would be curtailed. Finally, there is at least implicit support for serious efforts to conserve the existing stock of housing and established neighborhoods.

Does all of this require a radical change in American life styles and values, for example, smaller families and slower population growth? Does it imply that we curb our consumer appetites for more gimmicks and gadgets? Does it spell more ways of taking leisure and far more social responsibility for public housekeeping on the part of the individual? To those who take our environmental problems seriously, it means all of these things.

Equality of Opportunity

When we say "equality of opportunity," we mainly have in mind the housing problems of blacks, Chicanos, and Puerto Ricans. Women, Asians, Italians, Jews, and other ethnic minorities all encounter some discrimination in housing, but their difficulties pale in comparison with the plight of black Americans. Blacks comprised 11 percent of the population in 1970 but occupied one-fourth of all substandard houses in use. Blacks were highly concentrated in older neighborhoods and in the central cities. Black workers have access to jobs at the core but have less knowledge of or access to suburban employment. Black children attend schools that generally are physically less adequate than those in white districts and educationally inferior, in part because they are predominantly segregated. Because the intellectual tradition is less ingrained in black parents in comparison with some white groups (and this may be a realistic appraisal of the value of education by lower income blacks in terms of employment prospects), inferior education in the schools is reinforced by attitudes in the home and neighborhood. Such a pattern constitutes a culture of discrimination that is not likely to be broken by traditional American avenues such as individual freedom of choice.

That we have a national goal of equal opportunity is beyond question. That some groups have prospered in line with this goal is apparent; that blacks (and Chicanos, Puerto Ricans, and American Indians) have a long way to go is equally clear.

What do we mean by "equality of opportunity?" In the American creed, it means that each individual will be enabled to participate in voting, in seeking public office, and in the political process; that everyone will be judged on his merit in seeking a job; that all will have free access to public accommodations and housing markets; that each person will be enabled to secure a good education and to realize his maximum potential for self-fulfillment.

In 1960, the Goals Commission appointed by President Eisenhower addressed the goal of equality:

Vestiges of religious prejudice, handicaps to women, and, most important, discrimination on the basis of race must be recognized as morally wrong, economically wasteful, and in many respects dangerous. In this decade we must sharply lower these last stubborn barriers.[16]

The majority of the commission went on to urge that the government should enforce the principle that federal funds or contracts shall not be disbursed to employers who discriminate on the basis of race, with similar policies to be applied progressively to federal grants for universities, hospitals, airports, and federal housing programs. The U.S. Commission on Civil Rights had earlier recommended such measures by the federal government.

The federal courts had led the way in the 1950s with the historic reversal of the separate but equal doctrine in *Brown* v. *Board of Education.* Separate and segregated schools do not provide equal educational opportunities for black children, the Supreme Court held in that 1954 decision. Other federal court rulings chipped away at segregation in interstate transportation and some public accommodations.

But it is the President and the executive branch that not only must enforce such decisions, but must take the initiative in proposing legislation and using the executive powers to prohibit discriminatory practices. This President Eisenhower was reluctant to do; he thought that discrimination could be ended only by changing men's hearts, not by orders or laws. Yet he found himself ordering federal troops to Little Rock, Arkansas in 1957 to enforce a federal court edict requiring desegregation in that city's public schools.

John F. Kennedy, in contrast, viewed himself as an activist in the White House. During the campaign in the fall of 1960, he criticized President Eisenhower for failing to end racial discrimination in federal housing programs "by a stroke of the Presidential pen." He implied that this would be one of the earliest actions of his administration.

Kennedy's victory, however, was a narrow one; he had no general mandate and no firm control of the Congress. Forced to choose among his prime goals, he gave top priority to raising economic growth and employment, aiding economically depressed areas, and similar measures that enjoyed broad public support. No civil rights legislation originated with the Kennedy administration in 1961 or 1962. From Sorensen we learn that the votes were lacking in the House of Representatives to get such legislation through or around the conservative-dominated Rules Committee.[17] To try to do so would simply alienate moderate Southern legislators—men like Senator John Sparkman and Congressman Albert Rains, both of Alabama—and risk loss of their help on other measures.

What about the promised executive order? Executive Order 11063 on Equal Opportunity in Housing was issued in November 1962. It was a relatively limited order because Kennedy continued to be worried about political and economic repercussions. He had reason to be concerned because unemployment in late 1962 was still just below 6 percent. Housing construction had picked up, but no one could be sure of the effect of such an order on future starts. The order applied sanctions to new construction financed under FHA and VA programs and public housing—programs that comprised only 20 percent of total housing production. Conventional loans made by savings and loan associations, commercial banks, and other institutional lenders were deliberately excluded despite the fact that such institutions are regulated and insured by government agencies. Each federal unit with programs covered by the order was to police itself under the general guidance of a White House committee. As with many civil rights activities, enforcement was not vigorous. The agencies did not initiate actions to uncover patterns of discrimination. They waited for individual complaints and all told processed some 200 cases in the next five years.

Congress moved on the civil rights front between 1964 and 1968. The Civil Rights Act of 1964, which originated with Kennedy in 1963, prohibited discrimination or segregation in hotels and motels, restaurants and soda fountains, motion picture houses, and other places of public accommodation. The same act ruled out discrimination in programs and activities receiving federal grants or loans—hospitals, welfare, employment services, and schools. Under another title of the 1964 act, fair employment practices were required in hiring, job referrals, membership in unions, and apprenticeship and training programs.

In the Civil Rights Act of 1968, the Congress declared: "It is the policy of the United States to provide, within constitutional limitations, for fair housing throughout the United States." Under this act it became unlawful to discriminate in the sale, rental, or financing of housing. Landlords or sellers may not advertise "white only." A black family may not be told that a place has been sold or rented when in fact it is still available; and block-busting—a practice sometimes used in changing neighborhoods by unscrupulous real estate agents to frighten many people into panic selling—is precluded under the law. About three-quarters of the housing inventory of the country is subject to the fair housing law. To administer the new law the Department of Housing and Urban Development initially requested $9 million and received only $2 million. It seemed to be an ominous sign. But by 1971-72, the appropriation was about $8 million. The 1974 budget called for outlays of $10 million for fair housing and equal opportunity programs.

How broad is the American commitment to equal opportunity? In rhetoric it is an overarching goal of the United States. In law the coverage extends to most of the important areas. But governmental practices and community behavior in many places raise serious doubts about the depth of the commitment. In the area of employment, for example, federal program managers refused to apply sanctions, such as the withdrawal of contracts, against employers who continue to discriminate in hiring or promoting minority persons. William L. Taylor, former staff director of the U.S.

Commission on Civil Rights, has stated: "This argument against sanctions was based on a value judgment shared by most agency heads and contract managers, that civil rights objectives are subsidiary to their main mission—the efficient flow of goods and services to their programs—and that where the two goals come into conflict, civil rights considerations must yield."[18]

At the highest level of government, the Office of the President, there appeared to be a retreat from equal opportunity in the early 1970s on all fronts. Sensing an antiblack mood in the country, President Nixon came out against busing as a means of desegregating schools; he spoke against employment quotas for minority workers as "a dangerous detour away from the traditional value of measuring a person on the basis of ability."[19] In housing, his party rejected the use of federal aids to promote open occupancy. In the words of the 1972 platform adopted by the Republican party: "We strongly oppose the use of housing or community development programs to impose arbitrary housing patterns on unwilling communities."[20] White suburbs and neighborhoods could rest assured that the Nixon administration would not help black families to move in.

In 1955 Walter White, executive secretary of the National Association for the Advancement of Colored People, published a book called *How Far the Promised Land?*[21] "How far off is the day when the American citizen of Negro descent will walk beside his white fellow citizens in full equality?" Ralph J. Bunche asked this question in his foreword to White's book. Almost two decades later there was still a long way to go.

Redistribution of Income

The early American view was that income should be distributed in accordance with individual ability and effort, but that no one should starve. The contemporary view might be rephrased: but that no one should live much below the poverty line. Certainly there is no explicit commitment to equalizing income in the United States. Rather, there seems to be a propensity to narrow differentials in three ways: by reducing the number of people living in poverty; by providing more services such as health and higher education through the social sector at less than full cost; and by utilizing the federal revenue system to pay for an increasing proportion of public service costs. Since the federal tax system is mildly progressive, while state and local governments rely heavily upon regressive taxes (sales and property taxes), the net effect is to narrow somewhat the wide disparities in income.

The distribution of money income has changed little in twenty-five years. The highest fifth of all families receive 40 to 45 percent of the aggregate income; the lowest fifth obtain 4 to 5 percent. These ratios have not varied much since 1947. During the 1960s the top 10 percent of the families actually increased their share of the total, from 27 percent in 1960 to 29 percent in 1969, which may be associated with rising prices from 1966 on. During inflationary periods, there is a shift in income from those on relatively fixed salaries and pensions to professionals and business men. During the same period, the lowest tenth continued to receive only 1 percent of total money income, despite the introduction of the antipoverty program in 1964.

Those who live in poverty—some 24.5 million people by official estimates in 1972—are largely outside of the opportunity system. Two out of three are not employable: 8 million children, 5 million aged persons, 1 million sick or handicapped, and 2 million mothers with small children. "For these," said the Population Commission in its March, 1972 Report, "the answer should be an increased public responsibility for maintaining a decent standard of living." For the working poor—domestic workers, migrant farmers, and others with earnings below the minimal income standard—and those who cannot find work, the Population Commission recommended improved education and training and an end to racial and sex discrimination in employment.[22]

This was the programmatic thrust of the War on Poverty. The Economic Opportunity Act of 1964, which launched the effort, first set forth the purpose: "It is therefore the policy of the United States to eliminate the paradox of poverty in the midst of plenty in this Nation by opening to everyone the opportunity for education and training, the opportunity to work, and the opportunity to live in decency and dignity." The new programs created under the act included a new Job Corps for young people aged sixteen through twenty-one, patterned after the Civilian Conservation Corps of the 1930s; a work-training program also for younger persons; and a work-study program to help low-income young people attend college.

The aim of such programs was to instill self-esteem and work skills in potentially employable young people. In its first year the act was to aid almost half a million underprivileged young Americans. Another major element of the act was the community action program. This supported locally developed activities in such fields as education (preschool preparation such as Head Start), employment, job training and counseling, housing, and home management. President Johnson's first-year price tag on the antipoverty campaign was $970 milllon—1 percent of the federal budget. The new programs and related ones of other agencies were to be coordinated by the Office of Economic Opportunity and an Economic Opportunity Council composed of heads of departments and agencies.

Thus began a hopeful effort to reduce poverty in the country. It added up to a relatively modest redistribution of income. From July 1964 to June

1970, about $9.6 billion had been committed under OEO programs, almost half of this for community action activities. But it generated a consciousness of poverty in the country and in the Congress. As noted earlier, a housing program—rent supplements—was redirected to the low income group. Other programs in education, health, and manpower development were also launched under the War on Poverty banner.

In recent evaluations some of these programs have been given a low grade. Manpower training programs have not been able to assure the trainees of work at the end of the training period. The Model Cities program, an ambitious attempt to raise the quality of life in low income neighborhoods by integrating physical and social rehabilitation activities, seems to have fallen short of demonstrable success in most places where it was tried. Nevertheless, the War on Poverty did put the federal government on record as committed to eliminating poverty.

The nation continues to grapple with problems of poverty and welfare reform. There is a reluctance to recognize that the majority of people in poverty are too young or too old or too handicapped to work. Not that the unemployment problem is not real: especially among teenagers in the labor force where jobless rates were 17 percent for those sixteen to nineteen years old at the end of 1971; 10 percent for blacks, 7.5 percent for blue collar workers, and almost 6 percent for women twenty years old and over. Even in years of strong economic activity teenagers, blacks, and unskilled workers suffer relatively high rates of unemployment. In response, there is increasing consideration of the government as employer of last resort. The Emergency Employment Act of 1971 may serve as the prototype for future public policy. Recognizing the difficulties of low income persons, migrants, and the technologically displaced workers, it authorized federal funds for several hundred thousand public service jobs in environmental quality, health care, street maintenance, prison rehabilitation, and other fields.

For those who cannot work or cannot earn enough to live decently, some form of income maintenance remains to be devised. The Nixon administration's family assistance proposal as of 1972 would have established a national income standard of $2,400 for a family of four. States could supplement these federal payments up to then-current levels of welfare payments provided under programs such as Aid to Families with Dependent Children. Low income working families as well as welfare families would be eligible. It would also have provided training for welfare recipients and care for their children. The proposal has been criticized by such groups as the National Urban Coalition and the National Welfare Rights Organization for setting the allowance below the official Census Bureau poverty level and for failing to cover childless couples and individuals in need.[23] Even if set at the poverty level ($4,275 for a nonfarm family of four in 1972), it would not assure that low income families could secure decent housing within their budgets. For the poverty line is based on a minimal food budget rather than an adequate shelter allowance.

The Housing Goal

When Congress passed the comprehensive Housing Act of 1949, it set forth a declaration of national policy: "The realization as soon as feasible of a goal of a decent home in a suitable living environment for every American family." To a systems analyst, this could not be termed an operational goal because the time period is ambiguous—as soon as feasible, standards of decency and suitability are not specified, and the required volume of housing by price or rent level is unstated. But most home builders and public housers are not systems analysts. Year after year they went back to the Congress, pointed to the goal, and asked for more funds to carry out the commitment. Even President Kennedy, in his 1961 message on housing, made reference to this 1949 policy as one which the Congress had announced "with great vision." But he also appealed to a more encompassing objective: "Meeting these goals [of housing and community development] will contribute to the Nation's economic recovery and its long-term economic growth." Kennedy's message also pointed up other concerns: "a tragic waste" in the use of land, and the need to reserve open space for parks and recreation and to prevent building on flood plains. He also made a bid for more housing for moderate income families and an enlargement of the public housing program for low income families. The relationship of the housing effort to most of the larger goals discussed above comes through clearly in Kennedy's 1961 housing message and legislative program.

But we were not doing well enough. Production under the subsidized housing programs was relatively low. Riots and burning of property in Newark, Watts, Detroit, and other cities highlighted the wretched living conditions of blacks and poor people. The President's Commission on Civil Disorders, reporting its findings early in 1968, stated that nearly two-thirds of urban nonwhites live in neighborhoods marked by substandard housing and general blight. "For these citizens, condemned by segregation and poverty to live in the decaying slums of our central cities, the goal of a decent home and suitable environment is as far distant as ever."[24] In such districts, not only are many houses in substandard condition but they are also overcrowded, and rents are relatively high. "In nearly every disorder city surveyed," the Commission reported, "grievances related to housing were important factors in the structure of Negro discontent."[25] The Commission went on to recommend provision of 600,000 low and moderate income housing units within one year, and 6 million units over the following five years.

The idea of establishing official targets for housing in numerical terms had been gaining adherents since 1966. After five relatively good years for the home building industry, there came a sharp downturn in 1966 as credit was tightened to slow inflation. As noted earlier, housing starts fell by 20 percent—300,000 units—in 1966. No other major industry suffered a comparable cutback in output. Home builders and housing proponents felt that they had been made the sacrificial lamb by the administration's economic policy. Now they began to cast about for a way of protecting their interests when basic economic decisions are made by the federal government.

In November 1967, the National Association of Home Builders and its National Housing Center Council convened a planning conference on national housing goals. Representatives of more than forty private associations and public interest groups attended the meetings in Washington, along with observers and resource people from federal agencies, congressional committees, presidential advisory groups, and academic institutions. Strong support emerged for the setting of short- and long-term numerical goals in housing by the administration and the Congress. It was proposed that the President be required by law to make an annual statement of housing goals, progress toward the goals, and measures necessary to support the goals. The purpose of requiring quantitative targets, the conferees seemed to agree, was not to compel rigid adherence to a set of numbers but to keep housing continuously on the agenda of the top policy makers in government.

The numerical goal concept won the endorsement of two presidential advisory groups at work in 1967, the President's Committee on Urban Housing chaired by Edgar F. Kaiser, and the National Commission on Urban Problems headed by former Senator Paul H. Douglas. The Kaiser Committee was particularly influential in the determination of the quantitative targets actually called for in the Johnson administration's housing proposals.

The Housing and Urban Development Act of 1968 reaffirms the 1949 goal and "determines that it can be substantially achieved within the next decade by the construction or rehabilitation of twenty-six million housing units, six million of these for low and moderate income families." That act also requires the President to submit a housing report to the Congress each year. The report must compare actual results during the preceding year with the objectives set for that year. Recognizing the close dependence of housing activity upon federal economic policy, the legislation stipulates that the annual report provide an analysis of the monetary and fiscal policies of the government for the coming year that are required to achieve the objectives of the housing plan.[26]

Measurable goals are usually a problem for the program manager. They make him accountable in very specific terms to the legislators, the interest groups, and the public. The housing targets spelled out by the Congress and the Johnson people in 1968 became the responsibility of a new administration in the following year. President Nixon asked the country to lower its voice and reduce its expectations. The admonition certainly applied to housing. The incoming administration was far more concerned with restraining inflationary pressures than in expanding social programs like housing. Once again a tight monetary policy fell heavily upon housing producers. In addition, budget requests for housing and urban development were cut below the Johnson recommendations for Nixon's first full fiscal year (July 1969 to June 1970). As a result, housing production fell short of the housing targets. This was conceded in the Second Annual Goals Report, the first accounting required under law of the Nixon administration's performance in housing: "Construction of conventionally built and rehabilitated units during the 2 years [July 1, 1968 to June 30, 1970] totals only about 3 million units, which is about 17 percent less than the initial target for such units . . . Total subsidized housing production during the first 2 years of the goals period will fall more than 200,000 units or 30 percent short of the initial targets set a year ago."[27] This Goals Report also indicated that henceforth mobile homes would be included as a specific source of units to meet the ten-year goals. Prior to that time, statisticians in the Bureau of the Census and the Department of Housing and Urban Development had not included mobile homes in its tabulations on housing production. Inclusion of mobile homes, being produced at an annual rate of about a half million units in the early seventies, could make a large difference in the assessment of housing performance in relation to the goals.

Housing production was boosted in 1971 and 1972 as slack in the economy permitted a shift in resources to housing. A more detailed examination of performance during this entire period will be made later.

Concluding Thoughts

We have shown that there are primary ("meta") goals that transcend many sectors and interests. Lesser if important social objectives such as decent homes for all must be pursued within these major societal concerns. It is a matter of common knowledge, however, that some of the big goals have more clout than others. Economic stability and high employment have been more compelling concerns, it is clear, than a fair distribution of income.

Indeed, it is not even possible to demonstrate beyond a quarrel that a particular goal belongs in the primary category. We interpret the significance of laws, community behavior, and social history from a philosophical perspective. In the last analysis, it is a value judgment. Still, a good case can be made for the goals discussed in this chapter: full employment and stable economic growth; environmental protection; equal opportunity; and a fair distribution of income. They have been stressed here because there is a tendency to focus too quickly on "programs." Programs are means, how things are done. But we also must ask: What for? "Ours is a civilization," Merton has written, "committed to the quest for continually improved means to carelessly examined ends."[28]

How do we choose between the higher goals when they conflict—as between exploitation of lower cost energy (economic growth) and environmental protection? Or between a larger production of low income housing on segregated sites or a smaller or zero production in areas that would have a mix of income and racial groups? From political scientists we can get the idea of compromise and accommodation, from economists the notion of trade-offs and compensation for damages. But this is not an assignment for technicians; it is the responsibility of political leaders. To clarify the choices, the American public is more likely to turn to journalists and opinion makers than to social scientists. And a President may look to a commission of public men and women. These in turn may call upon specialists and technical experts. But even a presidential commission may not be listened to. Relatively few white Americans accepted the conclusion of the President's Commission on Civil Disorders that racism has been institutionalized in this country and therefore whites bear a heavy responsibility for riots and other manifestations of black discontent.

More recently, President Nixon refused to endorse his Population Commission's recommendation that abortions be made available on request to any woman who wishes to be free of the burden of unwanted childbearing.

The Population Commission faced some of the most delicate and difficult value and goal conflicts that any group may confront. Their words offer perspective on the kinds of questions raised in this chapter:

Given the diversity of goals to be addressed . . . how are specific population policies to be selected? As a Commission and as a people, we need not agree on all the priorities if we can identify acceptable policies that speak in greater or lesser degree to all of them.

We have come to appreciate the delicate complexities of the subject and the difficulty, even the impossibility, of solving the problem, however defined, in its entirety and all at once.

For our part, it is enough to make population explicit on the national agenda . . . to sort out the issues, and to propose how to start toward a better state of affairs.[29]

In that spirit we can conclude this section and get on with the task.

5 Government Housing Programs

Let us look more closely at the housing programs—what they are and how they work. In earlier chapters we have seen that housing programs evolved piecemeal and in most cases with several purposes in mind. The low-rent public housing program, for example, was intended to provide construction jobs and to clear slums as well as to improve the living conditions of low income families. The FHA mortgage insurance programs induced financial institutions to resume investment in mortgages on houses mostly for middle and upper middle income families. At the same time it stimulated home building activity and reinforced the shaky lending industry. As a result, about nine million families were helped to obtain new homes or apartments between 1935 and 1970. Housing was one of the objectives of the urban renewal program, along with the removal of obsolescent structures and the rebuilding of the city's tax base.

Federal housing programs are not limited to subsidies for moderate and lower income families nor are they all administered by "housing" agencies. While most of this chapter will be devoted to an examination of what are usually regarded as housing programs, it is useful at the outset to recognize other elements of the housing subsidy system.

Like Gaul, the housing subsidy system in the United States is divided into three parts: subsidies for the well-to-do, subsidies for moderate income people, and subsidies for the poor. Housing aids and subsidies are by no means confined to lower income families.

For the Rich and Well-off:

1. Property tax and mortgage interest deductions from the federal income tax. These helped more than twenty-seven million homeowners in 1971. Higher income homeowners benefit proportionately more than moderate and lower income homeowners, because these deductible items would otherwise be taxed at 50 to 70 percent as compared with 14 percent in the bottom tax bracket. The tax saving in 1971 from these tax deductions averaged $1,892 for each homeowning taxpayer in the $100,000 and over tax bracket compared with $130 for those in the $10,000-$15,000 class, $30 for the below $3,000 income class of homeowners, and zero for renters. In recent years, these interest and property tax deductions have cost the federal government between $4.5 and $5 billion in revenue each year.[1]
2. Depreciation allowances for apartment house owners including limited partners

who may never see the property but can take a pro rata share of the depreciation against other income.
3. High reserves against losses on bad debts for savings and loan associations; and exemption from corporate income taxation of real estate trusts that pass on the bulk of their earnings to share holders (although the dividends are fully taxable as personal income). Tax preferences to savings and loan associations and mutual savings banks reduced federal revenues by $400 million in 1971.[2]
4. Open space grants and sewer and water grants to suburban communities that enhance amenity and market value of houses.
5. FHA insures mortgage amounts up to $33,000 on single family, owner-occupied homes; it also underwrites mortgages on multifamily housing for those with market level incomes. Benefits are not easily estimated because FHA sets qualitative standards on new construction as well as making a national market for its insured mortgages, thereby holding down mortgage interest rates. In 1971 about $8.4 billion in mortgage loans were insured or guaranteed by the FHA, the Veterans Administration, and the Farmers Home Administration. If the net interest costs were reduced by only one half of 1 percent, the savings would have been $42 million the first year. (Indirect benefits to borrowers of conventional loans may also accrue, since rates on such loans might be higher in the absence of competition from the federal insurance and guarantee programs.)

For Moderate Income Families:

1. FHA provides insurance on property improvement loans up to $5,000 for single family homes. In 1970 FHA insured 319,000 loans totaling $617 million. The bulk of these loans probably went to borrowers with modest incomes, since lenders do not need insurance on less risky home improvement loans made to higher income families. The loans are expensive, bearing interest rates of 8.8 to 10.6 percent in 1972.
2. Rehabilitation loans at 3 percent and up to $12,000 are available to some families of moderate income (generally between $4,000 and $10,000 income) on properties in urban renewal and code enforcement areas. This is a relatively small program, involving about 10,000 units a year in the whole country. (Some of these loans may have gone to low income homeowners in conjunction with rehabilitation grants.)
3. FHA has recently been authorized to insure loans on mobile homes. It also provides mortgage insurance on mobile home parks. Thus far, FHA's participation in this half-million units a year activity has been negligible.
4. Interest subsidies for some homeowners, most with incomes ranging from $4,000 to $8,000. This program (Section 235) is discussed in detail below.
5. Interest subsidies for rental and cooperative housing serving some families with incomes between $4,000 and $7,000 a year. This program (Section 236) is also discussed in more detail at a later point.
6. Mortgage insurance is provided by FHA to families displaced by governmental action or by natural disaster and to other moderate and low income families. Mortgages may be up to $21,000 with very small down payments. This program [Section 221(d)(2)] enabled almost 92,000 families to secure existing houses and about 3,400 families to purchase new houses in 1970. The median income of

families purchasing homes under this program was $10,000; one out of four had an income under $8,000, which is close to the "moderate income" upper limit.
7. Grants are made to localities for rehabilitation or code enforcement in selected neighborhoods, usually those occupied by people of modest income. The federal aid may be used for minor municipal improvements in streets, lighting, tree plantings, and the like.
8. Rural residents of modest means are aided by programs of the Farmers Home Administration in the Department of Agriculture. Interest supplement payments can bring the interest rate down to 1 percent on new and rehabilitated houses as well as on existing houses in good condition. For the fiscal year ending June 1973, such aids were expected to help 133,000 moderate and lower income families in rural areas.[3]

For Low Income Families:

1. Public assistance payments by all levels of government were estimated to total $12.3 billion in the fiscal year ending June 1973. More than 16 million persons received the aid, including 12.6 million children and adults under aid to families with dependent children, 2.3 million elderly, and 1.3 million permanently disabled and blind persons.[4] If 33 percent of these payments were spent on shelter, approximately $4 billion in welfare funds went for housing. This is undoubtedly the largest "housing subsidy" program for the poor.[a] Unlike most other housing subsidy programs, however, welfare payments do not assure that the families will occupy decent housing; in fact, over 50 percent can find or afford only substandard or overcrowded dwellings.[5] These programs are administered by the Department of Health, Education, and Welfare and its state and local counterparts, not by HUD.
2. The low-rent public housing program, discussed below.
3. The rent supplement program, detailed at a later point.
4. An assortment of relatively small federal insurance and grant programs are limited primarily to low income families. These include mortgage insurance to enable families who are marginal credit risks to purchase homes (Section 237); mortgages on houses in older, declining urban neighborhoods (Section 223 e); and grants up to $3,500 to help low income families rehabilitate their homes (Section 115), a program that helped only 10,000 families per year. (Some of these families also received 3 percent loans and have already been counted in the Section 312 program described above.)
5. Relocation assistance to families displaced by governmental actions should perhaps be included here since many of the displacees are low income households. Under the Uniform Relocation Assistance and Land Acquisition Policies Act of 1970, such displacees could receive moving expenses; tenants could get up to $4,000 to help them in renting decent dwellings or in making down payments on homes; and up to $15,000 could go to displaced homeowners to assist in acquiring a decent, comparable replacement dwelling.

---

[a] I am indebted to Dr. Louis Rosenburg for calling this to my attention. Rosenburg is a collaborator with Professor William G. Grigsby and others at the University of Pennsylvania in a major study entitled *Poverty and Housing* to be published in 1974.

6. Grants for neighborhood facilities may be made in poverty areas for buildings that will house health, recreational, or social service activities. This program funded at about $40 million a year has helped finance about 100 centers a year in different cities of the country.
7. The Model Cities Program, supported at a level of about $500 million a year in 1971 and 1972. This program, in which about 150 cities were participating at the start of 1971, was intended to bring together physical and social rehabilitation activities in the poorest districts containing about 10 percent of the local population. Under a "planned variations" approach introduced in July 1971, Model Cities funds in 20 selected cities may be extended throughout the city rather than be limited to the districts with the highest incidence of poverty and other social problems; and local chief executives were given review authority over all federal aids prior to use in their cities.

These changes would seem to permit a diversion of funds from the poorest sections to less impoverished neighborhoods and to give city hall more opportunity to spread the benefits among a wider group of citizens. But this would become moot if the Nixon administration proposal to convert seven programs (including urban renewal and Model Cities) into a single special revenue sharing fund were adopted. Communities would then be able to use such funds according to their own priorities. The net effect would likely be a thinner application of aids in many areas, with the poorest neighborhoods losing some of their funds under priorities set by earlier legislation such as the community action program and Model Cities. Under an alternative bill passed by the Senate in 1972 but not enacted, Model Cities would have been retained as a separate program and not folded into a consolidated block grant.

It is not possible to tally up the "subsidies" to the high, moderate, and low income groups. What is evident, however, is that the well-to-do receive very substantial benefits in the nature of tax preferences. A heavy proportion of HUD and Farmers Home Administration housing payments go to families in the moderate income range of $4,000 to $8,000. The people in poverty who receive aid for housing get most of it through welfare payments rather than through recognized housing aids for those of low income such as public housing.

Housing Programs for Moderate and Low Income Families

1. Interest subsidies for home ownership (Section 235) are available to some families of moderate income. Incomes of eligible families range about a third higher than admission incomes for public housing in each locality. The median income of families receiving such a subsidy at the end of 1971 was about $6,300; only 4 percent of the aided families had an income below $4,000. Participating families have to pay a minimum of 20 percent of their income (less $300 per child) toward principal, interest, taxes, and hazard insurance. The mortgage loan is obtained through a private lender at the market rate (about 7 percent in 1972 plus 0.5 percent FHA insurance premium). The federal subsidy, paid to the mortgage lender, can bring down the interest cost to the participant to as low as 1 percent depending upon the amount necessary to keep the family's housing expenses at no more than 20 percent of income. (Costs of utilities and maintenance and repairs must be borne by the family.) A typical household aided by this program at the end of 1971 had purchased a new house valued at about $18,000 and had monthly mortgage payments of $175. The family paid perhaps $95 a month and received a subsidy of $80 a month. If the family's adjusted income increases by $50 a month after several years, the subsidy will be reduced by $10 a month. If a family's income rises to a level sufficient to meet the entire mortgage payment with 20 percent of its income, it may remain in the house but is no longer entitled to receive any subsidy.

Who initiates a subsidy agreement? The bulk of them are negotiated by knowledgeable developers and builders who purchase sites, plan the developments, and seek fund reservations from HUD. There is nothing, however, to prevent a resourceful purchaser from locating an acceptable house on his own and seeking a loan and subsidy through a bank or savings and loan association.

The 235 program has grown rapidly since it was introduced in 1968. More than 440,000 families were participating by the end of calendar year 1972. The projected production level for the fiscal year ending June 1973 was 165,000 units under HUD auspices. Another 107,000 new units were targeted for the same period by the Farmers Home Administration under a comparable program (Section 502) that operates in nonmetropolitan communities of 10,000 persons or less.[6]

The budget impact of such programs grows each year as more units are added to the aggregate requiring annual subsidy payments. By fiscal year 1973 the annual budget outlay for HUD's home ownership program under Section 235 was approaching half a billion dollars. Demand for such housing is far in excess of appropriations, according to HUD.[7] This is not surprising in view of the fact that some twelve million families had incomes in the eligibility range of $4,000-$8,000 in 1971.

2. Interest subsidies for rental and cooperative housing (Section 236) were also authorized under 1968 legislation. This is the principal federal program for direct housing aid to renter households with incomes above public housing levels but insufficient to pay the full market rentals on new construction. The 236 program was intended to replace two earlier ones—the below-market interest rate program [Section 221 (d) (3)] enacted in 1961 and the direct loan program for the elderly [Section 202] which dates back to 1959. The income limits are 135 percent of public housing admission incomes in the locality; but there are provisions for going higher in some circumstances as well as going lower by including families who receive rent supplements under another program. Families are expected to pay 25 percent of their adjusted income toward the full economic rent. The subsidy takes the form of a payment of part of the interest cost on the mortgage loan and varies down to 1 percent depending upon the tenant's income. Some lower income families may pay more than 25 percent of their income because the maximum interest supplement may not be sufficient to bridge the gap. The law assigns a priority to those displaced by urban renewal or other governmental actions. Older individuals and handicapped persons may be accommodated, as well as other families in the eligible income class.

The median income of families actually occupying such housing in the latter part of 1971 was about $5,000 (apart from those receiving rent supplements). The income range served varied from place to place and by size of household, but most families had incomes between $4,000 and $7,000. A typical two-bedroom unit in a Northern city had a full market rent of $210 a month and a basic rent (at 1 percent interest) of $140. The maximum subsidy in this case, $70 a month or $840 a year, was close to the national average.

Who are the sponsors or initiators? Nonprofit groups such as churches, labor unions, or hospitals may sponsor a 236 development; cooperatives may be formed for this purpose; and builders or long-term profit-motivated investors can take the initiative. Despite the difficulties in applying for a project and carrying it through to completion, many builders and other businessmen have lined up to participate because of the lucrative possibilities for rapid tax depreciation and other inducements. The profit-motivated developer is limited to a 6 percent cash return on the equity amount approved by HUD. But some are able to get the site cost approved at substantially more than the amount recently paid. More important, some investors are able to use or parcel out the accelerated depreciation allowances among limited partners whose high incomes from other sources make such offsets very attractive. To an equity investor in the 50 percent tax bracket, the average annual return on such a project over the first five years has been estimated to be 23 percent.[8] The project itself, if properly located and attractively designed, has a virtually guaranteed market because the rents are substantially below those in comparable properties for qualified tenants. Thus it is understandable that applications or preapplication inquiries exceed available funding by a ratio of more than two to one. Builders operating through limited-return companies have initiated roughly two-thirds of the projects, with nonprofit groups and cooperatives accounting for the rest.

Management of these projects has become a worrisome problem for HUD officials. The department put into effect in early 1972 a new set of project selection criteria, one of which is "provision of sound housing management" for multifamily housing. HUD presumably recognizes that a subsidized development generally requires larger management expenditures than conventional developments, especially in the early years when the pattern of management-tenant relations is being set. Some tenants may need social services and counseling; some tenants may not pay their rent promptly; others may abuse the property. And there may be a need to deal with tenants councils or militant neighborhood groups. But the subsidy formula does not provide any extra amount for management services, nor adjustments over the years for higher-than-estimated costs of maintenance and repairs. In fact, management fees have been set too low because they are based on rents paid by the tenants rather than the full economic rents.

Moreover, there is no large pool of real estate managers sensitive to the problems of lower income families as well as skilled in property management. Experience with the predecessor rental program, 221 (d)(3), suggests that weak management and inflexible subsidies (and relatively fixed incomes of tenants) may prove the undoing of many such developments, with eventual foreclosures and acquisition by the federal government.[9] The quick turnover of ownership of some 236 projects shortly after completion implies that certain developers have only a short-term outlook with respect to such ventures.

Site selection and tenant selection are almost as important in connection with moderate income programs such as 236 as with public housing. Projects that are located in all-black neighborhoods are not likely to have white occupants. Following the *Shannon* and *Gautreaux* decisions by federal courts in 1970 and 1971, HUD administrators stepped up their efforts to locate new subsidized projects outside of racially impacted areas. But the federal government cannot deliver suitable sites to sponsors, and localities and neighborhoods outside the black ghettos have been effective in keeping subsidized projects out, especially if they suspected a mixed racial occupancy. When subsidized developments are erected in suburban communities, they seem to be rented up quickly to people in the immediate area. While hard data are not available on the racial distribution of tenants by location of project, it appears that relatively few inner-city nonwhites have found their way into subsidized developments in suburban areas.

Despite these actual or potential difficulties, the new subsidized rental program under Section 236 picked up fast. Total production to the end of calendar year 1972 was estimated at 392,000 dwelling units. Most of these were new units but there were also some rehabilitated units. The projected production level for the fiscal year ending June 1973 was 175,000. The annual payments for all units produced under Section 236 through June 1973 are estimated at $400 million.

At the end of 1972 this program provided housing for only a fraction of the families in the income classes that were eligible. There were almost nine million families with incomes between $4,000 and $7,000. If every one of these families wanted a subsidized housing unit either under this program or the companion 235 program, each family would have a one out of ten chance of getting one.

3. Rent supplements. To understand this program, we must recall its legislative history. When President Johnson advanced the proposal in his legislative package for housing early in 1965, he referred to rent supplements as "the most crucial new instrument in our effort to improve the American city."[10] It was to be a relatively big program. The target set in the President's housing message was 500,000 units over the following four years. Who would be eligible? The new program was to be limited to families displaced by governmental action or living in substandard housing. It was aimed mainly at moderate income families.

Rent supplements were viewed as a substitute for the moderate income housing programs that required an extension of federal credit: 221(d)(3) and the elderly housing program known as Section 202. These two programs required capital loans by the government and loomed large in the federal budget. The Bureau of the Budget wanted them out and it had the support of a White House task force that had submitted its report the previous fall. The administration viewed rent supplements as a substitute for these programs but not for public housing for low income people, which was to be continued and expanded. The Johnson people proposed that the bottom income for rent supplements would be the maximum income limit for admission for low income families to public housing in each locality. For the country as a whole, this meant that the new program would serve nonelderly households with incomes between $3,500 and $6,000 and elderly with incomes between $3,000 and $5,000.

This seemed inconsistent with the Johnson administration's recently declared War on Poverty. It was Senator Paul Douglas, as we have noted earlier, who insisted that the housing needs of the poor were more compelling than those of the moderate income group. One chart submitted by administration witnesses showed that almost half of the five million renter households with incomes under $2,000 lived in substandard dwellings. The lowest income people in substandard housing were clearly more numerous than those in the $3,000-$6,000 income group. The housing subcommittees thereupon modified the proposal to make rent supplements available to poor families in the same income range as those eligible for public housing.[11] The Congress as a whole endorsed the change, although the margin for rent supplements was very slim.

Now the administration had to go before the appropriations committees and request funds to operate the programs. At this stage the opposition firmed. Suburbanites and small town people, North and South, viewed rent supplements as a tool by which the federal government might infiltrate lower class blacks into the white suburbs and all-white neighborhoods of cities and towns. So the appropriations committees gave the local people veto power over rent supplement projects by requiring that each community in which rent supplement developments were proposed must have a workable program for community improvement or grant specific approval to the proposed site. This meant that some localities that were rich enough or stubborn enough to refuse other federal aids such as urban renewal (for which the workable program was a prerequisite) could veto any rent supplement project by doing nothing.

Since its inception, the rent supplement program has received only a trickle of funds. By the end of calendar year 1970, after five years of operation, only 42,000 families were receiving payments through this program. The annual production level for rent supplement units ranged from 14,000 to 20,000 between fiscal years 1971 and 1973. In addition, some families lived in houses financed under other subsidy programs such as Section 236. About a third of all rent supplement payments committed between 1966 and 1971 were piggy-back payments with other aided housing. Payments are made to housing sponsors on behalf of these families to bridge the gap between the required market (or interest-subsidized) rent and 25 percent of the family's income. The median income of those assisted through rent supplements in 1970 was about $2,200.

4. Public housing is the Grande Dame of federally subsidized housing for low income families in the United States. It was started in 1937 and flowered for about five years until the war effort reduced such construction to a trickle. The program was given a boost by the Housing Act of 1949 which called for the construction of some 810,000 units over the following six years. But annual construction during the decade of the fifties averaged only 28,000. During that period public housing became less attractive to lower income working class families and the local housing authorities found themselves absorbing more and more problem families. As the Eisenhower administration closed at the end of 1960, there were 478,000 units of public housing under management in the country. While the larger cities contained the bulk of these projects, over a thousand communities, large and small, had local housing authorities. In 1960 blacks occupied 47 percent of all low rent units in the country. More attention was being directed to housing for the elderly. Some 17 percent of the 1960 occupants were elderly families or single persons.

This shift of public housing toward the elderly was a response to a real need; but it was also an attempt to reduce opposition to public housing in many localities. During the fifties the local housing authorities encountered increasing difficulty in obtaining suitable sites because of the identification of low rent housing with blacks and welfare families—the "undeserving poor." In 1960 there were 456 projects aggregating almost 79,000 units for which federal funds were reserved but not yet under construction.[12] Many of these projects were stalled by local or neighborhood opposition. In Cleveland and other cities, clergymen and elected officials were shouted off the platform when they pleaded with residents to let the proposed low rent housing be built.

In violence-prone Chicago, demonstrations, brick-throwing and arson took place over a number of months in 1953 and 1954 when the Chicago Housing Authority permitted four black families to move into an existing project known as Trumball Park Homes. At the height of the disturbances by whites in the neighborhood and white tenants of the housing project, as many as 1,200 policemen were needed to maintain a semblance of order. After nine months of living in fear, the pioneer black family (headed by a mail carrier and a World War II veteran) took the advice of the police and moved out. Not long after, Elizabeth Wood, the plucky executive director of the Chicago Housing Authority, was dismissed.[13]

Before we examine the experience with public housing from 1960 on, let us look at the formula and mechanics of the program. The local housing authorities that administer public housing are mostly quasi-governmental bodies authorized under state law to enter into contracts with the federal government to develop or operate low rent housing. Under an annual contributions contract with the federal agency, the local housing authority obtains a temporary development loan and subsequent to construction a yearly payment to cover the interest and amortization on bonds issued to raise the long-term capital funds. The bonds are attractive to higher income taxpayers because the interest is exempt from federal income taxation and repayment is assured by the federal government. Localities are expected to make a contribution by preferential treatment of the real estate. Commonly this takes the form of a payment by the housing authority in lieu of property taxes to the local taxing bodies of 10 percent of the shelter rent collected from the tenants. The rents charged tenants were expected to be sufficient to cover operating expenses, including heat and other utilities, management services, and upkeep and repair of the property.

Tenants were to pay no more than 20 percent of their income for rent. This was to pose a serious problem to the housing authorities when they were squeezed between rising operating expenses and relatively fixed continued occupancy limits. The stringent limits on income compelled the departure of some tenants with rising earnings who might have stayed and paid a higher rent and prevented some less-poor families from moving in. In the early years, the subsidy formula prevented the housing authorities from accepting any substantial proportion of very low income families since the rents collected from such people could not pay a pro rata share of the operating costs. In the 1960s the statute was amended to permit the federal government to pay extra monthly allowances on behalf of low income elderly, displaced households, and certain other categories of very low income households to enable the housing authorities to accept them without running at a deficit. Still, as the buildings aged, major replacements of heating plants and other systems became necessary and few authorities had reserves for such purposes. One by one they turned to the Congress for special appropriations to cover such outlays. Legislation enacted in 1969 and 1970 generalized the authority to provide federal funds for property improvements.

Passage of the Brooke amendment in 1969 presented a new difficulty. This stipulated that no family in federally-assisted public housing should pay more than 25 percent of its income in rent. No one could quarrel with this on grounds of equity but, since insufficient federal funds accompanied the requirement, a number of housing authorities found themselves forced into operating deficits. For fiscal year 1973 Congress provided $170 million in operating subsidies. The Senate Appropriations Committee said this would not be enough and directed HUD to submit a request for supplemental appropriations later in the year. Under pressure, the Nixon administration agreed in October 1972 to add another $100 million to help cover the operating deficits of local housing authorities, bringing the total to $270 million for fiscal year 1973.

Let us pick up again with the situation in 1961. The public housing program was then viewed by administration officials and many congressmen as a broken arrow. Kennedy requested authorization for an additional 100,000 units but he also asked for demonstration funds to experiment with alternatives. In granting this request, the congressional committees specifically assigned the demonstration program to the Administrator of the Housing and Home Finance Agency rather than to its constituent unit, the Public Housing Administration, which ran the public housing program. It seems clear that the Congress regarded PHA as too tired and beleaguered to come up with good alternatives to its regular program.

From 1961 through 1967 about 200,000 additional units were made available for occupancy, an annual rate of 29,000 housing units. From 1964 on the local housing authorities were encouraged by legislation and administrative actions to acquire existing houses and rehabilitate them or to lease good space from private owners for public housing tenants. This was particularly appropriate in local housing markets with a substantial volume of vacant dwellings. But the bulk of the additions to the public housing inventory continued to be new units. A new approach known as Turnkey gave a big boost to production. Turnkey permits a local housing authority to contract with a private developer to purchase or lease a given number of units when completed at a price agreed to before construction. This idea, which originated within the public housing staff in Washington, unleashed a much larger flow of production. From 1968 through 1970, about 224,000 units were made available for occupancy. About three-fifths of the 1970 production of new units came via Turnkey. Some 300,000 more units were projected from 1971 through fiscal year 1973. Of these, about two-thirds were to be new and owned by the local housing authorities; the remainder were to be leased units in accordance with a 1970 legislative requirement that 30 percent of the federal funds be allocated to leased housing. The average direct federal subsidy per year for new public housing in 1971 was about $1,500 per household.

At the start of 1972 more than forty-five hundred localities in the country were participating in the low rent public housing program. Some 993,000 units were under management and another 117,000 were under construction or rehabilitation. For a program that had been virtually written off ten years earlier, public housing was showing remarkable staying power. To lessen community opposition, the federal and local people tilted the tenancy markedly toward the elderly: from 17 percent in 1960 to 28 percent in 1965 to 38 percent in 1970. Much of the credit for this shift was due to the efforts of Marie McGuire, Public Housing Commissioner from 1961 to 1966. She also gave support to efforts to improve the esthetics of public housing and to humanize its relations with tenants.

What are the income levels and related characteristics of tenants in public housing? The median income for nonelderly families who moved in during early 1970 was about $3,100 and $3,600 for those in continued occupancy; for elderly, about $1,800. Nearly half of the nonelderly move-ins were receiving some form of financial assistance; among the elderly move-ins, about half received only old age, survivors, and disability insurance paid by social security, but most of the others received some combination of social security payments and other benefits or aid. While low income households displaced by urban renewal or other governmental action have a priority for admission, only 13 percent of the 1970 move-ins were displaced families. About 30 percent of recently admitted households had three or more minor children; in 1960 these larger families made up 42 percent of the total. The relative (not absolute) decline of larger families reflected the gains of elderly households.[14]

As with many social programs, public housing was introduced with unrealistic expectations. In the 1930s a number of studies had found high correlations between districts of bad housing and tuberculosis, prostitution, and crime. Substandard housing was thought to be the cause of many of these problems or at least a major contributor. The indicated social response was to clear the slums and place the former residents into sanitary and well-managed housing developments. As Abner Silverman has pointed out in a penetrating interpretation of the public housing program, this seemed to work in the golden years between 1937 and 1942.[15] But the first families of public housing were carefully selected from among the working poor. Many of these families moved out on their own volition or were forced to move under administrative orders laid down by Washington in 1945 to remove over-income tenants. According to Silverman, this "purge" reduced the proportion of ineligible families from about 25 percent in 1946-48 to 11 percent by mid-1950.[16] During the 1950s an increasing proportion of public housing tenants were recruited from among people who were caught up in the culture of poverty. They brought their problems with them into public housing and the problems did not go away. Thus ended the innocent hypothesis of environmental determinism—that good housing would reshape its occupants into socially acceptable people.

Some critics have seemed to argue a variation of this hypothesis: many of the public housing projects were so dense and so high that families with children could not live decently in them. A glaring example was the Pruitt-Igoe project in St. Louis, built in 1955-56. This was a complex of thirty-three eleven-story buildings containing 2,870 units standing on fifty-six gross acres of land in the core of a slum area. Originally about 10,000 people were housed in Pruitt-Igoe and half of them were under thirteen years of age. Children could not be supervised; crime and vandalism were rife in this area. By the end of 1972 only six buildings containing 650 units were still occupied and twenty-four buildings were entirely empty. In 1972, three buildings were demolished by decision of federal and local officials, their social death having cut short the potential economic life of the structures.[17] In 1973 it was decided to tear down all of the structures in Pruitt-Igoe.

In its formative years public housing attracted some unusually able and dedicated administrators and project managers, people like Ernest Bohn in Cleveland, Langdon Post in New York, Elizabeth Wood in Chicago, Warren Jay Vinton, Abner Silverman and Philip Klutznick in Washington, and scores of others. That generation is mostly gone from active roles in public housing (although some remain remarkably energetic in other fields). The new breed of public housers are perhaps less likely to participate in the political forum, but intuitively one senses that they have good technical skills and a good measure of commitment to the program. Those who initiate and operate public housing programs at the local level undoubtedly have a longer-term outlook than many of the limited-return builders of Section 236 housing.

To keep their projects and the program viable, however, will not be easy. Three-fifths of the present tenants are on low fixed incomes —virtually all of the elderly and many of the nonelderly residents. Almost half of the nonelderly families constitute broken homes and three out of ten are without a worker in the family. For such people, a combination of social services is required, an approach that was tried between 1962 and 1967 but without adequate coordination or sufficient funds. Efforts to enable tenants to have a voice in management policies and practices are being stepped up. Tenants need to feel that they have a stake in the neighborhood. Yet, as they become more assertive, they are bound to compound the difficulties of public housing officials and project managers.

A 1970 study in Baltimore, cited by Silverman, reached the conclusion that "welfare mothers whose grants are too small to pay the rent or buy enough food for the month cannot be salvaged by case work, however well intentioned."[18] But the Puritan ethic toward the "undeserving poor" is now deeply implanted in many working and middle class Americans. The main problem for public housers, quite possibly, is that America does not like its poor.

Production Levels and Goals

If Rip Van Winkle were a housing expert who fell asleep in 1960 and awoke a dozen years later, he would be astonished at the volume of subsidized housing produced or made available in recent years. He might recall that there were fewer than a half million public housing units in 1960 when told that there were about one million at the end of 1972, with 100,000 additional households being accommodated each year. He might be intrigued to learn about the interest subsidy programs for moderate income families, which generated more than 800,000 units from 1968 through 1972. He probably would not be surprised to hear that the Department of Agriculture had persuaded the Congress, historically rural-minded, to authorize similar interest subsidies for farm families and rural residents of communities of 10,000 or less. He would surely know that the bulk of the Census-defined substandard houses are in rural areas, and that the 300,000-odd homes newly added under the Farmers Home programs since 1968 made only a modest contribution to the housing needs in these areas. All students of housing, awake or asleep, probably experience some future shock in seeing subsidized housing production reach levels of nearly 500,000 a year.

Housing production, according to the President's Fourth Goals Report issued in mid-1972, was running ahead of the production path outlined in the Second Goals Report of 1970. Unsubsidized construction was said to be 17 percent ahead of schedule for the first four fiscal years of the goal decade. Subsidized construction was estimated at 92 percent of the target for the first four years, but subsidized rehabilitation was only 67 percent of the hoped for level.[19]

High housing production figures do not prove that good living arrangements are being provided. The President's Fourth Housing Goals Report expressed concern about the quality of the residential environments being produced: Where are they located? Are public services adequate? Will the new developments of rental housing be well managed? Can lower income home buyers take good care of their houses? There is also the issue of equity: Who is getting the subsidized housing since only a fraction of the eligibles can be served? And who should get it? The Housing Goals Report also raised questions about the adequacy of private efforts to maintain the existing supply of houses. These are matters that will be taken up in the following chapters.

A Word on Housing Finance

While the emphasis in this chapter has been on the direct aids for moderate and lower income housing, we must not lose sight of the large federal role in housing finance. Total housing starts were held below 1.5 million a year in 1969 and 1970 as the administration struggled to restrain inflation by means of tight credit. Interest rates on home mortgages soared to 8.5 percent with yields as high as 9.3 percent due to discounting in early 1970. Private funds were channeled away from housing-oriented thrift institutions in 1969 and early 1970 to Treasury bills and bonds and into corporate and municipal bonds. The crunch on housing would have been much more severe but for two reasons: the upsurge of subsidized housing production and the actions of federal agencies to direct funds into this sector. These took the form of mortgage purchases by the Federal National Mortgage Association and the Government National Mortgage Association, mostly in support of subsidized housing production; advances to savings and loan associations by the Federal Home Loan Banks; and mortgage loans by the Farmers Home Administration. Some $11.5 billion were thus channeled into housing in the first fourteen months of the Nixon administration. This federal support accounted for 45 percent of the total net flow of residential mortgage lending during that period.[20]

The turn came in the fall of 1970 as the economy moved into a recession. The Federal Reserve made credit more plentiful and families and businesses increased their savings. Savings and loans and other thrift institutions had record inflows of deposits in 1971 and were thus able to fuel the spurt in housing production. In short, total housing production is primarily dependent upon government policies affecting the overall availability and cost of credit. In periods of ample credit during the past decade, effective demand seems to have been strong enough to sustain a production level of 1.5 to 2 million housing units a year. For several years the new subsidy programs and revisions in the public housing program added 350-450 thousand units a year, bringing total starts to the 2-2.5 million level that housing advocates dreamed of in the early sixties.

Yet there was a good deal of dissatisfaction with the existing programs and efforts. At the start of 1973 the Nixon administration suspended new commitments for subsidized housing. After a six-month study, the administration announced tentative support for housing allowances as a substitute for production-tied subsidies. In 1973, the housing subsidy system was still in flux.

6 Some Alternatives in Housing Policy

On the title page of his basic book *Principles of Economics* Alfred Marshall inscribed the epigraph, "Nature makes no great leaps." Economic evolution is a gradual process, he believed, and what may appear to be a sudden structural change at the hand of an inventor or financial genius was in fact long in the making.

Standing back from the swirl of numbers and names of housing programs and personalities, we see that the housing system of today is essentially an extension of the past. We continue to provide the recognized housing aids to and through the lenders and builders rather than to the consumers and users. We favor homeowners over renter families. Substantial hidden subsidies are given to the affluent. Some moderate income families receive housing aids, but relatively little goes to the people in deep poverty. The focus of present aids is on new production and major rehabilitation rather than on proper utilization and maintenance of existing housing. The Census Bureau clings to anachronistic measures of inadequacy such as lack of indoor toilets, although most urban slum dwellers have them. It does not determine, however, whether the plumbing is in working order.

So we are not likely to jettison all present approaches or ways of thinking about housing overnight. Still, the present system leaves much to be desired. New combinations and modifications are being explored on paper and in the field. The President's Housing Goals Report issued in 1972 spoke of the need to examine housing policies at three levels: housing programs, housing strategies, and housing in an environmental context. This chapter is concerned with the second level of discussion. Some alternatives available to policy makers and the community are considered.

In an Ideal World

In an economist's dream world, all households would be self-reliant and well-informed, and have sufficient income to secure all their basic needs for a comfortable life including decent housing. The families would deal in responsive markets for housing services with effective suppliers of residential space of all types. Households could choose among various locations and degrees of commitment from ownership to short-term tenancy. There would be no arbitrary restraints on any family's choice on ethnic or racial grounds. Behind the final markets for housing services would be a network of well organized intermediate markets: in the financing of transactions of existing properties, in the financing of improvements and rehabilitation of older structures, and in the short and long-term financing of new construction. Housing would be viewed by all as a stream of services from a stock of capital [credits to Professor Irving Fisher's *The Theory of Interest* (1930) and Morton Isler (1971)], and there would be sufficient reserves accumulated to replace existing housing at the end of its economic life.[1] Much of the new production would be viewed as replacement of existing capital with the remainder responding to growth in population and households. A portion of the replacement allowance would be earmarked for removal of the spent structure from its site, with governmental overview to assure this action by the owner.

In the production of new residential structures, the supply of the main factors would be marked by effective competition: in building materials, skilled labor, buildable land, and management. Suppliers would be well informed about the present and future demand for their services and products. Improvements in building techniques and land improvement methods could be introduced when justified in terms of cost reduction or qualitative improvements or both, without arbitrary restraints by suppliers or local governments. If the individual firms could not capture the benefits of expenditures for research and development because of their small place in the total market, there would be pooling arrangements or support by public funds.

In the Real World

Few of these conditions obtain in the final or intermediate markets for housing. Many families cannot be served by the private market because of insufficient income. How to bridge the gap—through transfers of cash or of services—is a major question. This issue is complicated by another one: how many are self-reliant households whose only need is more money? And how many are, for the present at least, incapable of operating as effective consumers? Some people are presently outside the private housing system: migratory farm workers, Indians living on reservations, jobless blacks in rural districts like the Delta in Mississippi. An unknown number of migratory young people, members of a counterculture, are conspicuously outside of the conventional housing system.

In the cities the nonmarket people first came to our attention as problem families, families whose difficulties did not go away when they were moved from a slum house to a public housing project. Today many of these people, both in and out of public housing, are welfare recipients, unwanted as neighbors or tenants. For such people, housing is only part of an adequate social response. The elderly underhoused need medical and social services, the fatherless families need day care facilities and father-substitutes. The hardcore unemployed need adequate shelter but much more. These disadvantaged groups all need much more help than they are now getting. Some probably can become effective households and housing consumers if they receive adequate income maintenance or jobs, but many cannot.

This suggests a way of thinking about housing policies. We should identify family types and population groups and determine which are self-reliant enough to function in the private market. For the self-reliant households we can ask: do they have sufficient income to be effective consumers? The remaining groups are dependent people who need much more than shelter: health care, family counseling, job training, or some other combination of social aids. For some of these people, shelter may have to be in institutional settings such as nursing homes, child care centers, work camps, or special residences.

Now on the supply side we would recognize the importance of the standing stock of seventy million housing units in satisfying the needs, along with the two to three million new houses that we hope to see produced each year. We would be quite concerned about the effective maintenance and turnover of existing houses. And we would want to have new units produced and occupied for the lowest possible unit costs at the standards deemed acceptable.

A chart will help clarify this (see Table 6-1). The indicated public approaches are shown in relation to particular family types or population groups. For self-reliant families with good incomes, the main public responses are those that will improve the market and hold down the unit cost of housing, thus enabling such families to get a better buy for their money. (Of course, most of these families are also holders of substantial equities in existing properties; they want better information and lower transfer costs in dealing with such property, but they would not welcome a sudden innovation in construction technology that would produce new units at much below current holding prices, thus undermining their capital values.) Such families also seek superior municipal services and public schools and most are prepared to pay the necessary taxes for them. Superior local services are an important element in maintaining the quality of life for these people.

A subgroup within the category of self-reliant families are nonwhites with good incomes. Almost one out of four black families had incomes of $12,000 or more in 1972 and could afford good housing. They would benefit from improvements in the real estate industry and from higher levels of public services, but must look to much stronger enforcement of laws against discrimination to secure access to better housing outside of all-black neighborhoods. Since many will settle for existing properties in neighborhoods of relatively high turnover, such families also have a special stake in vigorous

Table 6-1
Family Types and Indicated Public Approaches to Housing

Family Type	Income Supplementation	Social Assistance	Improved Housing Industry	Housing Code Enforcement	Equal Opportunity Enforcement	Improved Municipal Services
Self-Reliant						
Adequate income	—	—	XX	a	a	XX
Below market income	XX	—	X	XX	b	X
Dependent						
Elderly ill	X	XX	X			
Hardcore unemployed	X	XX	X			
Parentless children	X	XX	X			
Other dependent types	X	XX	X			

XX Means relatively heavy significance for the particular group.
X Denotes some importance for the particular group.
a Denotes importance for middle class black families.
b Denotes importance for below market income black families.

enforcement of housing codes that prevent overcrowding or misuse of housing.

For lower income families who are essentially self-reliant, the most important public response, some experts assert, would take the form of income supplementation. We can defer for the moment the question whether such added income should be in the form of a housing allowance or general income support. In this view, payments in cash are preferable to payments in kind, such as subsidized apartments, on grounds of self-respect and unrestricted choice by the family of housing and other budget items.[2] If subsidized housing is available, lower income families could have the option of taking some of their income support in this form. But one condition must be met: equity demands that all families in the same circumstances be treated in the same way. Income supplementation in cash ought to be across-the-board and adjusted to actual income. Under current housing programs, only a small proportion of the eligible families can presently be accommodated.

If these aided families are to get their money's worth as more effective competitors for existing housing, there must be much stronger enforcement of housing codes than is now the case in most cities. Minority families will find their income supplements partially dissipated unless fair housing laws are more vigorously administered. All such families, white and black, will benefit if the costs and prices of housing are lowered through a more efficient housing industry and housing market. And of course the income transfers can be lower, the lower the cost of securing decent housing. Improved municipal services including schools are of substantial importance to this group; to the extent that the value of the services exceeds the taxes such families pay, they would be receiving additional income in kind.

Then there are the dependents of our society. These are the people who cannot now cope for themselves and may not be able to for a long time or ever. They obviously need shelter, but as a service linked to other socially-provided services. Income transfers to or in behalf of such people, including dependent children, will be necessary, but they cannot be expected to function as effective consumers or households in the private market system. Improvements in the housing industry will affect them only indirectly in that the cost of facilities and operating expenses would be reduced or better accommodations and housing services could be provided to them for the same or less money.

There has been much discussion in recent years of housing allowances or housing-based income maintenance programs as *the* answer to the "housing problem." This has frequently been coupled with the derogation of direct housing aids for lower income families. A housing allowance or income maintenance plan would be a valuable approach but it could not do the whole job. Income supplements are at most a necessary but not sufficient condition to a comprehensive and effective housing approach. For lower income families who are self-reliant, housing allowances would have to be joined with measures to increase housing production and lower costs, to maintain existing neighborhoods, and to improve municipal services. For dependent people, those outside the market economy, measures that simply bolster effective demand are not going to be enough. Such people need much more before they can become self-reliant consumers. And all too many will never make it.

Why Government Assumes Responsibility

Why does government have to take on such a large role in a field like housing? There are three main reasons:

1. To make up for lack of information or competence among the members of the community. This is the basis for providing consumers and producers with information about safe building materials, the true charges on mortgages or installment loans, and changes in the cost of living.
2. To prevent or ameliorate inequitable arrangements such as wide disparities in the distribution of income, opportunity, or power. On these grounds, public education at the primary and secondary level is provided free of charge, welfare aid is extended, displaced workers are retrained, and subsidies are provided for housing lower income families.
3. To deal with the interdependence in the welfare of members of the community. Only by joining with others can the people who share a common territory provide themselves with mutually beneficial improvements that no one could obtain on his own, such as a transportation system. Similarly, people pool their efforts through government in preventing actions that are harmful to all, such as air pollution, the spread of communicable disease, crime, or neighborhood blight due to the failure of some owners or renters to maintain their properties.[3]

In our country the predominant view is that each family should be allowed to disburse its income as it sees fit. This suggests that measures to put a floor under the standard of living would involve cash transfers to lower income families. But some goods or services are deemed so important from the community's standpoint that they are singled out for subsidy or provided directly: public schooling for the young, medical care for the elderly, food for the poor. Housing makes the list, unchallengeably in the granting of tax preferences to homeowners, somewhat grudgingly in the case of rental housing for poor families.

Government involvement with housing has been justified not only on income grounds but because of the interdependence of all people who live in a limited space. Fires may spread from abandoned houses to occupied ones, rats may overrun adjoining blocks, and bad housing may contribute to ill health and lower worker productivity. Children have suffered toxic effects from nibbling at chipped paint containing lead. Workers and others who live in the vicinity of airports and expressways report getting insufficient sleep or rest.[4] Unpleasant and overcrowded housing contributes to the discontent of lower income people, which eventually may boil up in riots and looting—this was a conclusion reached in 1968 by the President's Commission on Civil Disorders based on interviews of riot area residents. While the links between inadequate housing or neighborhood facilities and social misbehavior and worker productivity are not definitively established, the public seems to have acknowledged a connection. The general principle of interdependence and spillover effects of bad housing and slums is broadly sensed and is one of the justifications for slum clearance and neighborhood rehabilitation efforts, building and housing codes, and controls over land use.

Thus government intervenes, but not always in a carefully studied way, sometimes in ways that enrich the operators and business interests more than the intended beneficiaries, and on occasion opening the door to graft and bribery. Criticisms and complaints are plentiful and sometimes come from surprising sources. In 1969 President Nixon publicly castigated his own employees as bureaucrats who seek more and more control, and called for federal revenue sharing in order to restore power to the local folks. Washington hands may dismiss such statements as rhetoric, although these remarks hardly help to raise the morale and efficiency of the federal civil service.

Another kind of criticism by the administration should be taken more seriously by the student of policy because it raises questions about the effectiveness of the main housing subsidy programs. The Fourth Housing Goals Report refers to the interest subsidy programs as "highly complex and completely untested" when they were adopted in 1968, and increasingly expensive.[5] An estimate by Donald Kummerfeld, a former Budget Bureau official, places the *annual* budget cost of HUD's subsidized housing (including public housing) at $8 to $10 billion by 1978, under conservative assumptions if the 1968-78 goal of providing six million additional housing units for lower income families is to be realized.[6]

One reason the subsidies are relatively high is that they are applied mainly to new units built to good standards. An alternative would be to rely on subsidies that make more use of existing housing. But the savings might be offset if prices of existing housing are bid up in a tight market or if they are more expensive to maintain. In addition, the bill would have to be higher to accommodate the lowest income people rather than those in the moderate income levels. Let us examine some of these issues more closely.

Who Should Get Subsidies?

It would seem to be axiomatic that a humane society like ours would provide help to all of its low income citizens. If the subsidy recognizes the need to maintain some minimal standard of living, it would have to allow for the cost of housing, which comes just behind food as the second most expensive budget item. Contract rent and utilities require on average about 16 to 18 percent of the budget of a four-person urban family on a very modest living standard, according to estimates of the Bureau of Labor Statistics. Adding in expenses for household operations and house furnishings brings the housing costs to almost 21 percent. For an elderly couple, the BLS estimates that housing expenses up to 35 percent are bearable because of lesser family obligations and less need for house furnishings.[7]

The President's Committee on Urban Housing (the Kaiser Committee) recommended in 1968 that government assistance should be provided to all persons who need help to afford the cost of modest, decent, safe, and sanitary housing—regardless of family size, age, marital status, or health.[8] Present housing programs generally overlook nonelderly single persons (other than college students) and have a disproportionately low number of units for very large families. While recent production levels under these programs have been impressive, in the aggregate they currently accommodate only a small fraction of all eligible households. If the Kaiser Committee's objectives were to be achieved, adequate housing would have to be provided either directly or through income transfers to enable all families and individuals living alone to purchase the minimum-decency living package.

Who are the underhoused or those paying a disproportionate amount for housing? They include but are not limited to the 25 million persons living below the stark poverty line. Studies by the Urban Institute indicate that there are closer to 45 million individuals involved, grouped into 13 to 17 million households. They are not a representative cross section of the population. Thirty-five to 40 percent of the households are single persons. Another 15 percent of these households are large families of six or more persons, containing 35 percent of all the individuals in the group (15 to 16 million individuals).[9] A disproportionate number, we can be sure, are nonwhites, households headed by women, and older people.

Not all of these households live in physically deficient houses. Some are in standard units but are overcrowded; the rest pay an excessive proportion of income for shelter. Low income homeowners figure prominently in the latter group, including many elderly homeowners.

By the end of 1972 about 15 percent of the households requiring aid lived in subsidized housing. If the ten-year goal of six million subsidized units were achieved today, almost half of the households in the income gap could be directly accommodated, while others might benefit indirectly as a result of the expanded housing supply.

In 1972-73 public assistance payments were going to some sixteen million persons. All of these people would probably require additional aid, and another thirty million or so would get housing benefits in one form or another.

How Much Should Families Pay for Housing?

The answer to the previous question presupposed the response to this one. The people who need subsidies from the government are those who would otherwise be compelled to spend too much of their income to secure adequate housing or would have to settle for unsatisfactory living accommodations. The old rule of thumb was that a family should spend no more than 25 percent of its income for housing. But for a very large family of moderate or low income, that could mean having to skimp on food, medical care, or other basics, let alone recreation or education. When the public housing program was getting started in the late 1930s, 20 percent of income was deemed a fair housing expense ratio for low income families. This was a good deal for families admitted to public housing in the early years since most of them had incomes under $1,500 a year and families in that range typically spent 27 to 30 percent or more on housing and household expenses.[10]

Current housing programs generally require occupants to pay 20 or 25 percent of income for rent. The higher ratio is stipulated for the rent supplement program and interest-subsidized rental housing (Section 236). In the latter program, income is figured before taxes and withholding of all adult members of the household from all sources, but excludes nonrecurring income and earnings of minors; also, 5 percent is disregarded to allow for payroll deductions and the base is further reduced by an allowance of $300 for each minor child. In practice, some families in this housing actually pay more than 25 percent because the maximum subsidy is based on a 1 percent interest rate on the mortgage and the resulting rent may still exceed a fourth of the family's income.

Even at 25 percent the rental burden is heavy for many households, especially large families of moderate or low income. This ratio is more than most families except the poorest actually spend for housing. A 1969 survey by the Survey Research Center of the University of Michigan found that contract rent was about 18 percent for the $3,000-$4,999 families, 15 percent for the $5,000-$7,499 group, and below 11 percent for families with incomes of $15,000 or higher. This is consistent with the standard family budgets prepared by the Bureau of Labor Statistics. The BLS modest budget for a four-person family in 1969 estimated rental costs, including heat, utilities, and insurance on household goods, at 16 percent of the total budget. The ratio was below 20 percent in all but two of the forty metropolitan areas studied by the BLS. The typical family budget was about $6,500, a level which would qualify a household for Section 236 housing in many localities.[11]

What these figures suggest is that current housing subsidy programs are not overly generous. Higher income families who rent typically spend much less than 25 percent of income on housing. Families with children, in modest circumstances but above the poverty level, can assign no more than a fifth of income to housing without cutting into other requirements. Only retired people can afford to spend as much as a third of their income on housing, according to BLS estimates.

How Much of a Subsidy?

The amount of the subsidy under most plans depends upon four factors: the market price of adequate shelter, the household size, the family income, and the proportion of that income assumed to be appropriately allocable to housing expenses. Whether the housing is new or used, the payments must be sufficient to cover annual charges on the capital cost plus operating expenses, including utilities, maintenance costs, and property taxes. Such costs for adequate housing vary from community to community and by size of unit. Most formulas recognize this in some degree by relying upon determinations for each locality of going prices for units of different sizes.

The next consideration is what proportion of income a family should be expected to pay for housing. As noted above, most formulas on current programs require the family to pay at least 20 or 25 percent. Designers of housing allowance plans commonly use the same ratios for families with children and go up to 35 percent for the elderly.

With the exception of the rent supplement program, virtually all established housing formulas were designed to cover a portion or all of the annual charges on capital costs. The task of the housing managers was to select occupants whose incomes were sufficient and steady enough to cover through their rent payments all operating expenses and residual charges on capital costs. Housing managers and sponsors tried to maintain the financial solvency of their projects by selecting families near the top of the admission income range.

If operating expenses such as heating fuel, janitorial services, and repair costs rise steadily over a period of months, it becomes necessary to raise the rents. Many of the occupants of subsidized housing have fixed or lagging incomes. Thus, their rents tend to rise as a percentage of income during periods of rising prices such as the years since 1965. Pressure then builds up to change the basic formula, as happened in the case of public housing: operating subsidies became necessary to enable many projects to meet their operating expenses. (When this happens to older private housing, if rents cannot be raised sufficiently to cover operating expenses, landlords may finally be compelled to close and sometimes abandon the properties.)

New or Existing Housing?

All housing proposals must come to grips with the questions: What is adequate shelter? Need it be new?

Present programs are largely keyed to new construction. This has compelled housing officials to pay close attention to development standards. The new units have to be built to last at least as long as the mortgage loans or bonds against them—thirty or forty years or longer. But since they are for people who cannot pay their own way, the housing must not be too handsome or have too many appointments, lest the nonsubsidized citizenry become too envious. Space inside the unit has rarely been generous: a master bedroom might be ten by twelve feet; and most apartments for father-mother-two children families probably fall well short of the minimum of 1,150 square feet recommended by a committee of the American Public Health Association back in 1950.[12]

In the 1960s FHA officials wrestled with themselves over whether to allow central air conditioning in housing built for moderate income families in the South—a feature most nonsubsidized families in this region who move into new housing insist upon. Public housing officials struggled to stay within the stringent cost limits imposed by the Congress, particularly in high building cost areas like Chicago and New York.

One of the stickiest facets of this problem has to do with the location and density of the developments. Good sites have always been hard to obtain, especially for public housing. Community resistance in many localities forced the housing authorities to locate their projects in racially segregated areas, thus reinforcing apartheid. Sponsors of interest subsidies developments (Sections 235 and 236) have had somewhat more flexibility in the choice of sites. For one thing, the original legislation in 1968 did not require specific approval by the local government. (This veto power would have been given to the local governing bodies in the omnibus bill drawn up by the House Banking and Currency Committee in 1972, but the complicated package failed to clear the House Rules Committee.) But even without this restriction, a large preponderance of these interest-subsidized units have been located in central cities or the older suburbs.

Despite the various restrictions on qualitative standards and development costs, the subsidies for new construction are expensive. Moreover, a substantial part of the total subsidy goes to an investor or owner rather than to the intended beneficiaries. New public housing units require average direct outlays of about $1,300 a year to cover interest and principal payments on the debt. In addition, the federal government now pays a special subsidy toward operating expenses for very low income tenants. The appropriation in fiscal 1973 for this purpose added about $270 a year per unit. The estimated local contribution through payments in lieu of property taxes is about $100 a year. The financing through federal income tax-exempt bonds reduces interest payments by about $525 a year in the early years (2.5 percentage points below the market yield on home mortgage loans x $21,000 per unit). But the revenue cost to the Treasury due to tax exemption is about $800 annually in the early years (assuming that the investor is in the 70 percent bracket). The total net subsidy per new public housing unit is $1,945 a year or $162 a month.

Take another program: rental housing subsidized by interest payments down to 1 percent (Section 236). Payments per unit averaged about $870 in fiscal 1971. In addition, the revenue cost to the U.S. Treasury in 1971 for new rental housing averaged about $660 a unit as a result of allowing depreciation for tax purposes at a higher than straight-line rate. High bracket taxpayers are particularly advantaged by these tax preferences. The cost to all other taxpayers thus comes to over $1,500 a unit for such housing, with a portion of the tax reduction recaptured in the event of early sale.

Federal housing legislation now permits some of the subsidized units to be in existing structures. Public housing authorities have been encouraged since 1964 to lease standard quality housing units or to purchase older structures and fix them up if necessary. A 1970 amendment required that 30 percent of new contract authority for annual payments to be used in housing leased from private owners. For fiscal 1973 it was projected that 35,000 existing units would be utilized by local housing authorities, of which 30,000 would be leased.[13]

The idea behind leasing of existing houses is that it is cheaper than new construction. It also avoids the tendency to compress too many low income, minority families into a single neighborhood as may happen with new developments, and it leaves the properties on the local tax rolls. Including administrative costs, the subsidy for a two-bedroom unit of leased, used housing ranges from $1,200 to $1,500, considerably below the $1,945 annual cost per unit of new construction.[14]

Some local housing officials report difficulties with leased housing. The local authority has to negotiate a separate lease for each one or a handful of units; it is harder to collect the rent; and the housing authority has no direct control over the tenant's use or misuse of the property. Some people would say this is to the good, arguing that local authorities have tried to exercise too much control over tenants and rob them of their self-reliance. But it would seem to be necessary to select the tenants for scattered-site leased housing very carefully and try to place in such units the families who are most likely to get along with neighbors, maintain the property, and pay the rent regularly.

Still, the notion of utilizing the existing inventory more extensively for people who need subsidy is tempting on cost grounds. In a number of localities adequate housing can be found at prices or rents that are much lower than the required charges for new construction. The median contract rent in 1971 for the whole country was in fact about $95 a month and lower than this in a number of Southern cities. Some typical median rents in 1970 were: $62 in Norfolk, Virginia; $71 in Buffalo, $80 in Detroit, $90 in Baltimore, $96 in New York City, $108 in Chicago, and $113 in San Diego.[15] The most typical rental apartment in the existing inventory contained four rooms.

Compare this with the Section 236 rentals. New two-bedroom units built under that program in 1970 had market rents averaging $185 (about the same as for new nonsubsidized rental units). The maximum subsidy brought these rents to the tenants down to $115, still higher than rents on many older units of the same size.

Why then the strong preference on the part of housing officials for new construction? Some say that they want monuments to which they can point. But there is a less idiosyncratic reason. It is essential, they argue, to add directly to the supply of good housing available to families of lower income. This is the only way to be sure that some of these families will get adequate accommodations within their means. And other families of about the same income who remain in older housing will also benefit, since the additional units take some of the pressure off others in the private market and encourage the landlords to compete for tenants by lowering rents, improving services or possibly both. On the other hand, simply to provide such families with more money for housing would lead to hIgher rents in many housing markets with little increase in the supply. According to this view, rent inflation could continue for a long time if more purchasing power were to be pumped into tight housing markets. Thus the rents on existing apartments reported above could rise sharply if a large housing allowance or leased housing program were introduced. It is conceded, however, that housing assistance payments might appropriately be used for existing housing in local markets with a sustained loose supply of standard dwellings.[16]

How About Housing Allowances?

A specific alternative to present housing programs for below-market families is the housing allowance. It is not a brand-new idea. Back in the

1930s when vacancies were high, some real estate men proposed that poor families be issued rent certificates applicable toward the market price on existing housing. Social work experts and federal policy makers opposed the idea on grounds that it would tend to maintain the profitability of the slums and retard their elimination.[17] Instead, they designed the low rent public housing program.

In the 1960s economists and government officials began to formulate general income maintenance plans, but Congress, the Nixon administration, and the country had not settled on an acceptable approach by the end of 1973.

Housing allowances fall somewhere in between rent certificates and general income maintenance. Income transfers would be made to low income families so that they could afford decent housing in the private market. Unlike most housing subsidies now in use, the aid would go with the family, not the project. If the family moved, it would not automatically lose its benefit, as now happens when a family leaves a subsidized housing development. Thus the family would presumably have a much wider choice of housing. But not a completely free choice: it would be a violation of the spirit or the letter of the law to continue to occupy or to move into a substandard house. And since the allowance would be pegged to going rents or prices of existing units in acceptable condition, the aided family could not afford a new house.

Indeed, the central premise of a housing allowance approach is that there is an ample supply of older housing in most central cities which is well-maintained or could be brought up to par with moderate outlays. Ira Lowry of the New York City Rand Institute estimated in 1969 that older apartments in that city could be restored to decent condition and kept violation-free for rents of $100 to $150 a month. In contrast, new units under aided programs in New York required payments (including the subsidy) of $220 to $300 per month. The subsidy per family in an older but well-maintained apartment would, by Lowry's estimates, require $400 to $700 a year compared with $1,700 to $2,700 in a new unit.[18]

Would lower income families really be able to obtain decent living accommodations under a housing allowance program? No one knows at this point. It depends on whether there is in fact a large, underutilized reservoir of basically sound housing which can be brought back and then maintained at reasonable costs. Advocates point to the fact that a majority of the largest central cities lost population in the 1960-70 period as did many of the smaller central cities. But they know it is more than a matter of fitting fewer people into the buildings. At least three conditions must obtain: the city governments must be able to enforce the housing code in all older neighborhoods on a regular basis. The aided families must be sufficiently self-reliant to seek out better housing, to insist that it be well-maintained by the landlord or be able to maintain the property in the case of owner-occupants, and to work with others in the neighborhood to prevent vandalism or misuse of housing. And finally, there must be a sufficient number of competent owners and managers of rental properties who are willing to go back into these areas from which many departed or were forced out by adverse social and economic conditions.

The people calling for housing allowances at least on an experimental basis are mainly academicians and research analysts. The skeptics include men and women who have administered rent control and housing programs. The 1970 Housing Act authorized HUD to experiment with housing allowances and these efforts were under way in 1973. Perhaps these field tests would indicate whether it would be worth adopting the approach —although researchers have a way of demonstrating what they set out to test.

This much is clear: a housing allowance program would be expensive. For it is predicated upon assisting *all* of the households who cannot afford decent shelter, and this is a large group. The Urban Institute, as previously noted, has estimated that the number of households who need help ranged from 12.8 to 16.8 million in 1969. The lower number assumed that most families could pay 25 percent of income for housing with the elderly paying 35 percent. The larger number of households is predicated on housing expense/income ratios of 20 and 30 percent, respectively. If every eligible household were to participate (an unlikely prospect since 40 percent are low income homeowners), the annual cost would range from $7.4 to $9.5 billion. The cost figures allow for substantial administrative expenses and a subsidy-induced rise in housing prices and rents.[19] Another estimate prepared by Henry Aaron of the Brookings Institution called for payments of $5 to $6 billion a year in behalf of 14 million households at the lowest end of the income range.

Are There Less Expensive Alternatives?

Present subsidized housing programs have projected annual costs of $8 to $10 billion by 1978 if the ten-year goal is met. Housing allowances would cost $5 to $10 billion a year. These are not unbearable amounts in terms of the nation's total income of $1,300 billion, but they are substantial when measured against other aid programs to the poor. The federal share of public assistance programs in fiscal 1973 such as aid to families with dependent children and old-age assistance was estimated at just below $7 billion.[20] The Nixon Administration's Family Assistance Plan submitted to the Congress in October, 1969 (but not enacted by the end of 1973) was estimated to increase federal costs of public assistance, including food stamps, by $5.6 billion in the first full year.[21] So one can be sure that the search is on in the President's Office of Management and Budget and in other places for ways of limiting the federal commitment to social sectors like housing. Let us consider a few alternatives in housing assistance that appear to have lower price tags.

As William Grigsby has pointed out, it helps to know the purpose of the aid.[22] Is it to add to the supply of new housing? To improve the quality of existing housing? To reduce the burden of housing costs? Or all or some of these things?

Shallow Subsidies

This approach is predicated upon new construction for middle income families. Offer them a bargain and they will vacate their present houses and release them to people lower down the income ladder. Since these families are just outside the market for new housing, the subsidy per unit is much less than new construction for low income households. Besides, these families as a group have fewer behavioral problems so builders and landlords can deal more easily with them as tenants as compared with the lowest income group.

This was the essence of the moderate income housing program innovated by the Kennedy people in 1961—the below-market interest rate program [Section 221 (d)(3)]. At 3 ⅛ percent, the forty-year mortgages reduced rents by about $20 a month for four-room apartment units, or 15 to 20 percent below rents on modest new apartments financed at market yields of about 5.5 percent in the early 1960s. The program took in families with incomes mostly between $4,000 and $7,000. Not too much filtering occurred because production levels were modest. In part, this was due to funding limitations—the entire capital cost averaging $12,000 or so was lent to the nonprofit sponsor and almost as much to the limited-return builder. And these items were in the federal budget! Thus the outlays by the federal government appeared very large and Budget Bureau personnel and Treasury people had palpitations when they thought about the "cost," even though the loans were fully repayable at the cost of money to the government. In all, about 180,000 units were built under the program before its phase-out and replacement by the Section 236 rental program.

Lending Treasury funds to sponsors at the cost of money to the government is much less expensive in the long run than making up the annual difference between private loans at 7 or 8 percent and 1 percent—the Section 236 formula. But the initial capital outlays by the federal government are relatively large. The Treasury people and the Office of Management and Budget are strongly opposed to direct loans of this type.

*Shallow Subsidies for Middle Income Families with
Allowances for Low Income Families.*

A proposal offered by Irving Welfeld would subsidize a substantial number of middle income families each year in new construction.[23] He estimates that a subsidy of $500 a year on average would induce middle income families to go for the bargain-priced new housing, for they would be paying but 18 percent of income for rent. Builders would gladly put up the units because there is a guaranteed market. One million new units could be added to the inventory each year at an incremental cost of $500 million. This would release much housing to lower income families, who would also be assisted in this proposal through some form of housing allowance or used house program. Since there would be many more middle income seekers than additional units, Welfeld would distribute the new housing by lottery.

Would the subsidy be less expensive? On a per unit basis, yes—$500 a year per middle income new construction versus $2,000 for a low income family installed in a new public housing development. But it would appear to be an expensive and inefficient way of getting low income people into better housing. For we would still have to subsidize some fourteen million or more low income households at $500 or $600 a unit. (Welfeld does not offer numbers of low income families to be subsidized or the cost per family.) Now we are up to $7 billion or so for this group plus a middle income subsidy mounting to $2.5 billion or more by the end of the fifth year. Nor can we be sure that the housing given up by the subsidized families will be available to or appropriate for the poor, given the segmented markets and impediments to movement in most metropolitan areas. The proposal suggests the aphorism: They stoke the horses to feed the sparrows.

Operating Subsidies for Low Income Homeowners.

If the main purpose is to reduce the cost of shelter in relation to income for those living in standard dwellings, we might consider payments to low income homeowners of all or a portion of their operating expenses such as local property taxes. The usual way would be to start with the elderly and later extend the benefits to the physically handicapped and other categories. In the Urban Institute estimates of households qualifying for housing allowances, five to seven million are low income homeowners. If one third of them are headed by an elderly person, roughly two million households would be eligible for the payments. Assuming a property tax of $300 per family, the cost would be $600 million a year. Since a number of states offer partial tax exemption or rebates to elderly homeowners, the federal outlay would probably be less than this. The payments could be adjusted to reduce the elderly family's housing expenses to perhaps 30 percent of income. For very low income homeowners, the subsidy could be extended to cover other operating expenses such as heating, utilities, maintenance, and repairs. The price effects would be minimal. As Henry Schechter has observed: "The recipients of the housing allowances would be expected to remain in their present residences, so that the allowances would not give rise to new demands and inflationary impacts in the housing markets."[24]

In the interest of fairness some will suggest that we take account of the assets position of the subsidized family. For many families the principal asset is the home itself, which is an illiquid holding that the elderly may cling to. Some years ago Sidney Spector, then a federal official with the Housing and Home Finance Agency, advanced a plan for supplementing the cash income of elderly homeowners by converting their residential assets into annuities. Using actuarial estimates of life expectancy, the government could calculate the payments to older persons against their equity in the houses they occupy. Conceivably, an annuity plan of this type could be devised to augment the current income of the participants. The plan could stand on its own or be adapted to an operating subsidy program, thus further reducing the cost to the taxpayers. There is not too much interest, however, among elderly homeowners. Those with low incomes and low value houses would get only small annuities; those who could get larger annuities have little need for the extra income.[25]

Can the Older Houses Be Maintained or Rehabilitated?

The challenge of maintenance and rehabilitation of older housing is so important that it seems wise to discuss it as a separate issue rather than as a "cheaper" alternative to present production-linked subsidies or housing allowances. The Fourth Annual Housing Goals Report (1972) indicated concern in federal circles about the level of maintenance of the housing inventory. Total expenditures for maintenance, repairs, and improvements of residential property came to $8.5 billion in 1970 or $124 per unit. The Goals Report suggested that almost twice this amount needs to be spent, if people were to follow the rule of thumb that 1.5 to 2 percent of the cost of property should be allocated for these purposes.[26] It is likely that these reported figures understate the actual amount of repairs and replacement outlays. (How many of us have gone down to the Buildings Department and sought a permit or, if we have obtained a permit, reported the full amount of a major alteration or improvement?) Still, there may indeed be a serious undermaintenance of the nation's housing stock, concentrated in all likelihood in that portion of the supply occupied by moderate and low income families. For in a period of sharply rising operating expenses such as the years 1966-73, lower income homeowners defer expenditures on a faulty furnace or a weathered roof. Landlords of properties occupied by low income people do the same because it is difficult to cover such outlays out of current receipts or by raising rents. The ultimate consequences of postponing these expenditures may be extraordinary replacement and repair costs that induce some owners to close down the property and possibly abandon it.

Federal efforts to encourage conservation of older housing and rehabilitation for moderate and low income families have met with discouragement. The ten-year goal for rehabilitation of substandard dwellings was reported to be at 67 percent of the targeted level by mid-1972, with only 152,000 units rehabilitated under subsidized programs in the four years 1968-72.[27] Meanwhile, thousands upon thousands of units have been abandoned in cities from Boston to Birmingham. And many times the number of actual abandonments are houses falling into disrepair in the twilight zones of American cities, as the reader knows if he or she has driven the older streets from downtown to a near suburb of any large city. Saving these older neighborhoods and the central city itself is a much bigger challenge than salvaging the structures alone, and we shall discuss it in the next chapter. But let us look at some of the housing aspects at this point.

Location.

According to an old saw of real estate, there are three determinants of value: location, location, and location. The houses that we are concerned with are in the "wrong" part of town. Who wants to live in Cleveland's Hough area, the near North side of Kansas City, or almost any part of Newark, New Jersey? The answer: only those with no real choice in the area's housing markets. Those with better incomes, black families as well as white, opt out of the sections that are plagued with noise, crime, industrial odors, and parking problems. Only the poor, the older people, and the discriminated-against remain. There was a time when many of these sections were well situated from the standpoint of access to jobs in the downtown or industrial areas, and had churches, synagogues, and settlement houses for the immigrants. Some still are. But in many urban areas the jobs are increasingly in outlying places and the older-style community centers have lost their relevance or moved with their now-affluent members or their children. Yes, there are portions of the old city that have become fashionable and have been improved for the wealthy and near-wealthy—Georgetown in Washington, Society Hill in Philadelphia, and Brooklyn Heights in New York. But these are tiny islands in a sea of drabness or impending blight. Middle and upper income families, particularly those with children, have been moving out of the solid old neighborhoods for several generations and they are not likely to return.

Standards.

If most of the older sections are to be occupied by moderate and lower income families, what standards of housing should be considered acceptable? Every dwelling should be weathertight, be adequately heated (and cooled?), and have a decent kitchen and bathroom in working order. But is it necessary to replace a tub on legs with a sunken fixture? Or to perform radical surgery on everything except the frame? When costs of upgrading approach those of new construction, it is difficult to justify such high-grade rehabilitation on economic grounds. Yet this is what some local housing authorities are inclined to do when they take over older buildings, apparently in the hope of allaying early replacements and high repair costs. Private owners have frequently been encouraged by local renewal officials to do the same thing. But if the added costs substantially exceed the added value that the owner can later realize in the market when he desires to sell, he has made an unwise improvement.

There are different levels of housing improvement. We need not settle, in the policy choices we make, for all or nothing. A field study conducted by the writer in the late 1950s considered three possibilities: modest fix-up to code level including exterior cleaning, painting, and rewiring of the electrical system; all of this plus modernization of bathrooms and kitchens; and extensive reconstruction and alterations to high standards. Generally speaking, the highest level of renovation did not appear to be economically feasible, even with attractive financing terms, if the moderate income class of tenants were not to be displaced. The intermediate level of modernization did seem to have some warrant for many of the structures, although the resulting rents might work a hardship on some of the occupants.[28] More recent experiments and analyses seem to bear out these findings.[29] Much depends upon the design and condition of the structures, and their location and potential attractiveness to families with some options.

Subsidies of various types are clearly necessary. Public officials must consider the trade-off between high-standard renovation of some units versus modest improvements of a larger number, and between expenditures on the houses themselves and neighborhood improvements. There is a clearer case for rehabilitation when acceptable living accommodations can be provided at unit costs (including acquisition and improvement) that are significantly below the costs of new construction.

The Rehabilitation Industry.

If an "industry" exists for rehabilitation, it has escaped the attention of both government officials and consumers. In mid-1967 Robert C. Weaver, the first Secretary of the Department of Housing and Urban Development, told a Senate committee:

> Our review . . . makes it clear that a rehabilitation industry has not yet developed in sufficient size or scope to attain the economies of scale needed for the improvement of deteriorating housing at costs that low-income occupants could afford . . . No matter how we evaluate the degree of achievement or potential success of each of the programs, we cannot escape the inevitable fact that, as yet, the scale of rehabilitation activity does not match the needs of the nation.[30]

That statement still holds true. And in the ensuing half dozen years, federal and local officials who pushed rehabilitation efforts have suffered frustration, anguish, and even scandal over low production levels and excessive costs. Many responsible builders stay away from housing rehabilitation because costs are difficult to estimate; the jobs are in scattered locations and difficult to aggregate to secure scale economies; and the work often must be done under combat conditions. In North Philadelphia, a mechanic working alone in a property told observers that he always kept the doors locked for fear of intruders. It was not a matter of irrational racial prejudice: the neighborhood was black but so was the mechanic. A rehabilitator reported that unoccupied houses which are partially renovated or fully restored and awaiting occupancy are targets for vandals and thieves. If anything, then, rehabilitation has become a more perilous and expensive business in recent years. Operation Breakthrough, a highly publicized effort by HUD between 1969 and 1972 to stimulate the development and application of modern design and technology in the housing industry, seems to have by-passed rehabilitation and concentrated almost exclusively on new production.

Insurance in Urban Core Areas.

In the 1960s, property insurance became increasingly unavailable or prohibitively expensive in the inner cities. A 1967 survey by a presidential panel in six large cities disclosed that over 40 percent of businessmen and nearly 30 percent of homeowners in poverty areas had serious property insurance problems.[31] Insurance companies in Boston, New York, Cleveland, Detroit and other cities redlined certain blighted districts as poor risks and refused to sell coverage in such areas. An agent for an insurance company told the presidential panel about underwriting practices in Omaha, Nebraska:

"There are sections in the older part that are taboo. If you get any coverage you are real lucky."[32] This was typical of much of the testimony presented after the riots of 1967.

Without insurance against fire, theft, and other disasters, it is difficult if not impossible to sell real estate or to secure loans to rehabilitate it. A savings and loan association official described the situation in the Watts area of Los Angeles in 1967: "Real estate activity is practically at a standstill . . . The sale of these properties is dependent upon financing through reputable financial institutions, which are reluctant to do so because adequate fire insurance coverage is not available . . ."[33]

In 1968 the Congress responded to this situation by authorizing HUD to reinsure private insurance companies against excess losses resulting from riots or civil disorders. In return, the insurance companies must agree to cooperate with state insurance authorities in developing statewide plans to assure "fair access to insurance requirements," known by the acronym FAIR. It was hoped that such plans would eliminate most of the redlining of inner city neighbrohoods where property insurance has not been readily available.

By the end of 1970, FAIR plans were reported to be operating in twenty-six states, the District of Columbia, and Puerto Rico, with $13.6 billion of basic property insurance in force. Coverage has been extended to vandalism and malicious mischief. According to HUD, "The program has helped significantly to stabilize the property insurance market . . . There are fewer reports of widespread policy cancellations. Also, many property owners who previously could not obtain coverage can do so now."[34] Not all reports are as rosy, but the property insurance situation has evidently improved somewhat in older districts.

Financing Older Housing.

When the savings and loan associations and mutual savings banks and other institutional lenders stop making mortgage loans in a particular section, that district's days are numbered. The only hope then is that the vacuum will be filled by governmental action. FHA has been criticized for concentrating too much on new construction and neglecting established neighborhoods and existing housing. In fact, about 60 percent of all homes insured by FHA between 1935 and 1970 were existing or refinanced units (6.2 out of 10.4 million homes). The ratio was even higher from 1961 through 1970—76 percent were existing houses. It is probably true that FHA underwriters were disinclined to insure houses in declining neighborhoods since these are risky loans and foreclosures are bound to be relatively high. But by the middle 1960s it was Washington policy to move into such neighborhoods, and the FHA statistics for programs keyed to such areas (such as Section 221) clearly show a rising level of support from 1964 on. A special program for high risk areas [Section 223(e)] introduced in 1968 was pursued in a serious way in the next several years.

But programs like these are difficult to administer and open to miscalculation, abuse, and sometimes venality. In some poor neighborhoods people were bilked by speculators who got overvaluations through FHA. Example: Smith buys an older house for $6,000. He has it painted and redecorated at a cost of $1,000. Smith then resells the property to Jones for $12,000, netting $4,000-$5,000 on the deal. Jones paid 3 percent down or $360. Now he finds that the plumbing system must be replaced and there are other defects that all together will require $2,000 to repair. After several months Jones stops making his mortgage payments. Within the year he abandons the property. FHA is compelled to pay off the mortgage lender and acquire the property. After repairing the house, FHA stands to lose $7,000 or more when it attempts to sell the property.

This is a nationwide phenomenon. It has been documented by a House committee which held hearings on the situation in Detroit. FHA's inventory of acquired homes in that city rose from 800 in June 1968, to approximately 8,000 by April 1972. Another 18,000 to 20,000 properties were in default or foreclosure in Detroit on December 1, 1971, and were likely to be acquired by FHA.[35]

Nationally, foreclosures and assignments on FHA home mortgages rose from less than 1 percent in 1960 to almost 4.2 percent by 1970, with programs designed for moderate and lower income families showing about twice this rate (8.4 percent for Section 221 in 1970).[36] This is, of course, a cause for concern from the standpoint of costs to the taxpayers, although FHA insurance funds will cover some of these losses. More serious, perhaps, are the consequences for the tens of thousands of lower income families who have lost their equities and credit standing, and the large number who are on the brink of such losses.

There has been much finger-pointing, with administrative officials saying that they were merely carrying out the legislative intent and legislators denouncing the HUD-FHA administrators for lax administration, including failure to inspect the properties and for inadequate evaluation of applicants or counseling of home buyers. In fact, there must have been loose administration in some offices and corruption as well, as subsequent investigations, indictments, and convictions demonstrate. The broad legislative intent was to promote home ownership for families of low and moderate income; and to extend FHA home insurance to portions of the city that FHA area directors and underwriters had customarily redlined on an arbitrary basis. It was *not* intended to underwrite properties in violation of housing codes or failing to meet FHA's minimum property standards; in fact, the federal law specifically requires that eligible properties must meet "the requirements of all State laws, or local ordinances or regulations, relating to the public health or safety, zoning or otherwise . . ." [37]

It is another case of lack of empathy or feeling of responsibility for the poor and the blacks on the part of many middle class Americans. Experienced FHA personnel must have been aware of the situation, even if they were not on the take. Certainly the real estate men and mortgage brokers who handled the transactions and originated the loans knew that overvaluations were being made. Indeed, fee appraisers, retained by FHA but not federal employees, swapped high valuations in each other's districts. In fairness to FHA administrators, they did not have an adequate staff to do the necessary screening of properties and applicants even if they wanted to. Yet, Lawrence Katz, former FHA director in Milwaukee, was evidently able to do a much more responsible job of inspecting properties and counseling prospective buyers than his counterpart in Detroit and probably many other offices.[38]

Perhaps the most important lesson is that home ownership is not good for everybody. Some families have incomes that are too low or too irregular to make mortgage payments and also maintain the property. Some families are not effective consumers and are easily misled. Some households have too many personal problems (the dependent types referred to earlier) to take on additional responsibilities of home ownership. Former Secretary Robert C. Weaver recognized this and resisted efforts in 1967 to press home ownership indiscriminately on poor and moderate income families. But the political pressure became too intense, and the Johnson administration went all out for home ownership in the big 1968 legislative package. It remained for a new administration to carry out the law, with the results to date as described.

Consumers would be protected or indemnified under legislation proposed but not enacted in 1972. No mortgage or loan could be insured unless HUD found *by inspection* that the property met the requirements of all state and local health and safety laws, and was free from structural or other defects affecting the use and livability of the property. The federal department's present authority to correct or compensate the owner for defects in existing Section 235 homes would be extended to other programs utilized in older urban areas [such as Section 221 (d)(2)]. A one-year warranty would have to be given by the builder or rehabilitator to the buyer or homeowner against substantial deviation from approved plans and specifications in connection with FHA assisted rehabilitation. These protections are clearly needed. Whether the administration would give support and Congress would appropriate sufficient funds to carry out these well-intentioned measures is not certain. It would take not only new program money but a bigger administrative budget to increase HUD's staff of inspectors, appraisers, and counselors.

Weighing the Pros and Cons

Housing is a slice of life for which there are no neat solutions. Present housing programs stress production of new housing. During the four years 1969-72, the volume of production was impressive but it was a costly approach. These costs could mount to $10 billion a year by 1978 if the ten-year housing goal were to be realized. Could we spend this money more efficiently and fairly?

The principal challenge to the production-tied subsidy system is a housing allowance approach relying heavily on the use of the existing housing supply. Its adoption in the form proposed by its academic sponsors has one undeniable virtue: it would treat everybody in similar circumstances in a similar way. This is a cardinal principle of taxation and it is equally valid as a principle of income redistribution. What we cannot be sure of is the effect of housing allowances upon the supply of housing or the price of housing. Its advocates believe that most of the added money would go for improvements and rehabilitation; the skeptics think the main consequences in most localities would be substantial price and rent increases. All agree that it would not be self-executing in the marketplace. Local governments would have to do a much better job of policing the housing inventory against violations of codes, providing market information to consumers, and enforcing laws against racial discrimination.

The families who would receive housing allowances are not politically influential in their localities. It is difficult to visualize the majority of them becoming effective consumers or politically assertive in their own interests. The writer recalls surveys taken in New York City in the late 1950s in connection with rent control. Tenants in the luxury housing districts knew their rights and virtually every family in this group was paying the legally permitted rent and not one dollar more.[39] In contrast, the Puerto Ricans and blacks of the West Side and Harlem were commonly overcharged by substantial amounts. On the basis of his own studies, Chester Rapkin concluded that the minority family living in a single room was paying more per square foot for its miserable living quarters than wealthy families occupying plush apartments.[40] More recent surveys indicate that 54 percent of welfare households live in substandard or overcrowded places. Such findings do not bode well for plans that would put substantial rent certificates in the hands of the poor.

There is little doubt that millions of people live below the decency level in America. By a housing-poverty measure they number about 45 million persons, somewhere between 13 and 17 million households. It is probably wiser both from a humanitarian and a political viewpoint to aim for a general income maintenance system than for cash transfers linked to the provision of housing. The level of income payments should of course take into account the cost of decent shelter for households of different sizes, but it seems arbitrary to insist that a specific amount be spent on housing. A family with five children might prefer to spend relatively more on food and clothing and accept less space than the prescribed standard. Indeed, it is unlikely that such families could find large enough houses anyway except at exorbitant rents—this is what a field experiment in New Haven indicated to Housing Agency officials in the mid-sixties.[41]

From the standpoint of political acceptability, we are probably farther from a housing allowance than a general income redistribution arrangement. At least one side of the Congress was willing to adopt a minimal family assistance program. The closest thing to a housing allowance is the rent supplement, which Congress adopted in 1965 when the country was temporarily poverty-minded. When it was realized that rent supplements might enable some low income families to move into middle income neighborhoods and some black families into white areas, Congress declined to fund the program at more than a token level. The controversy over busing of school children from one neighborhood to another to achieve some racial balance indicates that housing is too emotionally charged to carry the burden of a massive income redistribution plan. As a matter of political tactics it seems wiser to fight for more and better housing and for a fairer system of income distribution as separate issues.

But if housing allowances are not the answer, neither is the present subsidy system politically secure or programatically balanced. Despite a large quantitative target adopted by the Congress in 1968, public support for housing subsidies is thin. (With one exception: deductions of mortgage interest and property taxes from the federal income tax, which cost the Treasury $5 billion a year but are not regarded as a subsidy at all.) There was no great hue and cry from the country when the House Rules Committee denied an up-or-down vote on the 1972 housing package. Most people probably did not know what was in the bill. With budget commitments rising each year on new construction, and with foreclosures and losses mounting on FHA-insured older housing, housers must give thought to tidying up the present system.

7 The Older City and Urban Renewal

The city, wrote Louis Wirth, is a relatively large, dense, and permanent settlement of socially heterogeneous individuals. People know intimately a much smaller proportion of those with whom they have contact than do small town folk and therefore are less accountable to each other. Bonds of kinship are weak and the family is less important. Tight living of individuals with few emotional or sentimental ties breeds a spirit of competition and mutual exploitation. To keep these forces from destroying the noncommunity, formal controls must be imposed—legal recourse, housing codes, traffic regulations, and professional ethics.[1]

What do people seek in this regulated anonymity? They go after more money, more gadgets, more status. As young families raise their incomes, they seek more residential space in better neighborhoods and districts served by good schools. The areas they move into are likely to be more or less stratified in terms of property values, age groups, and race. Most upwardly mobile American families have become owners of free standing houses, gaining thereby ground-level dwellings with private yards, tax savings worth 8-10 percent of monthly housing expense, and an unquantifiable enhancement of status. As David Riesman wrote in *The Lonely Crowd*:

> People look for nice neighborhoods in which their children will meet nice people . . . and the better schools that go with them. Since many others, too, will also be shopping for better neighborhoods, this pressure, combined with the rapid shift of residential values and fashions characteristic of American cities, means that no one can ever settle down assuredly for the rest of life.[2]

Since the 1940s this search for the good life has been largely outside the boundaries of the central cities. In the decade 1960-70, about two-thirds of all new housing units put up in metropolitan areas were located outside the central cities. The suburban development included not only a preponderance of single family detached houses but a hefty proportion of townhouses and other multifamily structures as well.

What about the central city dwellers? In 1970 they numbered 64 million people, almost a third of the nation's population. For the most part, they are people with less income and fewer options than the suburbanites. They live in older houses and their children attend less modern schools than those in the outlying communities. Elderly people are overconcentrated in the central cities. And so are the blacks, who make up 21 percent of all central city residents but only 4.7 percent of those who reside in suburbs. The core cities contained almost two-thirds of the metropolitan people living below the poverty line—$4,275 for a family of four in 1972; and a substantial share of the families below the minimum-decency budget of the BLS—about $7,800 in the same year.

To give shelter to the immigrant, the disadvantaged, and the poor is not a new responsibility for the core city. As we noted in Chapter 3, refugees and beggars gravitated toward Boston after the Revolutionary War; destitute Irish immigrants concentrated in New York, Philadelphia, and Boston in the middle of the nineteenth century; freed blacks settled in Northern cities before and after the Civil War. And between 1880 and 1920 came a flood tide of immigrants from Russia, Austria, Hungary, and Italy. These outlanders and foreigners clustered in the older cities, found jobs, sent their young to the public schools, and became Americanized.

But the situation of the central city in the late twentieth century has changed fundamentally from 50 or 100 years ago. In consequence it is relatively less capable of absorbing the migrants and caring for the poor than it used to be. In earlier times, the core city held not only the workers but virtually all the places of employment: the factories, the warehouses, the shops, as well as the office buildings. As recently as 1960 the central cities of the fifteen largest metropolitan areas accounted for almost two-thirds of the jobs in these areas. By 1970 they had little more than half the jobs and further shrinkage could be expected in the seventies.[3] Moreover, the mix of jobs is changing with less demand for manual labor and more for brain workers and technicians. The core cities have an oversupply of adults who are unsuited to the newer skills. Many of the underskilled are young blacks, Puerto Ricans, or Mexican-Americans. Despite all these handicaps in the competition for jobs and income, expectations are high among the disadvantaged. They see the good life on TV and in magazines. They want it too—and now.

For a decade or so after 1950 the mayors and federal officials hoped that the tide would turn. Losing the well-off to the suburbs, they banked on physical improvements to make the central city more attractive to people with good incomes. They hoped to rebuild the central business districts and create new urban environments for luxury apartments, cultural centers, universities, and research industries. This would generate the local tax revenues needed to refurbish the older neighborhoods, replace outworn facilities, and later to do something more for the poor and minority families.

But for many older cities it was too late for such a strategy. It was just too easy and too attractive for business and well-off families to locate elsewhere. Revenue gains from new industry and commercial investment were disappointing. Only in office activities have the core cities continued to dominate over their suburbs. Even in this sector, new office buildings have been concentrated in a relatively few cities which serve as national and regional headquarters for corporations. Overall, there appears to have been an erosion of private capital in the central cities in retail commercial structures and probably in manufacturing plants as well. More directly, there was a net loss of jobs in the decade of the sixties in cities like Detroit, Chicago, St. Louis, and New York. In Detroit, for example, the number of persons working in the central city dropped by 156,000 between 1960 and 1970, while metropolitan employment rose by 170,000. Clearly, the employment opportunities have been moving away from the city people. The strategy based on changing the physical environment for potential users of city real estate has not reversed the tide.

The People Problem

The older cities, along with declining rural areas, are the places where the nation comes face to face with its most serious domestic ills. They are problems of people living in degradation and despair, and surrounded by physical deterioration. Do the unfortunates make their own problems or are they the victims of their environment? Even the philosophers of benign neglect and those who draw distinctions between the virtuous future-oriented citizenry and the slothful present-oriented lower class acknowledge that there are some problems that our society cannot ignore.[4] Here are a few indicators:

1. Unemployment among persons sixteen through nineteen years old ranged between 12 and 17 percent from 1961 through 1971. In some districts and some cities it is much higher than this national average.
2. Unemployment among blacks and other races at 6.4 to 12.4 percent has been consistently about twice the rate for whites from 1961 through 1971. Part-time or irregular work, known as subemployment, is much higher. It was 23 percent in the low income neighborhoods of eight large cities surveyed by the Department of Labor in the fall of 1966, in addition to the 9.3 percent unemployment rate in these same neighborhoods.[5]
3. The poor pay more in the central city ghetto than do people in other parts of the metropolitan area. Part of this reflects higher selling costs to the merchants due to smaller average purchases, pilferage, higher insurance rates, and other factors. But some of it is attributable to exploitation. A Federal Trade Commission study of furniture and appliance stores in Washington, D.C. found that prices in ghetto stores averaged $255 for each $100 of wholesale cost; elsewhere in the city the ratio was $159 to $100. At the same time, the net return to retailers seems to be lower in such areas and many are getting out. Nobody gains in such an outcome.[6]

4. Health care and nutrition of the children of the poor tend to be inadequate. These factors contribute to poor performance in school; it is hard to concentrate or study on an empty belly. Adults as well as children suffer from inadequate health care and diets. Life expectancy for blacks, Indians, and some other minorities is significantly below the average for whites. In 1968 life expectancy at birth for blacks was 63.7, for whites 71.1 years.
5. Crime rates in the larger cities are high and rising. They are highest in very low income black districts. According to the Commission on Civil Disorders, "Most of these crimes are committed by a small minority of the residents, and the principal victims are the residents themselves . . . Just as most crimes committed by whites are against other whites." The bulk of the major crimes are committed by persons under twenty-five years of age. And during the 1970s the number of young blacks aged fourteen to twenty-four will grow rapidly in the central cities.[7]
6. Sanitary conditions in slum neighborhoods are sickening. There are lots filled with junk and garbage, abandoned cars and houses, broken bottles and scattered debris. Poor house- and neighborhood-keeping by residents, neglect by landlords, and indifferent service by city sanitation departments may all be to blame, in the view of the Douglas Commission.[8]

Almost any one of these problems could constitute a full-time challenge to the next generation, as President Johnson once said. Flashing back to the early sixties, it is obvious that pressure was building up to do more about the needs of the present occupants of the city. A new strategy began to emerge, placing more emphasis on changing the social environment rather than the physical aspects of cities and providing additional direct services for the disadvantaged. But this is an expensive approach, in the short-run at least, for it does not quickly generate additional local tax revenues. Thus the mayors and other local officials have had to look elsewhere for fiscal help, and elsewhere means the statehouse and Washington.

The Fiscal Bind

It is important to recognize the fiscal plight of the central cities for what it is. To economist William Baumol it is not a case of missed opportunities or the penalty for bad management; it is the inevitable consequence of long-term forces that are beyond the control of the local elected officials or their technicians.[9] Inept administration could have contributed to but not caused the fiscal problem. As cities grow in size and density, the social costs rise at a greater than proportionate rate: traffic congestion, air pollution, and perhaps crime. These require larger expenditures by local governments just to keep things from getting worse. Meanwhile, the city's neighborhoods become more crime-ridden and facilities become obsolescent. Those who can seek safer and more pleasant environments outside the city. Once the exodus begins it triggers a process of cumulative deterioration, for it does not pay landlords and other investors to keep up their properties as well for a lower class of users. Inevitably the tax base of real property is progressively eroded.

But the municipality must continue to increase its employees in an effort to offset the deterioration of the environment. Municipal activities are largely labor intensive: there are no ready capital substitutes for teachers, policemen, firemen, and social workers. Yet local government must meet the competition for labor from other sectors, such as manufacturing, where worker productivity is on the rise due to new technologies and deeper capital per worker. Wages and salaries of municipal workers thus rise faster than the increase in their productivity. Unions of public employees help see to that.

In brief, urban social costs and expenditures are rising inexorably without offsetting gains in the local tax base or worker productivity. These trends may be slowed but they cannot be reversed. If Baumol is correct —and the facts of rising public employment at the local level and rising expenditures per resident seem to bear him out—there is no internal solution. Baumol concludes with an endorsement of more federal aid for cities such as the general revenue sharing plan advanced by Walter Heller and Joseph Pechman, a version of which was advanced by the Nixon administration and passed by the Congress in 1972.

This is a sobering analysis but not a cause for utter despair. We should bear in mind that the largest component in the budgets of local governments is education—about 40 percent—and this is a form of investment in the future. Education is a good candidate for federal and state support because the localities do not reap the pay-offs when well-trained people move out of their areas, but the country as a whole realizes a brain gain. And if the core cities are losing some of their comparative advantage to the outer cities, they still have important transportation and freight distribution facilities, access to a portion of the metropolitan area's trained labor pool, cheap factory space for incubating new industries, and the central business district itself. These continue to offer external economies to some firms and public and nonprofit agencies—that is, they lower the cost curves of the individual firm through no specific effort of its own. And the central city is still the best location for a symphony hall, the theatre district, and a major art museum. In most metropolitan areas only one such facility or complex can be supported, and the logical location is in the core.

But the economic, fiscal, and social problems of the older cities are serious. Let us look at one of the major approaches by which the cities have tried to cope with them.

Urban Renewal

Functional obsolescence and depreciation are in the nature of things in a dynamic economy. Changing technology makes available new and better products: refrigerators replace ice boxes, high fidelity record players relegate the old victrola to the attic, private autos take the riders from the trolley cars. Similarly, new housing developments have drawn families from the old neighborhoods. Consumer preferences change and rising income enables many consumers to make their demand effective.

American cities grew rapidly in the post-Civil War period, as people streamed in from abroad and from the farms and small towns of this country. Tenements were thrown up for the immigrant and native-born working class, many below the standards of decency the day they were opened. Many buildings lacked central heating and toilets in each apartment, and some had windowless rooms. But they were quickly filled and some remained in use for decades because working class people kept coming to take the place of those who had bettered themselves. Here and there the old housing was replaced by commercial structures that could make better use of strategically located sites. In Manhattan and a few other places, replacement occurred under private auspices in response to an intense demand for close-in space by firms and some wealthy families. In most sections of the older cities, however, replacement did not pay because undeveloped land became available through improvements in transportation. These new sites were often more attractive in setting and almost invariably they were easier for the builder to assemble than developed property.

By the 1930s there was a growing awareness that many of our people lived in slums and many thousands of urban blocks were in a state of deterioration and blight. It was in this period that the concept of publicly-aided urban redevelopment was formulated and gained adherents. The supporters were a strange alliance of welfare workers and real estate developers, mayors and downtown merchants.

Underlying Assumptions.

As a child of the Depression, urban redevelopment was influenced by the notion of secular stagnation. It was thought that investment opportunities for private enterprise were declining over the long-run. It followed that more public investment would be necessary to utilize the savings of society and thus maintain full employment. Population growth had slowed down and there were vacancies in urban real estate. Automobile ownership had leveled off and many workers relied upon public transportation to get back and forth each day. The suburban style of life had evolved but it was then affordable only by businessmen and professionals. In short, urban redevelopment was predicated upon the assumption of a bounded city, with strong potential demand for the close-in sites served by public means of transportation. The impediments to reconstruction were believed to be mainly on the supply side—the difficulties of assembling the land from many private owners and providing the necessary public facilities.

What Are the Main Tools of Urban Redevelopment?

1. Public power of eminent domain. Take properties in slum areas from their present owners and assemble them for new development. Present owners are compensated and tenants helped to relocate.
2. Write-down of land cost. Reduce the resale price of the sites to their fair value for private development in accordance with the community's redevelopment plan.
3. Municipal investments in public facilities to create well-serviced and attractive environs.

Another tool associated with urban redevelopment is code enforcement to prevent some property owners or tenants from diminishing value or livability of other properties in the same neighborhood. Tax preferences may be used to encourage improvements, and penalties imposed to deter or to pay for deficient maintenance and repairs. In general, the methods of urban redevelopment include any measures that improve the relative attractiveness of particular properties or districts to private investors for new fixed improvements or reconstruction.

The states and local governments have the power of taking land for a public purpose under the Constitution, but only the federal government has the means of raising the substantial funds needed for write-downs of land costs. Urban redevelopment was conceived in the 1930s, but it was not until 1949 that the federal government adopted it as a program. Under the Housing Act of 1949, federal loans and grants were authorized to be made to local public agencies that were empowered under state laws to clear slums and to carry out urban redevelopment programs in their communities. Federal grants were to cover two-thirds of net project costs; localities could count their public improvements in the area toward their one-third share of the costs.

Whose Neighborhoods?

Then came the tough questions. Whose areas would be designated for clearance? What reuses would be permitted under the official plan? Who would benefit and who would suffer? The clearance areas had to be predominantly residential before acquisition or, if not, predominantly residential in the redevelopment. This much was clear: under the law the new housing did not have to be for the former residents of the slum clearance area. As it turned out, most of the early projects were designated for middle and upper middle income housing or commercial and industrial activities. But 52 percent of the families living in ninety-nine of the earliest projects had incomes so low that they were eligible for low-rent public housing. And 65 percent of all families displaced by these urban redevelopment projects were nonwhites.[10]

From Redevelopment to Renewal.

After five years of experience it was evident that urban redevelopment was a painfully slow process. Moreover, large parts of the older cities were not being treated at all. By 1954 some 200 localities were engaged in the program but only 60 had reached the land acquisition phase.[11] Of $500 million authorized for grants in 1949, $348 million were "reserved or earmarked" by the start of 1954 but only a small fraction of this amount had actually been disbursed.[12]

The Congress then determined to enlarge the scope of the program to promote conservation and rehabilitation of the entire inventory of housing instead of spot clearance of rock bottom slums. In line with this change in emphasis, the program was given a new title: urban renewal. A new mechanism was devised to make sure that the local effort would be based on a broad perspective, systematic consideration of local priorities, and consultation with civic groups and residents. The new requirement was called the "workable program." It had seven cardinal elements including a community plan, housing and building codes, sound fiscal arrangements, a relocation plan for displaced families, and citizen participation in the decisions about urban renewal.

Because private investors continued to perceive developments in urban renewal areas as risky ventures, new FHA insurance aids were made available with mortgages insured up to 90 percent on replacement cost rather than estimated value, and FNMA stood ready to purchase the residential mortgages at or near par. Later, as the properties seasoned and the redeveloped areas stabilized, private institutional lenders took more of the mortgages.

By the end of 1960, 475 communities were participating in the federally-aided urban renewal program. About 114,000 families had been relocated and almost ten thousand acres of land actually acquired by local public agencies. Completed projects since 1949 numbered forty-one for the entire country. Progress for a program like urban renewal is difficult to measure, but it seemed to be painfully slow. The Housing Agency's annual report for 1960 reflected a concern about "projectitis" and the need to continue to search for ways of stemming the spread of blight. The Urban Renewal Administration was trying to get the localities to engage in comprehensive community renewal planning.[13] It is difficult, however, to find in the official statistics and statements a conviction that urban renewal was, after ten years, making a major contribution to the improvement of life in the older cities of America. And the Census of 1960 revealed continuing erosion of the population and economic base of many older cities and widening disparities between the central city and the newer suburbs in household income, the value of housing per family, and per capita outlays for schools and other public amenities.

Urban Renewal under a New Administration.

The program got a new shot in the arm from the Congress and a new administration in 1961. The authorization to make contracts for urban renewal grants was raised by $2 billion that year, bringing the total authorization to $4 billion. More emphasis was placed on economic revitalization by a provision permitting up to 30 percent of the federal capital grant funds to be used for commercial and other nonresidential reuse of blighted areas that were previously not predominantly residential. A small mass transportation program was initiated and other measures were provided to help restore the health of older cities. Not least, there was an infusion of new enthusiasm and hope among mayors and local renewal officials, which was fully matched by the optimism and drive of the federal urban renewal people led by Commissioner William L. Slayton.

Urban renewal surged forward in the next several years. Virtually all cities of 250,000 population or more had active programs and many smaller towns were beginning to participate. At the start of 1963, some one thousand communities had certified workable programs, indicating their eligibility to engage in federally-aided urban renewal. An increasing number of projects were reaching completion, thus giving tangible evidence of the benefits. In cities like Hartford, Philadelphia, and San Francisco the downtown skyline was being transformed as new office buildings and civic structures rose on urban renewal land. Upper middle income housing developments were now joined by new moderate income rental housing on urban renewal sites financed by FHA under a provision of the 1961 Housing Act. The University of Chicago, the University of Pennsylvania, Wayne State University, Yale University, and a score of other land-bound urban universities were now expanding or being insulated from encroaching blight under generous terms of federal law that credited their expenditures in urban renewal areas as local contributions toward urban renewal projects.

It was a heady time for mayors and their renewal officials and city planners. Real estate developers were scouting for investment opportunities, churches and labor unions were now doing their part as nonprofit sponsors of moderate income housing for senior citizens and families with children. FHA, long known as a hardnose agency that insured in economically sound areas, was taking on social-purpose housing projects and rehabilitation activities. As federal and local urban renewal officials cut ribbons on the new developments, they told each other that the city was being saved.

The Black Revolt.

Being saved for whom? Within the shadows of Philadelphia's emerging Penn Center, Hartford's Constitution Plaza, and San Francisco's proposed Western Addition lay the black slums simmering with discontent. The inner city blacks could see the gleaming towers but it was not their world. They could hear the bulldozers making inroads on their neighborhoods for the expansion of universities that their children were not likely to attend and for expressways that accelerated white suburban commuters through the black parts of the city. In 1963 and 1964 a series of serious disorders broke out in Chicago, Cleveland, Philadelphia, New York, and other cities. The following years were marked by riots and disorders in Los Angeles, Tampa, Cincinnati, Atlanta, Newark, Detroit, and scores of other cities. In each city there was a reservoir of grievances the deepest of which, according to the Commission on Civil Disorders, were police practices, unemployment and underemployment, and inadequate housing.[14] How much urban renewal contributed to the reservoir of discontent among blacks is anybody's guess. Blacks and other minority groups made up three-fifths or more of all families displaced by urban renewal programs. And many blacks evidently viewed the program at its worst as a deliberate effort to dislodge them from their footholds and at its best as an inadequate form of federal assistance.

In 1968 the Commission on Civil Disorders recommended that the urban renewal program be continued but reoriented to the needs of low income people. Wrote the Commission:

Urban renewal has been an extremely controversial program since its inception. We recognize that in many cities it has demolished more housing than it has erected, and that it has often caused dislocation among disadvantaged groups. Nevertheless, we believe that a greatly expanded but reoriented urban renewal program is necessary to the health of our cities. . . . but a reorienting of the program is necessary to avoid past deficiencies. The Department of Housing and Urban Development has recognized this, and has promulgated policies giving top priority to urban renewal projects that directly assist low-income households in obtaining adequate housing. Projects aimed primarily at bolstering the economic strength of downtown areas, or at creating housing for upper-income groups while reducing the supply of low-cost housing, will have low priority, unless they are part of balanced programs including a strong focus on [employment] needs of low-income groups.[15]

A Thin Market.

Along with the growing resistance from minority groups, urban renewal faced another difficulty in many cities: a thin market for higher priced housing. Places like San Francisco, Chicago, New York, and Washington had relatively strong demand for such housing because of the importance of accessibility to the core among executives and professionals in headquarters cities. Not so in St. Louis, Cleveland, Buffalo, and numerous other cities. In such places it was difficult to market the land for the high value uses anticipated in the redevelopment plans. The lack of interest among private developers for many sites meant that localities were becoming large landholders. By 1964 about 27,000 acres of land had been acquired by local public agencies but more than 12,000 acres were not yet committed to any reuse; and redevelopment had not yet started on another 5,000 acres of committed land.[16] Moreover, there were serious difficulties in renting some of the market-priced housing completed prior to 1963 on urban renewal land with FHA financing under Section 220. Almost 30 percent of the mortgages on these multifamily projects were in foreclosure, default or in modification, the latter term meaning that FHA was permitting the owners to defer repayment of principal on loans and only meet the interest payments.[17]

Thus market realities were a major factor in the reorientation of the urban renewal program. Housing Administrator Weaver could argue on economic grounds as well as humanitarian considerations that more of the urban renewal land should be allocated to moderate income housing.[18] In 1965 about a third of the residential reuse of urban renewal land went for such subsidized housing.

New Priorities for Urban Renewal.

Congress also responded to the demands that the program should be made more sensitive to the needs of disadvantaged and dislocated families. Under the leadership of Congressman Albert Rains of Alabama, the Housing Subcommittee secured passage in 1964 of a number of changes designed to humanize the urban renewal program. It authorized federal support for local programs of intensive code enforcement in areas of incipient blight; established a new relocation adjustment payment to lower-income displaced families and elderly individuals to cover a portion of the increased rents most of these households have to pay when compelled to move; and authorized a new program of low-interest rate loans (3 percent) to finance rehabilitation of dwellings and business properties in urban renewal areas. At the urging of the ranking minority member of the Subcommittee, William B. Widnall of New Jersey, the measure specifically prohibited federal support for any clearance project where rehabilitation is feasible. In consequence, the annual increase in families scheduled for relocation by urban renewal agencies leveled off at about 20,000 over the next several years. About 5,000 families a year received relocation adjustment payments averaging about $370 per family.[19]

In 1968 Congress stipulated that a majority of the total number of housing units in a locality's residential urban renewal projects approved after August 1 of that year must be for low and moderate income families or individuals; at least 20 percent of this total must be for low income families and individuals. Relocation adjustment payments were increased and a new provision added for displaced owner-occupants to enable them to purchase replacement dwellings.

Measuring Performance.

The urban renewal program continued in operation in the early 1970s with a commitment level of about $1 billion a year. HUD stated that it was emphasizing urban renewal activities carried out under the neighborhood development program—smaller and shorter-term projects that are reviewed and funded each year.[20] Smaller scale projects probably bring less uncertainty and fear to the residents than the older style urban renewal projects that typically take six to nine years to complete.

What has been accomplished by this program in the two decades that it has been operating? Here are some quantitative measures:[21]

1. Capital grants through 1970
    approved: $9.3 billion;
    disbursed: $4.4 billion.
2. Land purchased by June 1970
    53,000 acres
    =   one city the size of Seattle, Washington.
3. Dwelling units completed or under construction by June 1971 on urban renewal land

250,000 units
= 8/10 of 1 percent of 32 million dwellings built in the United States during the same period.
4. Nonresidential buildings completed or under construction by June 30, 1970 on urban renewal land

   315 million sq. ft. of gross floor area
   = approximately $5 billion or 1.4 percent of the total value of such construction in United States during the same period.
5. Total redevelopment value of improvements on urban renewal land by June 1971

   $12.4 billion.
6. Estimated receipts from local property taxes on value of improvements on urban renewal land by June 1971

   $300 million
   = 8/10 of 1 percent of estimated $38 billion in property tax receipts as of same date.

Proponents of urban renewal can take only small comfort from these figures. From the standpoint of the older cities, the investments that did take place as a result of urban renewal were probably larger than would have occurred without the program. But some economists could argue that most of this investment would have taken place anyway, albeit probably outside the older cities.

The Douglas Commission scored the program for moving away from a major intent of the Congress in 1949 to provide housing for the poor and near-poor. It was also critical of relocation practices under urban renewal, especially prior to 1965, for failing to view relocation not as part of a ground-clearing operation but as a step toward a decent home and a suitable living environment for every displaced household. The Douglas Commission noted with disappointment the Census Bureau finding that gross rent to income ratios of households relocated by urban renewal agencies in 1964 rose from a median of 25 to 28 percent. On the plus side, 94 percent of the families were relocated in sanitary housing.[22] Among the achievements credited to urban renewal, the Douglas Commission included:

1. Improvements to the physical appearance of hundreds of cities;
2. The increase in land values and the tax base in the business districts;
3. Attraction of some affluent and well-off people to gracious living areas within the central cities;
4. Civic improvements by universities, hospitals, and other institutions;
5. Carrying out the projects honestly and without graft or scandal.[23]

Have the older cities become more livable as a result of urban renewal? For some groups—yes: for commuters and residents who use a renovated central district such as Boston's Government Center; for those who enjoy a performing arts center, such as Lincoln Center in New York; and for students and faculty at the University of Chicago and other universities which are in renewal areas. But urban renewal officials in many cities tended to be too responsive to private developers seeking profitable ventures and too indifferent toward their low income residents. They wanted the well-to-do people to come back and the poor to disappear. It is an old American attitude, as shown in Chapter 3.

Some Lessons from Urban Renewal

Urban renewal promised too much. It was supposed to make the cities beautiful for the beautiful people, restore the tax base, raise up the poor. It could not do all of these things or perhaps any of them all by itself. In the beginning it may have been necessary to promise so much in order to sell it to the Congress and the public. But that was a quarter century and 500 legislative programs ago. Is it too much to hope that the Congress and the country will support socially desirable legislation without being told that *this* is the one that cures everything?

Urban renewal is not the way to fiscal salvation for the cities. The net gain to the real estate tax base from urban renewal improvements has been small. And this has come only after long years of planning, hassling small businessmen and families occupying renewal sites, and frequently slow rent ups of the new commercial and office space or the creation of excessive vacancies in older buildings that are still usable. Mayors and city finance officers now realize this. They are wise in pressing for additional direct aids from the federal government in the form of block grants or revenue sharing.

Land subsidies are not necessary for viable commercial redevelopment projects in the central business districts. Only the power of eminent domain is required to assemble the land if the project is deemed to have a clear public purpose. A large commercial and hotel complex known as Franklin Town was started in the early 1970s in Philadelphia's central district without any land write down. It is likely to demonstrate that land subsidies are simply unnecessary when the market is strong. Land subsidies should be limited to projects that will house lower income families and for supporting facilities (including shopping) in such neighborhoods. Perhaps land write downs can also be justified in connection with industrial investments that will provide jobs for underemployed inner city people.

Urban renewal is best thought of as a set of tools rather than an end in itself. Techniques of land assemblage for public purposes were advanced in the United States through experience with urban renewal. Few urbanists would throw away these tools. They can be utilized, for example, in shaping new development patterns and helping to build new communities. Indeed, one of the nation's best known urban renewal officials, Edward Logue, transferred his skills to a public development corporation in New York which is mainly building on raw land outside of the cities.

For the inner cities, however, the biggest problem in the 1970s is to keep them livable for moderate and lower income people and to increase the employment and educational opportunities of the disadvantaged. In the Housing and Urban Development Act of 1968 Congress placed a high priority upon meeting the housing needs of low and moderate income people. And the urban renewal officials in HUD under former Secretary George Romney evidently made a genuine effort to carry out the spirit of the 1968 Act. In 1969-70 about 70 percent of the 25,000 dwelling units completed on urban renewal land were for low and moderate income households. This is a less dazzling and more difficult assignment for urban renewal than clearing land for shopping emporiums, but it is a responsibility that mature administrators will not avoid.

8 Model Cities

The problem of the older city is people. What happens to real estate is secondary. If the people who dwell in the core cities have enough basic income or earning power, they will be able to live decently and maintain their homes and neighborhoods. Without adequate income for the residents—and the amount is relative to what other Americans have, not the subsistence level in India—there is little hope for the central city.

In the mid-sixties the Johnson administration saw the need for new approaches to help the poor and the near-poor. Who are these people? They include:

1. Men and women working but not bringing home a decent week's pay;
2. Youngsters who see no light at the end of the school tunnel;
3. Elderly persons who cannot work but deserve some dignity in their twilight years.

Out of concern for such groups came the antipoverty programs, the manpower development efforts, and Model Cities.

Model Cities was designed to help localities seek innovative ways of improving the quality of life in poverty neighborhoods. The program provided funds to selected communities for a wide range of activities not otherwise or adequately supported by existing federal aids in such areas as education, health, job expansion, and economic development. It was also an effort to increase the capability of local governments to plan and coordinate public services for the people who live in the most impoverished conditions.

The Model Cities proposal incorporated the latest thinking of policy planners in the middle sixties. The mayor or chief elected official was to be strengthened by being given the main responsibility for the program. In addition, heavy reliance was to be placed on comprehensive planning and programming techniques such as five-year plans and cost-benefit analysis. At the same time, the residents of the affected neighborhoods were to have a substantial if not determining voice in the design and conduct of the programs.

In 1972 almost 150 localities were participating, including virtually all cities of 300,000 population or larger. The actual federal outlay on Model Cities for the fiscal year 1972 (July 1, 1971 to June 30, 1972) was $500 million. The projected outlays for fiscal years 1973 and 1974 were at the level of $600 million a year. [1]

Conceptual Roots

There was an evangelical ring to Model Cities when it was first announced. "Nineteen sixty-six can be the year of the urban turnabout in American history," a presidential task force told Mr. Johnson in the fall of 1965. It urged a new approach that would completely eliminate blight in the poorest neighborhoods and create in their place high quality environments and living opportunities. Piecemeal approaches and conflicting activities would be replaced by closely coordinated physical and human resource programs. The efforts would be concentrated in target neighborhoods comprising perhaps 10 percent of the city's population. All of the talents and techniques of modern technology would be utilized, including cost-reducing methods of construction and systems analysis. [2]

The task force proposed to set up a nationwide contest among cities and towns. From among the applicants, sixty-six localities were to be selected to participate. After an inexpensive first year of planning, annual costs to the federal government would range between $750 and $900 million for three years, then taper off. How could so much be done for so little? All other relevant federal aid money would be channeled into a common account from which the selected communities could obtain funds. A federal coordinator was to be assigned to each city to provide liaison with all federal agencies and to review the city's plan before it could receive money under the new program.

The concept of Model Cities emerged from a task force of experienced men. What perceptions of reality led them to this new approach? Looking at older programs, they reasoned along the following lines:

1. The functional approaches—housing, health, education, and others—are too piecemeal. A coordinated approach, a meshing of activities, is essential if we are to make a dent.
2. Social programs and physical renewal efforts should go hand in hand.
3. There should be a premium on innovation. Old established ways of doing things are not working well enough.
4. Elected officials must be strengthened relative to career functionaries and independent authorities. Unearmarked funds or "glue" money should go to the mayor or chief elected official as one way of aiding him in the struggle with independent or quasiautonomous bureaus, commissions, and other agencies of local government.

5. Resident participation in some degree is desirable and necessary, but the mayor and elected officials must hold the upper hand.
6. Earlier efforts have been spread too thin. They should be concentrated. How? By focusing on a target population (actually a geographic area containing the group) of deprived and disadvantaged people.
7. There are new problem-solving techniques which hold high potential for rationalizing urban decision making. Cities should be encouraged to use them.

From Proposal to Legislative Enactment

Neither Congress nor the established clientele groups were enthusiastic about the proposal. The idea of a large role for the resident poor did not sit well. The new militance of the underclass, which put pressure on the schools, hospitals and other existing institutions, was associated with the Community Action Program. The establishment people and the mayors wanted no new federal programs to underwrite agitation among the poor. As a result, the congressional committees deemphasized citizen participation and assigned primary authority to local elected officials.

A policy declaration in the administration's bill stated that housing aided under the act should be aimed at eliminating racial discrimination. This was deleted by the Congress. Racial fears also surfaced in connection with schools: the Secretary of Housing and Urban Development, who was to administer the program, was specifically prohibited from requiring busing of children into integrated schools as a condition of assistance.

Some members of Congress have always conjured up images of federal czars reaching into the localities and destroying local autonomy. To allay these fears, the congressional committees eliminated the administration's proposal to have federal coordinators in each demonstration city whose task would have been to pull together all relevant federal aids.

Other changes in the administration package were also necessary to secure sufficient support. Local officials of urban renewal agencies argued that the new program would have the effect of diverting federal funds for urban renewal to the cities selected for demonstrations at the expense of cities not chosen. To meet this valid argument, the administration and the Congress agreed to increase the total authorization for urban renewal. Further, the President's request for a five-year authorization of program funds was reduced by the Congress to two years.

Even with these changes, the Model Cities bill was passed only by a narrow margin. Later, to broaden support in the Congress and the country, the administration decided to increase the number of participating communities to about 150.[3]

Conflicts and Pitfalls in Program Design

Model Cities was loaded with built-in conflicts.

1. The mayor's political dilemma: could he favor the poorest 10 percent of the city's people without alienating the residents of working class and lower middle class neighborhoods? Some local officials viewed this designation as an invitation to political suicide.

2. Responsibility for coordinating all the programs was placed on the mayor. But as noted in Chapter 3, the "good government" people of the early 1900s did not trust their mayors and had set up independent boards and commissions to provide certain public services such as public education, welfare, correction, and health. These arrangements have been carried down to modern times in many localities. Thus, the chief elected officials were given responsibility without clear authority, particularly in the areas of social development that were so heavily stressed by Model Cities.

3. The monkey and the elephant herd: how could a small monkey (with only 500 coconuts) tease compliance from the elephant herds and all the other animals who already roamed the urban turf stocked yearly by the Washington wardens with 10,000 coconuts? In budget terms, the cities and towns were receiving something in the order of $10 billion a year through 400 or so federal aid programs in the first few years that program money became available under Model Cities. The bulk of these funds came through the Department of Health, Education, and Welfare, not HUD. The budget request for Model Cities in fiscal 1969 was for $500 million in new obligational authority. Less than half of this amount was actually obligated that year because of slowness in local planning, detailed federal reviews, limited local capacity to carry out the activities, and in some places lack of cooperation from existing agencies such as school districts. But even if all of the money had been put out, the Model Cities people could hardly be expected to establish authority over other federal agencies and their local counterparts with resources aggregating fifteen to twenty times the new Model Cities money. All of these categorical aid administrators continued to insist upon compliance with the rules and regulations of their programs as a condition to funding in Model Cities neighborhoods.

4. How could the residents be involved without developing a political machine that would seek control in the neighborhood and pose a direct threat to the mayor and the local political organization? The designers of the Model Cities program wanted more than lip service to citizen participation such as characterized the earlier workable program and urban renewal, but they knew that the Congress and the country were in no mood for more federally-supported confrontations between the minority poor and the local governments. They evidently underestimated the determination of

resident groups to have a major role, including a share of the funds for staffing the citizen groups with technicians and administrative personnel. In Philadelphia, the citizens group known as the North City Area Council demanded a separate budget and considerable decision-making authority. The city rejected these demands and was taken to court, along with HUD which supported the city's position. A federal appeals court ruled in favor of the citizens group.[4]

The conflicts designed into the Model Cities program made it an administrative nightmare:

1. plan with people vs. plan comprehensively;
2. be creative but follow every step in the guidebook;
3. involve residents in jobs but use labor-saving technology; and
4. show quick, visible results but change traditional institutions.

Choosing the Model Cities

With all these booby traps down the road, Model Cities enlisted a large number of talented and dedicated people to make the program go. Some of them shifted over from the antipoverty programs, people volunteered from other HUD programs, a few people even came from the State Department, and a number were recruited from private life. In its formative period, Model Cities was the kind of movement that attracted men and women who might have gone into the Peace Corps, the Community Action Program, or an Environmental Protection Agency. The citizens groups also tapped leadership from the poverty neighborhoods.

The localities spent the first year preparing their applications and negotiating with the HUD administrators for a ticket of admission to the program. The public saw little, but behind the scenes there was a struggle for power among the old-line bureau chiefs and the people appointed by the mayor to set up the program. Delicate negotiations also commenced between city hall and spokesmen for the poverty neighborhoods tentatively designated for inclusion in the program.

HUD's new Model Cities Administration sifted and evaluated the applications over the summer and fall and selected 63 cities in November 1967. The following year 84 more communities were brought in and 3 more subsequently included to bring the total to 150. As of December 31, 1970, 4 cities were no longer participating. All 27 cities of half-million population or more were named, along with 56 cities in the 100,000-500,000 range, 46 in the 25,000-100,000 class and 21 cities with less than 25,000 population.

Performance under Model Cities

Seventy-five cities completed their first year of planning and began entering the action phase in 1969. Most of the other participating communities commenced the action phase in 1970. The experimental nature of the program and close scrutiny of local proposals by the Model Cities Administration held the commitment level for supplemental grants below the amounts that could have been obligated. Actual expenditures were of course below the amounts approved in the early action years. Expenditures in fiscal year 1970 were $86 million, rising to $328 million in 1971 and $500 million in the year ending June 1972.

What was the money used for? Education took 20 percent of the funds; environmental protection and development (including urban renewal) accounted for 17 percent; housing activities received 16 percent; and 11 percent went for health programs. Other substantive areas supported with relatively smaller allocations were manpower and job development, social services, economic development, recreation and culture, and crime prevention and juvenile delinquency. About 60 percent of the Model Cities funds have been for social development, the remainder for physical development.[5]

The supplemental grant under Model Cities was an open-ended contribution in the nature of a block grant for improving living conditions and opportunities for people residing in the poorest part of the community. It could be used to enrich activities or projects that were already receiving federal support under an existing program. Some of the grant money could be spent on novel or experimental activities for which there was no other federal support.

The Model Cities grant was supposed to have a multiplier effect with respect to funds coming into the model neighborhoods. For each dollar of Model Cities money, three to four dollars were to be generated from other sources. This did not happen. Many federal programs are governed by fixed allocation formulas and could not be modified. Even where administrators of other federal programs had some discretion in the disposition of funds, they were reluctant to cooperate. To give up control over one's program money is to accept a loss of power or influence. It took persistent maneuvering to get the functional bureaus and offices to earmark a portion of their funds for Model Cities. An intensive effort with the Department of Health, Education, and Welfare resulted in channeling an estimated $150 to $200 million of grant funds to Model Cities between fiscal years 1968 and 1971. Less than half of this money would otherwise have gone to the model neighborhoods, in the opinion of Sidney Gardner, a former HEW official.[6] In any event, only one dollar of other public funds was generated by each dollar of Model Cities grants in the first two action years.

Some Accomplishments

Despite these limitations, some individual accomplishments can be cited. HUD had always had the reputation of being a developer- and lender-oriented department. With Model Cities, it could give more attention to the people of the slums, the citizen groups, and to the mayors and elected officials. Among the root problems of the slum population are unemployment and subemployment. One sector of potential employment is public service. In New York, Detroit, and several other cities, civil service regulations were modified to place less emphasis upon formal education and written examinations as the basis for hiring. The number of jobs made available in this way to model nieghborhood residents has not been ascertained.[7] In Portland, Maine and Toledo, Ohio city demonstration agencies negotiated the hiring of model neighborhood residents with third-party contractors in a variety of industrial sectors.

If one job could be generated for each $10,000 of Model Cities program money, 50,000 to 60,000 jobs might have been opened up to the residents of the poverty neighborhoods in different parts of the country. Model Cities was not the lead agency in the field of manpower development, but here and there it helped muster public support for the population groups with the greatest need for jobs.

Educational handicaps of children from poverty neighborhoods have also been dealt with through Model Cities programs. In Lancaster, Pennsylvania, for example, tutoring services during and after school were made available to children from the model neighborhood. Some improvement in reading scores resulted. In Providence and Chicago, Model Cities funds were used to provide preschool preparation for tots in low income neighborhoods; the public housing authorities made space available in their buildings for this activity. In Baltimore, Washington, D.C., and several other places, parents were given the opportunity to help shape the educational programs in their children's schools. These were only beginnings, but they indicated what might be done if funds were made available for continuing such programs on a long-term basis.

Crime rates are highest in the poorest sections. But police practices are a matter of bitterness among many poor people, especially racial minorities. As with other functions of government, Model Cities did not have the main responsibility for crime prevention or the improvement of police-community relations. Nevertheless, Model Cities programs in several cities were credited with stimulating the employment of young men from the model neighborhoods as community service officers. In this capacity, they served as paraprofessionals in the police department with the possibility of qualifying for regular appointments.[8] Typically, however, police departments resisted Model Cities efforts to perform significant operational or evaluative roles in their departments.

Economic development in the ghettos and barrios of American cities by community groups and businessmen also received support through Model Cities. By the end of calendar 1970 an estimated $32 million of grants under this program had been committed to economic development, mostly through community development corporations. Citizen pressure for economic development apparently induced the reluctant Model Cities administrators in Washington and the localities to enter this field. This may have been due to different expectations about the economic potential of inner city areas. The government officials have studied the trends and they are bleak; but the residents, watching private industry and merchants leave the area, see a void to be filled through self-help and resident ownership and control. In Seattle, East St. Louis, Portland, Oregon and other cities, community development corporations or similar organizations received funds from Model Cities.[9]

On the whole, economic development efforts have met with little success. Conditions which drove existing business firms out of poverty neighborhoods continued to plague the new enterprises. Problems were, in fact, compounded by the inexperience of new entrepreneurs. The lesson seems to be that working through the general economy, as in the case of Leon Sullivan's Opportunities Industrialization Centers, is a sounder approach than attempts to rebuild the ghetto economy as a self-contained entity.

These activities initiated in various places suggest the limited success of the Model Cities program. Even when an activity has proven its worth, it has often been impossible to get the funds to keep it going on a long-term basis. This may be a basic defect of any demonstration program, but those which attempt to help the poor are particularly vulnerable since the poor do not have much political influence in their communities.

Measured in dollars, Model Cities outlays have been small relative to the scale of problems at which they were aimed. Nor did the leveraging of Model Cities dollars through other federal programs take place at the three or four to one ratio as was originally hoped.

In the critical area of employment, such data as are available for the inner city population do not suggest any significant gains. In the view of a White House task force set up to review Model Cities in late 1969, the program was, in concept, "a long step in the right direction," but in practice only a short step.[10]

Model Cities: An Interim Judgment

Model Cities assigned a high priority to making life more bearable and hopeful for the weakest and most unprivileged urban Americans. For securing a national mandate from the Congress for this purpose, it deserves a high mark. But that was in 1966. Whether the commitment to help the poor and disadvantaged will continue to be honored is by no means certain. In the early 1970s, many Americans were inclined to be less generous, to lock the doors, and to beef up the police.

Model Cities gave a boost to the beleaguered mayors—a little more money, a little more authority vis-à-vis the functional bureaucrats in education, health, manpower and other social sectors. Under an experimental approach termed "planned variations," the mayors of selected cities received the authority to review, comment, and sign off on federal categorical aids prior to use in their communities. This was in line with a general propensity of the Nixon administration to allow more discretion to the localities in the use of federal funds. While this might improve the administrative effectiveness of local governments, it could also weaken the national commitment to assist the least influential claimants for local services—the undereducated, underemployed, and disadvantaged groups.

This demonstration program also helped to initiate or continue the process of city hall-community group dialogues. Citizens had one more way of voicing their complaints and demands and letting off steam. It is better than letting the pressure build up until the lid blows. And many of the grievances are legitimate. Indeed, through Model Cities clients and consumers gained increased representation on housing authorities, hospital boards, and similar agencies that affect their daily lives. This may be one of the lasting accomplishments of the program.

The end products of Model Cities are not massive, startling, or unusually innovative. Some of the new activities are helpful improvements in public or social services. Mainly they have enabled the communities to cope a little better with their difficulties. The time has been too short and the resources too thin to make marked gains in the quality of life in poverty neighborhoods. Even a Robert Moses or a Leon Sullivan could not transform the social environment for the 300,000 people of North Philadelphia at $80 per person.

Whether new institutions evolved under the impetus of Model Cities is uncertain. One change that coincided with (but was not necessarily caused by) programs like Model Cities may be noticed in a number of places. This was the tendency to disestablish the old-line white liberal leadership of some organizations and replace them with younger, more group-conscious minority directors and boards. This has occurred in connection with housing associations and economic development groups in some cities.

A modest block grant approach was pioneered by Model Cities. Supplemental grants from this program could be used for a wider range of activities than the typical federal categorical aid program. The national purpose was recognized, but local circumstances could be taken into account in the use of the money. Whether poverty neighborhoods will receive a comparable priority under the new revenue sharing arrangements emerging from the Congress and the Nixon administration is doubtful. But this brings us to the next major public response to the needs of local government.

9 Revenue Sharing

The costs of local government have raced ahead of internal fiscal resources in recent times. Since World War II, pressures have been building up in the core cities to do more about decaying neighborhoods, to replace outworn municipal plant and equipment, and to raise educational standards. In the sixties, increased welfare needs and rising expectations among the poor developed at the same time that the general public was demanding more police protection and environmental controls.

In 1966 the general inflation hit the cities in the form of increased salary demands from municipal workers and teachers. In some large cities wage increases in the municipal sector ranged between 6 and 12 percent a year from 1966 to 1970. In Philadelphia, for example, actual expenditures rose about 14 percent a year during that period, reflecting not only wage increases but also service improvements, rising debt charges, and increases in other costs.[1] Other large cities had similar increases in expenditures. Between 1965 and 1971, pay per municipal worker in the United States rose at a rate of 7 percent a year and by 50 percent over the six years.[2]

What is a mayor to do? As individuals, a large number have left office or been turned out by the voters. But those who hold the responsibility have four options to consider individually and in combination:

1. Increase efficiency.
2. Reduce service levels.
3. Increase local taxes or charges.
4. Seek more money from the state and federal governments.

Few municipal experts expect large savings through more efficient operations, at least not in the near future. Local government is a labor-intensive industry and is likely to remain so. There are no techniques at hand for multiplying the output of policemen or teachers to a significant degree.

Cities are trying to hold the line on service levels and costs but some of the increasing costs are built-in: debt service, pensions, and employee benefits. There will be demands to cut services but which ones? Police? Schools? Health care? In fact, all of these services are likely to be expanded in the seventies. In Philadelphia, outlays for schools and municipal services were expected to increase by about 7 percent a year between 1970 and 1975 without allowing for inflation. Taking into account the rise in prices, the total city budget was projected to grow from $750 million to more than $1.5 billion in a matter of five years.[3]

To meet the increased demands for public services, local and state governments have had to boost their tax efforts almost every year. State and local revenues, exclusive of federal aid, rose from 9 percent of the gross national product in 1961 to almost 12 percent by the end of 1971. These governments raised $600 for each man, woman and child in 1971 compared with $257 in 1961. (In dollars of 1961 purchasing power, state and local taxes per person rose from $257 to about $375 in 1971.)

The large central cities with their high-cost populations and relatively static economies have been most hard-pressed. In Philadelphia, again, locally-collected taxes in the early sixties took 6 percent of total income earned by city residents but were up to 8 percent by the end of the decade. Per person these local revenues ross from $165 to $287 between 1961 and 1970. These local levies would have been substantially higher by 1970 if not for a tripling of state aid for Philadelphia schools during the decade.

Growth of Federal Aid

In 1961, the year Kennedy entered the White House, federal aid to state and local governments amounted to $7 billion. In 1971, it was $30 billion. During the sixties Congress added some 400 programs, most of them in the Johnson period, bringing the total to 530 by 1970. In relative terms, the biggest gains were registered in the fields of education and manpower, health, and community development ahd housing.

Virtually all categorical programs required some state or local contributions in cash or kind, varying from 10 to 50 percent or more. By offering federal dollars, a categorical program seeks to induce state or local agencies (and in some cases private groups) to undertake activities that are presumably important for the nation as a whole. Seven out of eight dollars of federal categorical aid have gone initially to the states, only one out of eight directly to localities. In the latter group were urban renewal, Community Action, and Model Cities. But much of the federal money ends up in urban areas, after administrative massaging by state agencies.[4]

How much of this federal money goes for the urban poor or near-poor? Only a crude estimate is possible. For the fiscal year ending June 1973 the U.S. budget called for $31.5 billion to be laid out in metropolitan areas. An inspection of individual program outlays by purpose suggests that about half of the federal money was supposed to be for the poor and near-poor.

These programs are intended to supplement the incomes of the poor, put people to work in decent-paying jobs or increase their employability, improve the life-chances of children from impoverished homes, make the families healthier, or provide better living arrangements.

How adequate are these programs? The largest single outlay—$6 billion—was for public assistance. Other large outlays were for child nutrition and food stamps (almost $2 billion), medical assistance ($2.1 billlon), and elementary and secondary education ($1.5 billion). Of the latter program, a White House task force wrote in late 1969:

> We believe that city and state officials are as capable as federal ones of reading the laws that Congress passes and of interpreting them correctly. We believe that in general they can be trusted to respect the intentions of Congress . . .

To which was added this curious footnote:

> We say this despite the deplorable record of the cities in cheating their poverty areas of a fair share of the [then] $1.3 billion spent for improving elementary and secondary education.[5]

In the critical area of employment and manpower development, about $2.5 billion were included in the 1973 budget. But unemployment rates for inner-city employables are close to 10 percent in large cities. Subemployment, meaning men and women who are working but at wage rates too low to live decently (below $3.50 per hour in 1972), is a fact of life for 60 out of 100 inner-city workers. Moreover, recent surveys of federally supported manpower training programs have found that graduates who find work typically earn only $3,000 a year—a poverty income.[6]

In a word, the federal aids for the core cities and their poor have helped—but not enough. The Nixon administration, with a substantial degree of support from working class people, was resistant to any large increases for income maintenance or job creation programs for the poor as urged by the National Welfare Rights Organization, the National Urban Coalition, and some members of the Congress. Most people did agree, however, on the need to consolidate some federal programs—there were just too many to manage and coordinate. Thus, the stage was set for two new forms of federal aid backed by the Nixon administration: general revenue sharing and special revenue sharing.

General Revenue Sharing

Congress recognized the fiscal plight of the cities by passing a general revenue sharing act in October 1972. This legislation, titled the State and Local Fiscal Assistance Act of 1972, authorized the distribution of $5.3 billion in calendar 1972, with annual payments rising to $6.5 billion in 1976. One-third of the money goes to the state governments, two-thirds to local governments. The allocations among the states are determined under a formula that considers population, relative tax effort, and per capita income inversely weighted. The same factors are used to determine the distribution among general purpose local governments. The funds received by local governments may be spent on a wide range of functions with two notable exceptions: operating expenses for education and welfare payments. Social services for the poor or aged, however, are eligible expenditures. Generally, the funds may be used for both operating expenses and capital outlays.

The main advantages of general revenue sharing are:

1. Predictability: local and state governments know how much they will get each year and can plan accordingly.
2. Periodic increases: the federal government's unique ability to tap a rising income stream makes this possible.
3. Absence of strings or matching requirements. State and local governments can spend the money according to their own priorities.
4. Distribution recognizes need and tax effort of each jurisdiction.[7]

It should be noted that revenue shares under the 1972 act are not completely unconditional. Funds received under this program may not be applied against other federal aid programs as the matching funds required of state and local governments. There is a prohibition against discrimination in the use of the money on grounds of race, color, national origin, or sex. Prevailing wages must be paid on construction projects that are assisted with these funds—the well-known Davis-Bacon Act proviso that the building trades insist upon. And acceptable accounting and auditing procedures must be followed by participating governments, so that the books can be examined to assure full compliance with the law and absence of hanky-panky in the use of the money.

How much of a contribution will general revenue sharing make to the overall needs of state and local governments? Total expenditures of these governments have been increasing at an average rate of 10 percent a year. The payments under general revenue sharing will cover about 3 percent of aggregate outlays between 1972 and 1976. But all federal aids, including this new source, will account for 20 to 25 percent of state/local expenditures in the same period.

What does it do for a large central city? Philadelphia's share for the first twelve-month period came to $44 million. Outlays for schools and municipal services during the same period were running at an annual rate of close to $1 billion. Thus, the first full-year payment under federal revenue sharing covered little more than 4 percent of Philadelphia's total expenditures. For New York City, the $202 million revenue share was slightly more than 2 percent of a $9 billion budget in fiscal year 1972.

When he signed the measure into law, President Nixon told the assembled state and local officials in a paraphrase of Winston Churchill's words: We have given you the tools, now you go do the job. It was a rather small tool.

Special Revenue Sharing

This is the companion to general revenue sharing in the plans of the Nixon administration. And it involves more money. The administration's budget for fiscal 1974 called for the replacement of seventy existing categorical aid programs by four special revenue sharing programs.[8] The categories and dollar amounts for the first full year of budget authority were:

Special Revenue Sharing	*Billions*
Urban community development	$2.3
Education	2.5
Manpower training	1.3
Law enforcement	0.8
Total	$6.9

The idea is to give state and local governments wide discretion in the use of these funds. The federal agencies that heretofore have allocated a substantial amount of aid on a program-by-program basis and in some cases project-by-project, would recede from the scene. Within the broad framework of congressional intent, state and local governments would decide on that all-important question: Who gets what? Federal representatives would no longer have an affirmative role in influencing priorities of localities or state governments. They would have to see that the civil rights laws are being observed; also, federal auditors would check the financial accounts. And federal technicians would be on call to give advice. But that is all.

The implicit assumption of special revenue sharing is that there is a close correspondence between national needs and local priorities in such sectors as urban development, education, and manpower training. Therefore, it is unnecessary—indeed, counterproductive—for federal agencies to participate actively in shaping and overseeing local efforts to revitalize old neighborhoods, improve school programs, or prepare workers for job opportunities.

For the urban sector the Nixon proposal is titled the "Better Communities Act." It calls for the termination of such programs as urban renewal, grants for water and sewer facilities, public facility loans, open space land grants, neighborhood facilities, rehabilitation loans for older housing, and Model Cities. State and local governments were to begin sharing in a pool of funds in mid-1974. The 1974 budget indicated that $2.3 billion would be available for allocation under this new approach the first full year.

The special revenue sharing approach would not require detailed applications from the communities. The bulk of the money would be distributed virtually automatically to general purpose governments in metropolitan areas on a formula basis. The allocation formula would consider population, the degree of overcrowded housing, and the proportion of families living below the poverty line. There would be no local matching of funds and the locality could use the money as it saw fit. It would simply have to publish a statement of community development objectives and projected use of funds for the year.[9]

The notion of consolidating community development programs and streamlining the approval process had been gaining support for several years. There were too many specialized programs, too many forms to fill out, too many consents to be negotiated. Model Cities was designed to rectify this situation in poverty neighborhoods but it never secured control over other relevant programs. There is no dispute, however, about the need to pull related programs together, to allow more flexibility to local administrators in the use of federal funds, and to expedite federal determinations about funding local efforts.

The heart of the matter is whether local officials can be expected to pursue national objectives that are locally unpopular or politically dangerous. Would a city council or county board assign as high a priority to poverty neighborhoods as did the Congress when it passed antipoverty and Model Cities programs in 1964, 1965, and 1966? Would a policeman-turned-mayor permit federal funds to be used for legal services for the black kids in trouble with the law? Congress mandated in 1968 that a majority of housing units in a community's residential urban renewal projects must be for low and moderate income people. Would not many cities, released from this federal requirement, be tempted to favor higher income housing? Should federal funds be available to affluent suburbs to enable them to clear out slum pockets of poor or black families without any assurance that such families will be adequately rehoused within the locality?

Special revenue sharing, as proposed by the Nixon administration, would evidently remove what little leverage the federal government has been able to exercise over localities in behalf of the poorest, weakest, and least influential members of the community. And it might tempt localities to pursue beggar-my-neighbor policies of exporting their poor, closing recreational facilities to all but town residents, and declining to participate in areawide agreements on sites for moderate and lower income housing.

Community Development Grants

If there is support for consolidating some programs, there is less willingness in the Congress to remove the federal presence in community development and redevelopment. Senator Sparkman, for one, said, "I do not believe that the Congress or the American taxpayer would want a plan of Federal distribution of funds to local communities without knowing how the money is to be used." As an alternative, he proposed a multiyear block grant for community development. Each locality would be entitled to a basic amount each year, just as in special revenue sharing. But unlike the Nixon plan, the Sparkman bill would lay down requirements for federal aid, including a local program to meet housing needs of low and moderate income families and to carry out systematic code enforcement. "My intent," stated Sparkman, "is to facilitate the delivery of Federal assistance to localities, and at the same time to retain adequate control of Federal funds to assure that they are spent in a manner consistent with national development objectives."[10]

On the House side, a Housing Subcommittee was shaping a block grant proposal similar to Sparkman's. By September 1972 a wide-ranging bill had emerged from the parent Committee on Banking and Currency (H.R. 16704) that was intended to consolidate, simplify, and improve a number of laws accumulated over the years relating to housing and urban development. Included was a new program of block grants for community development. This bill was denied clearance by the House Rules Committee on grounds of complexity and lack of time for adequate consideration. But the proposed measure had bipartisan support and was resubmitted in essentially the same form in the following Congress.

The 1973 Sparkman bill would provide contract authority over two years in the amount of $5.9 billion, more than twice the annual commitment level in the administration's proposed Better Communities Act. Communities would be assured of some continuity in funding over several years, unlike the start-and-stop experience with a number of federal-aid programs.

The bulk of the funds (75 percent in the Senate bill, 80 percent in the House bill) would go to general purpose governments in metropolitan areas. They would not get the money almost automatically and without requirements as under the administration's proposal. In their report on the 1972 bill Congressman Patman and his co-sponsors explained why:

The committee considered but emphatically rejected the administration's revenue sharing approach which would have required no application or preconditions to receiving funds. Instead, the committee's block grant approach makes the receipt of grants contingent on the [HUD] Secretary's approval of an application which demonstrates that the applicant's activities will be a part of a meaningful development program, and in accordance with accepted Federal objectives.[11]

What would a community have to do to get its money? If the congressional committees have their way, every eligible locality would be expected to meet high standards of planning and performance. Some of the requirements are familiar ones—identifying objectives, providing residents with an opportunity to participate in the preparation of plans for their neighborhood (a Model Cities requirement), and compliance with civil rights laws. The committees also say to each community: You have a responsibility to provide housing not only for your present residents but also for low and moderate income people who work there or may reasonably be expected to reside or seek housing in the community. This presumably includes not only factory workers but policemen and their families, teachers, and even sanitation workers. Municipal employees in many suburban communities have been unable to find homes within their means in the places where they work.

In exchange, the localities may share in a larger pot of money than they have previously had access to. Some would be entitled to substantially more under an allocation formula that takes into account the community's population, extent of overcrowding in housing, degree of past participation in related federal aid programs, and extent of poverty weighted double. All metropolitan cities would be "held harmless"—receiving at least as much as before under relevant programs and without time limit.

This contrasts with the amounts that many larger cities would get under the administration's proposal. That bill would protect most cities against cuts for the first two years. Thereafter many would experience sharp drops in federal money under the administration's proposed distribution formula and funding level. Almost two out of three of the ninety-one largest cities would face reductions by the fifth year ranging from 3 percent to 77 percent. Thus, Cincinnati would receive $18.8 million a year for the first two years but only $9 million in the fifth year. Other losers under the Better Communities bill are such cities as Boston, Atlanta, Indianapolis, and San Francisco. Gainers under this formula would be cities that had not participated as actively in urban renewal or other community development programs or whose previous grants had not reflected their population size (or possibly the incidence of poverty or overcrowded housing). Big gainers in relative terms would be places like Dallas, Phoenix, Miami, Memphis, Omaha, and Long Beach.

Many more local governments including some urban counties are likely to receive aid under either the administration's Better Communities bill or the alternatives offered by the congressional committees. With this broadening of participation and some local governments entitled to big increases under the several formulas, only a substantial boost in federal funding could cover the total entitlements without absolute reductions for some of the cities with the deepest problems of physical decay and family poverty. Such an increase is provided in the Senate and House proposals.

Funds from community development block grants may be spent on the same types of activities previously permitted under the consolidated programs. These include slum clearance, code enforcement, construction of public works and neighborhood facilities, and land acquisition for open space and recreation. There are also some new wrinkles: provision of solid waste disposal facilities; the acquisition of land necessary for the guidance of urban development (land reserves for future public and private development as in Sweden?); and health, social, and cultural activities supportive of other approved community development activities.

Community development grants under the Sparkman bill would cover 90 percent of net program costs (but could cover the full costs of rehabilitation grants and relocation payments for dislocated persons up to specified limits). The remaining 10 percent would have to be provided by the locality in cash or kind. Localities could not be kept dangling indefinitely while their applications were being processed. Under the Sparkman bill the Secretary of HUD would have to give written notice of his approval or disapproval within 90 days after submission of the application.

The block grant for community development is an imaginative approach to carrying out urban renewal, providing public infrastructure, and conserving land within a metropolitan framework. For the first time, growth communities might be induced to consider their housing needs in relation to job opportunities within their boundaries. Suburban communities would be offered incentives for lowering the barriers to low and moderate income housing. They could not pursue no-growth policies or engage in snob zoning practices and still receive federal funds.

Older cities would benefit over the long run as their less advantaged residents gain access to housing and employment in the growth parts of the metropolitan area. In the near term, mayors and elected officials would be recognized as having primary responsibility for community improvement as against the special purpose agencies that sprouted in response to federal categorical aids. And within the national objectives, they could more readily tailor programs to their particular local silhouette than under the existing assortment of federal aids.

For the urban poor and near-poor, block grants for community development would not bring salvation. But they would be a move in the right direction.

Prospects for the Older Cities

The older cities of the nation are in deep trouble. As municipal governments, they are finding it more and more difficult to meet everyday services and pay the bills. Costs keep mounting faster than internal sources of revenues; federal and state aids must be increased each year on an emergency basis. As families and individuals, many of the residents of older cities live in quiet desperation. But they receive little sympathy for they are widely regarded as lazy or useless people, indeed parasites. Yet the large majority of those who can, do in fact work, but at wages below the decency level of $3.50 an hour and $7,000 a year. So they are stuck in the older districts, as are elderly people on small pensions and social security and welfare families with children. These people and the cities they inhabit have a common prospect. And it is not bright.

This remains true despite substantial increases in aid from the federal government in the past decade. Federal help to "save the city" was first provided through the urban renewal program. Land was cleared, buildings were built, some districts were reclaimed. But many neighborhoods continued to deteriorate as they lost attractiveness for those who could afford to keep them up. No one today expects urban renewal to do what was once promised—to restore the cities to fiscal solvency.

In the sixties federal support was extended to human resource development—a head start for preschool tots from disadvantaged homes, job training for adults and teenagers, homemaker counseling, and more health services for older persons. It was called the War on Poverty. These efforts have touched the lives of millions of people; many are the better for them. But joblessness remained high, crime rates rose, and riots and disturbances erupted in scores of cities. Perhaps too much was expected from this antipoverty effort both by taxpayers and potential beneficiaries.

Model Cities was a big idea but a small fund. Model Cities tried to put it all together for the poor—neighborhood rehabilitation and people rehabilitation: concentrate all the aids in a particular section of town, interlink everything into a "system," and use computers to print out progress reports. It was Scientific Management harnessed to a humane purpose. We can see many examples of useful activities stimulated by Model Cities. But the systems approach, not surprisingly, remained on paper. Nor were the Model Cities administrators able to induce or compel cooperation from a number of established functional agencies. Had all of these difficulties been overcome, Model Cities, like other programs overtly for the poor, had an Achilles' heel: it was bad local politics.

How can a mayor or chief executive select out a tenth of the city's population for special help without seeming to shortchange the rest? The usual way is to provide something for everybody and a little *less* for the poor neighborhoods. In connection with a program like Model Cities, the mayor must show that it is all new money from Washington that the Feds insist on spending this way. If the national administration makes clear that it is no longer committed to such a program, as the Nixon people did by proposing to replace Model Cities with a special revenue sharing fund, few local politicians will be able to give a high priority to the poorest neighborhoods.

Local politics versus national priorities underlie the struggle between the Nixon administration in calling for special revenue sharing and those who favor block grants for urban development, as proposed by Senator Sparkman and Congressman Patman and a majority of their committees. It boils down to whether a federal presence will be maintained in support of national objectives such as housing for moderate and lower income families, legal services for the poor, and open access to parks and recreational opportunities for minority families.

As the seventies unfold, it has become clear to many in the Congress that the cities cannot possibly pay their own way and must be permanently included in the federal budget. General revenue sharing under the 1972 law is but a first installment, for it covers only 30 percent of the annual increment in local expenditures projected over the next five to ten years. Urban services cannot be cut and savings from increased efficiency in the performance of local services will be modest at best. The main alternatives to increased federal support are agreements of suburbanites to share their tax base or a substantial increase of aid from state governments. In both possibilities the votes of suburban people or their representatives would be determining. Having divorced themselves from the city in the past decade or two, the better-off metropolitan families are not likely to raise the alimony.

More is involved than money. When the nation looks at the inner cities and their inhabitants, it is looking at its main domestic problems. "Their" problems become "our" problems. And their discontents can be ignored only at peril to the majority. For crime will mount, we shall have to hire more and more police, and build more prisons. But jailers also lose some of their freedom.

Americans have been capable of great generosity to victims of floods, former enemies, to each other. But they have also yielded at times to pettiness, hatred, and fear. The years ahead will be a time of struggle for the American soul.

10 New Development

Why do families move from old areas to newer developments? The answer may be the key to understanding the urban development process. So Catherine Bauer Wurster suggested back in 1951.[1] Whether it is *the* key or *a* key, the American's propensity to move is a force to be reckoned with.

There are two kinds of moving—migration and mobility. Migrations have commonly been impelled by adversity, such as religious persecution, political oppression, or economic decline of an area. If you look at a table of farm population in the United States, you will see a long column of minuses over many decades. People found that they could not make a living on farms and left the land for cities and towns.

The other kind of moving is the shifting about of urban people from one part to another of the city or metropolitan area. Many move to get more space or a better school district, to become homeowners, or to get away from racially changing neighborhoods. Usually it is for a number of reasons. It is the interplay between such motivations and the environments supplied by nature, builders, and local governments that interests us here.

More than half of man-made America has been developed within the lifetime of a thirty-year old person. Over forty million homes and apartment units were built between 1946 and 1973, with schools, roadways, shopping centers, and industrial plants to match. Most of this construction has been in metropolitan areas but outside the older cities. The suburban and exurban developments are not monolithic—they vary from modest tract homes to sumptuous estates. In comparison with the central cities, however, they are much more spread out. The city of Washington, D.C., for example, contained 750,000 people in 1972 within its sixty-one square miles. A major suburb, Montgomery County, Maryland, with 500 square miles, had 550,000 residents. In all areas, the newer forms of residential development and highway networks consume enormous amounts of land.

Into these suburbs and exurbs have come the families with stable employment and good incomes. Most are not wealthy, just well-off. Many will not stay in one place too long. The company will transfer some of them and others will find better opportunities on their own. Those who move will likely get more than they paid for the house but will trade up to a better house elsewhere.

This buoyant demand has stimulated the growth of the home building industry. There are hundreds of home builders and thousands of subcontractors in each large metropolitan area. A successful builder will put up perhaps 100 to 200 units a year but not enough to dominate the markets in which he operates. Few builders are in a position to bargain from market strength with landowners, labor unions, materials suppliers, or local governments. Home building is still a small-scale, high-cost industry. As costs go up for land, labor, materials, or construction money, most builders are forced to accept the increases and pass them on to consumers. Thus prices of new housing rose by 6 to 8 percent a year between 1966 and 1973.

The structure of government in metropolitan areas is also a factor in rising public and private development costs. The existence of scores and in some areas hundreds of local jurisdictions makes it virtually impossible to secure economical patterns of development. Sewer and water lines and transportation arteries are thus longer than necessary. In the private sector, the builder is confronted with different rules and standards in different localities relating to zoning, street widths, sewer requirements, and building materials and methods that may be used. The home builder has to get permission from many different public agencies initially and at several stages before he completes his development. This is a time-consuming process that adds to his financing costs and ultimately to the price that families must pay. Obtaining local approval for moderate and low income housing developments is almost always difficult and often impossible.

A number of factors inhibit the rationalization of the development process in the United States. Many people have a stake in the status quo, not only producers but also present homeowners. For if new homes keep going up in price, so do prices of desirable existing homes, *their* properties. Since 1960 there has been a marked increase in federal and state efforts to secure changes in local institutions and private practices that affect residential construction. The beginnings of change were visible by the early seventies.

The Demand for Space

Each year about two out of ten Americans change their residence. In 1971 over thirty-six million people moved, two-thirds of them simply finding another place in the same county. The most frequent movers (apart from college-age persons) are young families with parents aged twenty-five to thirty-four. For many of these people, the move reflects an adjustment to the increasing size of the family. Older people are more inclined to stay put. This is especially true of those aged sixty-five and over, but even middle-aged parents with high school children move less often than younger families.

The new-home buyer is typically married and in his thirties, has one or two children, and has an above-average income. Those who purchased with conventional loans in early 1972 paid an average of $38,000 and invested more than $9,000 of their own money in the down payment. A family buying a house at this price would need an income of $18,000 to $20,000 or more to meet all housing expenses. Many of these families probably accumulated the sizable down payments through ownership of another house that rose in price.

The new-home buyer with an FHA-insured mortgage (but no other subsidy) was typically in his early thirties and had an income of about $13,000. He bought a house for about $24,000 with ten percent down and thirty years to pay on the mortgage. Chances are he will sell it within ten years for a third to a half more than he originally paid and buy a bigger and more expensive home. If he holds for fourteen years, the price is likely to double.

At least this is what happened to many who bought a new house a decade or so ago. For example, original settlers in Levittown, New Jersey, now Willingboro, have seen their houses rise in price from $12,000-14,000 to $24,000-28,000 between 1958 and 1972. This is the equivalent of 5 percent a year compounded. Thus, inflation produced a tidy capital gain to an owner when he sold. But another house cost more and required a larger down payment. Putting the capital gain from house number one into house number two within a year enabled a family to avoid a federal tax on the capital gain.

It is a reasonable assumption that most home buyers are aware of the possibility that they will get substantially more than they paid when they go to sell, providing the neighborhood stays nice, the schools remain good, and no blacks or lower class people move into the vicinity. Home ownership with inflation gives people a big stake in keeping things unchanged. It helps explain why so many Americans oppose new development or any alteration in community patterns. Builders call it LMI—Last Man In. I'm here so let's close the gates.

Structure of American Government

Some public concerns that are clearly national in scope or impact cannot be treated directly by the central government. Constitutional and historical patterns require that the federal government work through state or local agencies to carry out national missions. This has been the case in the alleviation of poverty and the training and redevelopment of surplus workers. It has also been true for housing and community development.

A second fact of political life is that state governments have traditionally been oriented to small town and rural interests, unresponsive and sometimes hostile to the needs of the big cities. As CED stated in 1970:

Few state governments have sought to collaborate with the major cities—or with other local units—in meeting critical local responsibilities.[2]

Redistricting of state legislatures to reflect the one-man one-vote ruling of 1962 (*Baker* v. *Carr*) has given a larger vote to metropolitan residents. The suburbanites have been the big winners. The population movements of the past two decades have enabled these people to gain political power relative to central city people and perhaps the rural population.

A third phenomenon that is much deplored by political scientists (and all but ignored as a problem by the general public) is the multiplicity of governments in urban areas. There are fewer than 300 metropolitan areas In the United States, but they contain some 20,000 local jurisdictions. In the country as a whole, there are 80,000 or so local jurisdictions. These political creatures trudge about their duties—some as specialized as the servicing of a single cemetery or sewer facility—seemingly impervious to the scholar's charge that they constitute a crazy quilt of governments.

One consequence of fractionated jurisdictions is that some parts of the regional community can pass their social costs on to other parts without being charged: the congestion, noise, and air pollution that suburban motorists impose on central city residents; the untrapped or untreated wastes that float by air or stream from Town A to Towns B and C. In short, the multiplicity of governments in metropolitan areas permits economic nonaccountability for social costs.

Another consequence is political nonaccountability. Many of the "governments" at the local level are special districts and authorities. They are not directly responsible to electorates or to general governments elected by local citizens. Drawing their revenues from charges or fees, such districts usually do not have to convince the general taxpayers of the priority of their services, unlike other claimants for public resources.

In sum, national objectives in community development and housing are dependent for their implementation on local governments and participants in private markets. Most state governments (New York and Massachusetts are exceptions) have historically been unresponsive to the housing and other needs of central city populations. And at the metropolitan level, problems that are areawide in scope cannot be dealt with effectively because of the absence of areawide policies and governmental machinery. Each locality within the metropolis does what it thinks is best for itself: social costs can frequently be passed on without penalty to neighboring communities, and undesired residents or activities can be excluded by the in-group.

Public Services in Suburban Areas

A major consideration in the decision to seek or maintain a residence in a new development or a prestigious suburban community is the quality of public services. Schools are especially important to some parents. In the

New York metropolitan region, advertisements of homes for sale sometimes list the school district as well as the attributes of the house. Other local public services such as libraries, recreational programs, and open space are also significant elements in the standard of life available to urban families. "When I pay taxes," said Oliver Wendell Holmes, Jr., "I buy civilization." On a less lofty plane, the suburban home buyer says: I'm a taxpayer and I expect good services.

But there are wide disparities in public service levels, not only between the central city and the suburbs but among various suburban communities within the same metropolitan area. For the well-off family with school children, it pays to live in the suburban area rather than the central city. The outer communities require lower expenditures per resident for welfare, health, and police and fire protection. And with higher average incomes, they can and do spend more per resident on education while taking a lower proportion of income for all local services.[3]

The affluent suburbs also spend considerably more on education per pupil than less prosperous suburban communities. In the Philadelphia region, plush communities like Jenkintown, New Hope, and Upper Merion spent $1,000 to $1,200 per pupil for education in 1969-70. Each of these places had at least $35,000 in real property at market value per pupil. (The richest community, Lower Merion, had $63,000 for each pupil but spent only $966 on each youngster in school that year.) At the other end of the range were a number of outlying communities that spent only $700-800 per pupil, although imposing as high or higher effective property tax rates and receiving more state aid for schools. The reason for these lower school outlays is that they have much lower amounts of real estate behind each student—typically $15,000-$20,000.[4]

Such disparities among nearby communities in taxpaying ability and spending for desired public services are found in self-reinforcing. The families that can afford Saks Fifth Avenue and the best of everything have their own exclusive enclaves. They form something of a club with membership open only to those who can afford an expensive house. Everyone who makes it has a stake in limiting new members to those of the same social and economic rank and restricting further development. Much the same applies to less affluent places with community associations built around a swimming pool and public services to match.

Many localities calculate break-even property values—the average price of a house necessary to pay for all public services required by a household. At recent costs of schools and other local services in some areas, even families with a $40,000 home may barely pay their "share." This is likely to be the case for families with two or more children in the public schools. Given the heavy dependence upon the local property tax for school costs, each locality is behaving rationally from a fiscal and service level standpoint, in seeking to exclude lower priced developments and families with lower incomes than those already in the community. In fact, on these grounds it may make sense to have no more residential development of any kind.

No-growth or slow-growth policies are in effect in a number of suburban communities. The reasons or rationalizations include:

1. desire to preserve the character of the community;
2. need for open space and breathing room for present residents;
3. inadequate public plant capacity in sewerage, schools, and other facilities;
4. environmental damage that may result from further development.

The environmental concerns are not always misplaced. Much of the postwar residential development, especially in the 1950s, failed to provide for adequate treatment of waste. Sometimes local governments had to install facilities later at considerable public expense. The environmental concerns of the seventies brought response at the state level. A number of state agencies imposed moratoria on new construction until sewerage facilities could be enlarged. There appeared to be a tendency, however, for localities to do nothing about needed sewage treatment plants or trunk lines or to drag their feet about participating in regional arrangements in order to avoid further development.

Exclusionary Land Use Practices

There are a number of ways in which suburban localities keep out lower priced homes and apartments. The traditional exclusionary device is zoning; it is still the first line of defense. But there are other methods: the subdivision regulations may require heavily paved streets thirty-six feet wide in front of each house where twenty or twenty-four feet would suffice; the developer may be required to dedicate exorbitant amounts of land to the community; minimum floor area requirements per house may permit only expensive homes; and in some places the number of bedrooms per unit in multifamily housing may be limited to keep out households with children of school age.[5]

Consider zoning. In theory, zoning is supposed to prescribe permitted uses and densities of development for vacant land in accordance with a plan for future growth. The legal justification for zoning is the power of a public body to regulate property rights for the public health, safety, and welfare of the community. In practice, according to the Douglas Commission, many localities initially assign very low densities to undeveloped land and then deal with each application for rezoning on an ad hoc basis. In Connecticut, for example, more than half of the vacant land zoned for residential use in the state in the late sixties was for lots of one to two acres.[6] Some localities make no provision in their zoning ordinances for multifamily housing.

These zoning practices result in an artificial scarcity of buildable land at any one time. Prices are pushed up on sites that are rezoned to higher densities from time to time. Not only does this open the door to chicanery among landholders, would-be developers, local lawyers, and public officials, it also rules out developments that cannot bear high land costs. Subsidized and lower priced housing developments are thus excluded through a seemingly undeliberate and impartial local process. Suburban zoning is a clear example of benign neglect.

It is a tough system to beat. Individual developers are reluctant to take local zoning authorities to court. Smaller builders cannot afford to litigate and larger ones risk reprisals by the community officials on later projects. Even if a favorable ruling is handed down, the locality has ways of delaying the builder. With land loans or development loans at rates of 10 percent or higher a year, the developer can hardly afford to wait around.

The famous Girsh decision is a reminder that a builder can lose even when he wins in the courts. Joseph Girsh, a builder, applied for rezoning of 7.7 acres of land in Nether Providence township, a suburb of Philadelphia. He proposed to build not subsidized or lower priced housing but two luxury apartment buildings on this site. That was in 1964. He was turned down by the locality and took his case to court. After six years of litigation, the Pennsylvania Supreme Court ruled that the township's zoning ordinance was deficient in not providing for any apartment house construction. Under pressure from the court, the locality in 1970 created an apartment district and classified several vacant parcels for apartment development. But it did not include the Girsh property in this rezoning. In 1972 the new owners of this site still could not obtain a building permit to erect apartment structures so they went back to court. Faced with another Pennsylvania Supreme Court order, the local officials of Nether Providence initiated steps in April 1972 to condemn the former Girsh property for a park. Attorneys for the Pennsylvania Builders Association wrote:

The Girsh case suffers from the fatal defect of allowing the local government another or maybe even a series of other opportunities to harass the prospective developer. To be even more concrete, Joseph Girsh won his case but never did live to see his apartments built. The project that was originally proposed in 1964 has still not been started (late 1972).[7]

Still, there has been some movement against exclusionary land use practices of localities as a result of decisions in state courts. Class action suits have been brought in behalf of potential residents who are screened out as a result of arbitrary zoning or related measures. The Pennsylvania court in the Girsh case observed that "it is intolerable to allow one municipality (or many municipalities) to close its doors at the expense of surrounding communities" or the central city. And it suggested that ideally planning and zoning would be done on a regional basis.[8] In New Jersey, a state court told Madison township that its zoning ordinance was invalid for failing to consider regional needs, especially for housing of low income families. The court said: "A municipality must not ignore housing needs, that is, its fair proportion of the obligation to meet the housing need of its own population and that of the region."[9]

One of the most hopeful things about these legal actions is that new coalitions have been formed to represent the interests of classes of people who have up to now been effectively excluded from new suburban developments because of race or low incomes. The New York-based Suburban Action Institute, headed by Paul Davidoff, was organized expressly for this purpose. The National Committee Against Discrimination in Housing, directed by Edward Rutledge, has long been active in this fight. And so has the Legal Defense Fund of NAACP. The home building industry also has a big stake in securing access to suitable land on which subsidized and lower priced housing can be built. Thus the National Association of Home Builders and some of its state and local affiliates have joined in these legal actions. And in 1972 the state government in Pennsylvania aligned itself with an unusual coalition of parties in a court action against some of its own political subdivisions—Bucks County and a number of local zoning jurisdictions within the county—for allegedly engaging in exclusionary zoning.

Costs of Development and Occupancy Expenses

These institutional practices help explain the high cost structure of housing. Let us take a closer look at the elements of housing cost. First we must distinguish between the costs of producing the structures and the annual or monthly expenses of occupying them. The initial capital outlays are ordinarily transformed into annual charges—interest and repayment of loans and return on equity capital invested by the owner or developer. To these must be added the expenses of servicing and maintaining the property, local property taxes, and related expenses. In the aggregate these determine the housing expenses of owner-occupants or the rents that must be charged to tenants.

Development Costs.

In 1972 a new single-family house in the Northeast or North Central region might sell for about $35,000. Row houses and walkup apartment units were produced at about $22,000. The main components of development costs in relation to sales price for a detached house and total development cost for a multifamily row house ("townhouse" in advertising parlance) are shown below.

Table 10-1
Components of Development Costs for Single-family and Row Houses

	Single-family House[a]		Row House Unit[b]	
Component	Amount	Percent	Amount	Percent
Structure	$20,300	58	$14,960	68
Site acquisition	3,150	9	1,760	8
Site improvement	3,850	11	1,540	7
Marketing	1,050	3	—	—
Financing	1,750	5	1,320	6
Overhead, profit, fees	4,900	14	2,420	11
Total selling price	$35,000	100	$22,000[c]	100

[a] 1,300 square feet of floor area.
[b] 1,000 square feet.
[c] Total development cost.

Percentage figures adapted from: Elsie Eaves, *How the Many Costs of Housing Fit Together*, prepared for the National Commission on Urban Problems (Washington, D.C.: U.S. Government Printing Office, 1969), pp. 44-45.

As the figures suggest, building costs of row houses are somewhat lower per square foot than for detached houses. But there are even greater savings per unit on site costs. Typically there is less land per unit in a townhouse development than in single-family subdivisions; and site preparation and utility costs are also lower.

These development costs become the capital base that must yield a return to mortgage lenders and equity holders (implicit in the case of owner-occupied houses) and must be amortized over a period of years. They are converted into annual or monthly charges which have to be paid by the occupants of the house whether the owner or renter. And the monthly charges will vary not only with the amount of the capital cost but with the interest rate and term of repayment, as shown below.

Occupancy Costs.

Let us look at the monthly expenses to the occupant—in this example a renter household. The figures reflect full market costs and rents for a unit in a row house with a total development cost of $22,000.

Table 10-2
Annual Costs and Rent for a Row House Unit

Item	Amount
Development costs:	
Building cost per unit	$14,960
Site costs	3,300
Overhead, financing, and fees	3,740
Total cost per unit	$22,000
Financial investment:	
Mortgage (90% of cost)	19,800
Equity (10% of cost)	2,200
Total	$22,000
Annual costs:	
Debt service (7½%, 30 years) = 0.085 x 19,800	$1,683
Equity (15% return)	330
Maintenance, operating, insurance, and replacement reserve	550
Real estate tax (assessed valuation/replacement cost = 67% × 30/1,000	442
Vacancy allowance (5%)	158
Required rent per year	$3,163
Required rent per month	$264

The monthly rent that an owner must charge for this new dwelling is $264. Almost 64 percent of this amount reflects amortization and return on the capital invested in the development. Operating expenses for heat and utilities, janitorial service, replacement reserves, and management are the next largest claim on rents—17 percent. The real estate tax takes 14 percent, and the allowance for vacancies makes up the rest.

Potential Reductions in Housing Expenses.

Working with this set of figures, we can see the changes in rents that would result from possible reductions in one or several components of cost. The most beneficial from the community standpoint would be reductions resulting in lower resource requirements without lowering standards. Such changes in the cost structure are usually associated with technological improvements or greater efficiency in producing or operating the facilities.

More commonly in the field of housing, the rent reductions have resulted from shifting some of the expenses from occupants to taxpayers. Let us consider some of the possibilities.

1. Changes in the Real Cost of Building. The capital cost can conceivably be lowered by reductions in the real cost of the building through technological advances or lower unit costs as a result of larger scale production. This is what former Housing Secretary George Romney tried to do through a program called Operation Breakthrough. Unfortunately, it was not too successful. Factory-produced units developed through this program typically came out at about the same unit costs as conventionally-built units.

2. Changes in Site Costs. These might be cut by technological improvements in the provision of utilities and service streets or site preparation. Raw land costs might be lowered through large-scale assemblage by public agencies or private developers. James Rouse acquired the land for the new community of Columbia, Maryland at a relatively low cost per acre. The land was purchased through a number of agents and the plan for a new town was not announced until the bulk of the land was in the control of the town builder.

3. Write-down of Capital Cost. The charges to the household can be reduced by public absorption of all or part of the capital base. This is called a write-down when applied to land (and sometimes structures intended for rehabilitation) under the urban renewal program. These are usually one-time capital subsidies.

4. Changes in Long-term Financing Arrangements. Monthly rents can be lowered by reducing interest rates or lengthening the repayment period. A number of federal and state housing aids do just this, including the federal programs that accounted for the bulk of subsidized housing between 1968 and 1972—Sections 235 and 236 that provided interest rates as low as 1 percent for certain eligible families. Under other programs, the federal government has lent long-term funds at or near its own cost of borrowing [the Section 221 (d)(3) program for moderate rental housing as originally enacted in 1961]. The savings to the occupants can be considerable, as shown below.

5. Reduction in Real Estate Taxes. The property tax takes a sizable bite of the house consumer's dollar—14 percent in the example given above. If alternative sources of revenue to the localities could be found, as suggested by the Nixon administration, the burden on housing expenses might be lowered (or, more probably, kept from rising). Actually, this is already done in some places in the form of a partial tax exemption or abatement to encourage housing production or rehabilitation for certain groups (middle income families in New York City) or to relieve the burden on the elderly homeowner (as in Florida). Public housing authorities in most parts of the country generally make payments to the locality that are in lieu of and lower than the property taxes that would normally be charged.

6. Lowering Operating Expenses. In theory such expenses could be reduced by greater management efficiency. Public subsidy of these costs is also possible. For example, under the 1969 Brooke amendment, local housing authorities are not supposed to charge their tenants more than 25 percent of each family's income. This limitation brought a number of local public housing authorities close to insolvency. Thus it has become necessary for the federal government to pay a portion of operating expenses for some projects, as well as continuing contractual contributions for interest and debt amortization on bonds issued to pay the initial capital costs.

Required Rents under Varying Assumptions.

Using our row house example as a base, *let us* see how much rents could be reduced by lowering individual components or combinations of costs.

Table 10-3
Required Rent for a Row House Unit under Different Cost Assumptions

	Monthly rent	Percent reduction
I. Full market costs and rent	$264	—
II. Same as I with 25% building cost reduction	218	17
III. Same as I with 50% site cost reduction	247	6
IV. Development costs same as I with 1% rate of interest, 40 yrs., 100% mortgage	145	45
V. Same as I with 80% real estate tax exemption	233	12
VI. II + III	202	23
VII. III + IV + V	109	59

Among the possibilities shown here, the single approach producing the deepest cut in rent to the family is a reduction in the interest rate to 1 percent with a forty-year repayment period and a loan-to-cost ratio of 100 percent. In our example, the required rent for a townhouse unit can be brought down from $264 per month to $145, a 45 percent reduction. This illustrates the potential of a federal aid that was widely used between 1968 and 1972. Under the Section 236 interest reduction program, nonprofit sponsors obtained 100 percent loans and limited-return sponsors could qualify for 90 percent loans.

Further rent reductions are possible if the site cost is lowered, as could be done through the urban renewal program, or if the housing is relieved of the bulk of the normal property tax. In combination with an interest subsidy at 1 percent, these devices result in a rental of $109 a month in our illustration, or less than half the rent that a private developer would have to charge at full market interest rates and costs.

HUD has tried to bring down housing expenses through improvements in the production and marketing of housing. While Operation Breakthrough has fallen short of its objectives, other research and development efforts may be expected under new names. Our example suggests that cuts in costs of production are worth striving for, although they are not likely to do away with the need for financial subsidies. If building costs and related overhead and fees could be lowered by 25 percent, rent savings of about 17 percent would be possible. Together with a 50 percent reduction in site costs, market rents could be brought down by about 23 percent. But savings of this magnitude through improved technology are not likely to be effected in the near future.

Trends in Housing Costs

What has, in fact, been happening to house production costs over the years? Between 1946 and 1966 they increased by 110 percent, well above the rise in wholesale and consumer prices. In the inflationary period 1966-72, building costs continued to run ahead of most other costs. In October 1972 the wholesale price index for lumber and wood products was 13.2 percent above the 1971 figures; wage rates of construction workers increased about 12 percent for the year; and construction loans, while not as high as in 1969-70, were still 9 to 10 percent.

Land prices are more difficult to gauge. Among the best studies are those by Grace Milgram, which indicate that residential land costs in metropolitan areas have gone up at least 10 percent a year on average since 1946.[10] Improved sites under FHA-insured homes increased about 8 percent a year between 1968 and 1971. On a square foot basis, these site costs actually rose 12 percent a year. It is evident that costs of improved land for single family homes have gone up more than any other cost components in the postwar years. In 1950 site costs were 12 percent of the sales price of new FHA homes, but 21 percent in 1971.

What have these cost increases meant for potential home buyers? Those who buy with FHA-insured mortgages tend to be the marginal purchasers, many of whom could not acquire a new home without FHA to stand behind the mortgage. In 1960 the purchasers of new FHA-insured homes paid an average of 23 percent of after-tax income to meet their housing expenses; in 1970 this ratio was up to 27 percent.[11] Millions of other families were simply precluded from buying a new house as a result of the sharp increases in costs.

Structure of the House Building Industry

Rising costs reflect the nature of the house building industry. House building is a highly localized and fragmented activity. The National Association of Home Builders had almost 68,000 members at the end of 1972. During any one year there are about 50,000 firms actively engaged in assembling finished housing on specific sites and another 200.000 special trade subcontractors. Some 4,000 to 5,000 firms produce 100 or more units a year but relatively few have a volume exceeding 1,000 units. Levitt and Sons was perhaps the largest builder of conventional houses in 1970 with over 5,000 units, but no more than 1,000 in a single location. These larger builders are responsible for about two-fifths of single family production but at least three-fourths of all multifamily units.[12]

There are at least four categories of producers of residential space. Every area has its small stick builders, so named because they follow traditional building practices and put up relatively few houses a year —perhaps ten or twenty. At least half of all firms in the house building industry fall into this group, but they account for no more than 10 percent of total production.

As volume rises to 75 or 100 units a year, we recognize the merchant builder. He is producing for general demand rather than for specific customers. Some merchant builders reach a scale of 500 to 1,000 or more units a year. These larger operations generally include a substantial amount of multifamily construction. Some of these firms expanded between 1968 and 1972 in response to federal housing programs such as turnkey public housing and the interest-subsidy developments. A successful merchant builder is likely to be found operating in a number of different communities within a region. Thus he may have to rely upon local subcontractors for much of the work, including excavators, masons, plumbers and electricians. As a consequence, even the large builder may not be in a position to exercise effective control over costs and quality of work.

Home manufacturers make up a third group. They include some large fabricators such as National Homes and divisions of Boise Cascade, General Electric and other large corporations. The bulk of the home manufacturers, however, appear to be relatively small operations with annual production of less than one thousand units a year. Indeed, it is difficult to draw the line between the factory-built unit and the factory-built components (such as roof trusses) which are sold to conventional builders. The image of the industrialized house is the three-dimensional module but this is less commonly produced than factory-made walls, floors, and roofs which are assembled on the site. In any event, all types of factory-built housing must be placed on foundations and connected to utility systems. In some places, home manufacturers will rely upon local contractors to do such work simply to win their cooperation in dealing with local zoning and building officials and construction workers.

Total production of manufactured units was estimated at 350,000 in 1971 by the National Association of Building Manufacturers. Growth since the mid-sixties has been incremental, despite efforts of HUD to stimulate such production through its Operation Breakthrough. The manufacturers have also been given a boost by California and other states which have passed laws that permit offsite certification of industrial units or components. Once approved at the state level, such housing systems or elements are held to meet the building requirements in all localities.

But rationalization of the house building industry is not just around the corner. Shipping costs are a problem—the maximum feasible distance for most plants is 200-300 miles. More important, securing consents from a multiplicity of public and private interests in each community seems to be getting tougher rather than easier, in cities as well as in suburbs. And the American consumer remains strongly resistant to the notion of prefabricated housing. Only a striking bargain might overcome this attitude and thus far the savings, at least on a monthly expense basis, have not been great.

Producers of mobile homes constitute a fourth group. Some builders refuse to recognize mobile homes as decent shelter and refer to them derisively as "trailers." But an industrial group that has expanded its shipments from 104,000 units a year in 1960 to almost 600,000 in 1972 cannot be ignored. Mobile homes are clearly filling a need. There were more than two million households living in mobile homes in 1970. About three out of five were in rural areas, and a relatively high proportion (42 percent) were in the South.

Typical purchasers, according to the 1970 Census, were young families with no children or one child and incomes in the $7,000-10,000 range. For mobile home buyers, the most popular type was 12 by 60 feet and provided 684 square feet of living space. Some mobiles are expandable units and double-wides which can provide as much as 1,368 square feet of space.

About half of the new units have gone into mobile home parks, the others onto sites individually owned or leased by the family. Many suburban communities automatically screen out mobile home parks. Thus most have been located in areas that do not have stringent land use or building controls. This freedom from local controls has probably helped keep unit costs low. A twelve by sixty foot mobile home could be purchased, already furnished, for $7,000-8,000 in 1972. But loan costs are high and the units depreciate much more rapidly than conventional houses. In this respect, they are not as effective a hedge against long-term inflation as mortgageable real estate.

The mobile home industry itself consisted of 350 to 400 active firms in 1970. The ten largest firms turned out almost half of the industry's total production that year. Not much capital is needed to enter this industry —perhaps $150,000 to purchase the equipment needed to produce one to six units a day. By the same token, many small firms go out of business each year.[13]

No one knows what to make of this burgeoning sector. Is it the forerunner of an increasingly industrialized housing industry with more and more units produced offsite at lower wage rates? If so, more of it would have to be brought in from the boondocks and small towns to the urban areas. Here the industry will be increasingly up against the same kinds of restraints that face the home manufacturers and conventional builders—building codes, zoning, and possibly property taxation—factors that would substantially increase occupancy costs. And the mobiles or modulars would have to be adequately served by schools, sanitary facilities, and recreational opportunities that urban families have come to expect. Barring major changes in community attitudes and institutional practices, mobile or postmobile homes are likely to have only a limited role in accommodating future urban growth.

For all segments of the house building industry, restrictive practices by suburban governments with the tacit (but sometimes noisy) approval of present residents is the institutional reality that must be faced. To many American industries, the entire country is a common market, but to the housing industry every metropolitan area is dotted with customs officers and barriers. No wonder firms in this industry remain small scale and development costs continue to rise.

The Emerging Pattern of Development

In all parts of the country population growth and new development continue to be concentrating in the urban regions. In Pennsylvania, for example, the Philadelphia metropolitan area and six other metropolitan areas accounted for more than 90 percent of net population growth between 1960 and 1970, two-thirds of the state's increase in jobs, and 68 percent of new housing construction. Slight or no increases in housing were registered in forty-four of the sixty-seven counties of the state. In the nongrowth counties, many families continued to live in obsolescent structures, many without adequate community services such as sewer systems.

Within the metropolitan areas, the suburbs have absorbed the lion's share of new industrial and commercial development. In the nation's fifteen largest metropolitan areas taken as a group, the outer areas between 1960 and 1970 gained more than three million jobs (a 44 percent increase) while the central cities lost almost one million (a 7 percent drop). During the same period, about three out of four new jobs in manufacturing and retailing went into the suburban parts of the country's metropolitan areas. The same was true of new industrial plants and shopping facilities. In the Philadelphia area, for example, the central city itself got only a fifth of the manufacturing plants (measured in dollars of investment) and a quarter of retail development. Only in office buildings did the city attract more than half of the investment activity in the area.[14]

The placement of highways has shaped the pattern of industrial development. Some 80 percent of the new industrial plants have been located within a mile of modern interstate highways or the turnpike system in the Philadelphia area, according to estimates of the Delaware Valley Regional Planning Commission.

Housing developments in many parts of the country appear to be taking place in more compact patterns. This seems to have been true of the development since the mid-sixties as compared with the previous ten to fifteen years. As land costs have risen, builders have sought to economize on this factor. Average lot sizes on new FHA-insured homes were in fact reduced between 1968 and 1971. And builders sought out previously passed over land. But the denser development pattern is largely attributable to the shift from single to multifamily construction. Larger multifamily structures of five or more family units accounted for about 38 percent of total housing units in 1971 and 1972, compared with an average of 33 percent in the 1964-70 period and about 20 percent in the years 1960-63. Many of these large apartment developments have been located to give residents ready access to major highway and public transportation routes.

But the location and pattern of residential development do not appear to be significantly influenced by any unified and deliberate process of planning or priority-setting by state or metropolitan public agencies—other than by the highway engineers who, publicly at least, eschew the role of comprehensive planners and insist that they simply follow the travel preferences of the public! Regional planning agencies are supposed to be developing a "housing element" in metropolitan plans, but somehow they do not seem to get done. Meanwhile, what to build and where to build housing are essentially determined by market demand and negotiations among prospective developers and builders, zoning attorneys, and public officials at the township, village or municipal level. In few if any metropolitan areas do local officials have to pay attention to regional plans for housing new families or rehousing people who live in substandard conditions.

Racial Segregation

New housing developments in Northern suburbs have generally been closed to black families. Despite civil rights laws that prohibit racial discrimination in housing, most suburban localities have—and most builders accept—unwritten rules against integrated housing developments. The exceptions are so unusual that they surprise the visitor. In Columbia, Maryland, for example, the prospective resident may see a film at a reception center that shows black families in the new community. Designed to contain more than 100,000 residents when completed, Columbia was home to more than 30,000 people at the end of 1973. The developer does not maintain statistics of residents by race, but an unofficial guess is that 10-15 percent of the residents are blacks and members of other racial minorities. This is well over the proportion of new housing that minority famllies were able to obtain in the nation's Northern suburbs in the 1960-70 period.

In fact, racial segregation in housing probably increased between 1960 and 1970. All of the net growth in the white population of metropolitan areas took place in the suburbs; but three-fourths of the increase in the number of metropolitan blacks was in the central cities and the rest mostly in the older adjoining suburbs. As a result of these moves, 59 percent of the metropolitan whites were suburbanites in 1970 but only 22 percent of the blacks, the same proportion as in 1960. In some metropolitan areas the degree of concentration of blacks in the central city was significantly higher than the national average. In Philadelphia, for one, the proportion of the metropolitan area's nonwhites living in the central city rose from 79 to 87 percent between 1960 and 1970.

The consequences of this growing separation of the races are likely to be ominous—but few white Americans want to face them. From an economic standpoint alone, the inability of the blacks to gain access to the outer areas spells serious trouble. The new job centers are going into the outer areas and city residents have a hard time getting to them or even hearing about the employment possibilities. In the central cities themselves, the cost squeeze on local governments and schools is getting tighter. With most of the well-to-do people living outside of the city, there is less and less willingness among whites to see the city's problem as their own or to help improve living conditions in the black poverty neighborhoods. Thus, poor blacks may have less of a chance to work and earn their way out of poverty. But not many whites are inclined to change this situation.

In 1968 the National Commission on Civil Disorders questioned whether American society could survive the conflict implied in having 21 million blacks penned in the central cities and more than 100 million whites living in suburban rings. That is where current trends will carry us by 1985:

If large-scale violence resulted [as a consequence of rebellion by Negroes], white retaliation would follow. This spiral could quite conceivably lead to a kind of urban *apartheid* with semi-martial law in many major cities, enforced residence of Negroes in segregated areas, and a drastic reduction in personal freedom for all Americans, particularly Negroes.[15]

Segregation of the Elderly

The last segregation is of our old people. A youth culture does not want them around so they are packed off to Tampa or Leisure World or just left in the old house. The elderly are not usually found in the newer developments other than special housing for "senior citizens" or nursing homes. The best new housing for the elderly is likely to be provided by church or synagogue-affiliated groups. Nursing homes run by profit-minded operators can be a racket.

In any event, the elderly tend to be underrepresented in the newer suburban developments and overrepresented in the central cities. In Pittsburgh, Pennsylvania, for example, persons sixty-five and older comprised 9.8 percent of the suburban population in 1970, but 13.5 percent of the residents of the central city. Older persons also constitute higher than average proportions of small towns and counties experiencing losses in jobs and population. In such places the living conditions of many of the elderly are apt to be pathetic.

For most older persons, however, the problem is not that the roof leaks or that the toilet is an outdoor privy. It is that they lead isolated lives away from young families with children. Western Europeans do a much better job of interspersing older people among the rest of the community. And to compound the problems of loneliness and isolation, elderly households commonly have to spend a large part of their income on rents or housing expenses. Many older people spend 35 percent or more of their fixed incomes for shelter, well above the average proportion for younger families.

New Development: Pluses and Minuses

Building by building, acre upon acre, a vast amount of urban capital has been accumulated in the postwar period. Most of this new construction took place in the outer parts of metropolitan areas on previously undeveloped land. The predominant residential structure in the early postwar years was the free standing single family house. Along with the new industrial parks, shopping malls, and highway networks, this form of residential development consumed enormous quantities of land. With rising land costs and some changes in household mix and consumer preferences, townhouses and apartment buildings became more prevalent in the late sixties and early seventies. But the overall pattern of new development could be aptly described as Spread City.

What affluent consumers wanted, they managed to get: pleasant homes, private space, physical separation from different types of people, local taxes used to improve local schools, local roads, and local recreational facilities.

But the outcome for the population at large and certain segments has left something to be desired. Construction costs and occupancy expenses for new homes have raced ahead of incomes, for the lower third of the population at least. House building remains a high cost, small scale industry. In part this is due to the multiplicity of jurisdictions and rules that govern construction in each metropolitan area.

There are wide disparities in per capita expenditures for schools and other desired local services from one community to the next within the same urban region.

For lack of areawide arrangements, public facilities such as sewer systems have been built too small to yield potential economies of scale and in some places are simply unavailable.

In the view of ecologists, much of the new development has been misplaced and not enough land has been set aside to protect the natural environment. Nor do we have sufficient space for regional parks and recreation within easy range of metropolitan populations.

The spread patterns have increased travel time for many workers, thus partially cancelling out shorter work days. But most people insist on the convenience of driving to work.

Not least, segregation of the poor, the elderly, and the blacks has increased during the past decade. The social cleavages in the society have been cemented by physical barriers. Increasing distance and lack of information have tended to shut out the inner city employables from jobs in outlying industrial parks and shopping centers.

A fierce localism undergirds these difficulties. Many local governments in suburban growth areas are geared to prevent changes in community composition and to maintain prevailing patterns of demand for housing and municipal services. People of lower income and minority races are kept out. The local jurisdiction guards its gates by limiting the production of housing and prescribing high standards for development. The principal means are local control over land use and development, plumbing and other building codes, and the provision or witholding of access streets, sewer plants and trunk lines, and other essential facilities. To many residents and suburban officials such policies are not viewed as evil but natural. For this society was nurtured on a belief in individualism and self-interest.

These trends and practices have not gone unnoticed and unchallenged. In his 1965 message on cities, President Johnson said: "We need to reshape, at every level of government, our approach to problems which are often different than we thought and larger than we imagined." Under legislation sponsored by the Kennedy and Johnson administrations, that reshaping process began in the sixties. Not only Washington but the states began to move. In the next chapter we look at some of the programs and proposals for coping with urban growth.

11 Shaping Urban Growth

For half a century at least such groups as the Regional Plan Association of New York have called upon us to shape urban growth. Since the 1920s city and regional planning has become a profession and thousands of men and women have been trained to practice this calling. Today virtually all metropolitan areas have planning commissions. The promotion of sound and balanced growth in metropolitan areas is a national policy by declaration of the Congress.

Yet it is still not clear that we can really shape urban growth in the United States. Maybe at best we shall have to be satisfied to cope with growth. For shaping growth implies that there is an essential harmony of interest among the various individuals and groups that make up large urban concentrations. If there are basic differences and conflicts among groups, all we can do is try to deal with them in a more or less equitable way.

Alan Altshuler has argued persuasively that comprehensive planning is not really possible for large urban areas. There are too many deep-seated conflicts within the metropolitan population. The modern American, moreover, does not make strong personal commitments to broad objectives such as "orderly growth."[1] The average man does not think in global terms so you cannot appeal to him on this level. What he responds to are concrete threats or specific opportunities. He may join with his neighbors to fight a link of Interstate 95 from coming through his neighborhood, but you will not turn him on with a plan for a "balanced transportation system."

There is something else that urban growth shapers must reckon with. It is the rejection of reform leadership in American political life. During the fifties and early sixties reform mayors sought and won office in a number of cities: Richard Lee in New Haven, Joseph Clark and Richardson Dilworth in Philadelphia, Arthur Naftalin in Minneapolis. Kennedy and Johnson took the White House with the promise of "getting the country moving again" and creating a good, even a "great society." Their successors include policemen and law and order men. The latter breed reflect the fear of change and the rejection of elite leadership by the lower middle and middle-middle classes.

How long this national mood will last no one can say. But it does not bode well in the years immediately ahead for those who propose sweeping changes in the way we pay for public schools, provide housing for the poor, or organize government in metropolitan areas. In fact, reformers may have their hands full trying to keep alive national commitments and policies adopted in the Kennedy-Johnson years. As an example, in 1972 Congress came close to giving local governments the power to approve or disapprove individual housing developments for lower income families proposed to be built with federal aid within their jurisdictions. This would have permitted localities to block many prospective projects for moderate as well as low income people. But the Nixon administration went much further. In early 1973 it announced its intention to halt further commitments for federally subsidized housing and to reevaluate all housing assistance programs. The question of local approval was now moot. At issue was the entire federal commitment, dating back to 1949 and reaffirmed with specific numerical targets by the Congress in 1968, to help provide decent homes for millions of poor and moderate income families.

But planners and reformers have something of a messianic instinct. They will keep trying. What will they be striving to do? On what precedents can they build? The conscious effort to deal with urban development as a related set of problems is a comparatively new phenomenon in the United States. But it has gained support among some business and civic groups. If truly comprehensive planning is not feasible, taking an areawide view of developmental problems and trying to deal with them more systematically makes sense to a lot of people. It may help the public discussion to clarify the objectives of an urban development policy. First, however, it is in order to indicate the directions of change.

Where Are We Heading?

Let us quickly set forth some expectations about the future.[2]

1. National population will grow over the next twenty-five years but at a lower rate than projected as recently as 1968. Instead of 300 million people, the American population in the year 2000 is likely to be closer to 265 million.
2. The metropolitan areas will continue to draw almost nine-tenths of this growth because these areas will contain the best jobs and educational opportunities. The metropolitan populations will total 190-200 million, about 50-60 million more than in 1970.
3. Per capita income will rise about 2.5 percent a year. Median family income will rise from about $11,000 in 1972 to more than $20,000 a year in 2000 (in dollars of 1972 purchasing power).
4. There will be an effective floor under income and welfare, but there will still be wide disparities in income between the top and bottom fifths of the families.

5. A larger proportion of national income will be allocated to the non-defense public sector (about 25 percent of GNP in 1972). Income in kind such as below-cost or free public services (education, health, and recreation) will comprise a larger proportion of total family income.
6. Service-oriented employment will grow relative to production-oriented activity. Public employment at the state and local levels will continue to increase relative to private jobs.
7. Work will be spread among more people through shorter work days and possibly shorter work weeks and/or longer vacations. A larger fraction of white women will be in the labor force (possibly 50 percent compared with 42 percent in 1971), but the proportion of black women in the labor force will remain about the same or taper off slightly (49 percent in 1971).
8. A larger percentage of high school graduates will go on to college (perhaps two out of three by the end of the century compared with one out of two in 1971). Adult education and refresher programs will also increase. There will be more emphasis on learning because of the rapidity of change and increase in information.
9. Technological advances will be made in manufacturing, communications, and transportation. There will be wider use of automation in industrial production, but lesser changes in housing production. Gains in productivity of public services and education will be modest due to the labor-intensive nature of these activities.
10. Alienation from the community and culture will remain a nagging problem as "science and compound interest" release men and women from the discipline of working hard for a living. The Puritan work ethic will continue to lose appeal. The feeling will grow that one cannot influence, let alone change, the system of government and corporate decision making.[3]
11. Life styles will place more emphasis on personal development and self-fulfillment through study, travel, participation in performing arts and athletics, and perhaps civic participation.
12. More and more blacks, Puerto Ricans, and Mexican-Americans will "make it" into the middle class and will move into the main stream; but a substantial proportion and number of these groups will be considered lower class and will still suffer from discrimination.

These are simply guesses about the future, premised upon perceptions of past events. If the population estimates (based upon 1972 projections by the Bureau of the Census) prove to be more accurate than earlier ones, the crunch on resources may be less severe than previously feared. Nevertheless, the massing of 50 to 60 million more people into metropolitan regions within the next three decades will put great pressure upon governmental machinery and institutions as well as upon land, air sheds, and water basins. But at the same time, we shall have more income per person with which to deal with the social and physical environment. That is to say, we shall have the means to make choices about the quality of life available to metropolitan man.

What Kind of Urban Development Do We Want?

If we knew what kinds of communities and living arrangements people want, presumably we could figure out how to design and build them. But there are difficulties in laying out community goals. For one thing, they are subjective—any listing will reflect my or your values and biases. We can try to get around this by looking at legislation that Congress has passed and by assuming that a series of consistent enactments reflect shared values and objectives of a majority of Americans. Another problem, recognized earlier, is that some desired ends are in apparent conflict with other desired ends. For example, many people are tired of government red tape and want more streamlined decision making and follow through by public authorities; but there is also an insistent demand that citizens be heard and residents be given a voice in public decisions— which has to cause delay and uncertainty. A related question is whether the objective is attainable. Is it wise, for example, to urge the development of neighborhoods or communities in which people of widely different income levels or different races will live willingly and comfortably together? If experience suggests no but the equalitarian ethos says yes, there is no obvious way to resolve this dilemma. Finally, there is the temptation to list every urban problem—and urban is almost everything. From there it is but a short jump to proposing a New Town which will solve everything. If that trap is not avoided here, at least it is not unrecognized.

What Are the Objectives?

1. Decent Homes for All. Congress enunciated this goal in the Housing Act of 1949, reaffirmed it and set quantitative targets in 1968. Many housing programs were enacted to carry out the goal. Experiments with leased housing and housing allowances were authorized in 1961, 1964, and 1970. The goal is to have sufficient new housing produced and existing housing properly maintained so that all new households, mainly young adults, can be accommodated and lower income families enabled to obtain adequate housing within their means. There would be reasonable freedom of choice for individual households with respect to location, price, style, and owning or renting. For those who need subsidies, *all* families and individuals in the eligible class would receive aid and to the extent possible have a choice of taking housing allowances in cash or securing space in subsidized projects.

2. Good Neighborhoods and a Suitable Living Environment. This became public policy by congressional declaration in 1949, the 1966 Demonstration Cities Act ("improving the quality of urban life"), and 1968 legislation. Good neighborhoods are places where people know many of the people who live and work nearby and feel some allegiance to each other. Frequently this cohesion is based on ethnic, racial, or religious ties. Sometimes people come together because of shared fears—of crime, of intrusion by lower income people, or racial minorities. Good neighborhoods have relatively clean streets and sanitary services, shopping facilities, play areas for youngsters, and gathering places for adults; and they are insulated from heavy traffic, excessive noise, and industrial fumes and sootfall. We do not really know how to create good neighborhoods, as the late Stanley Tankel used to say.[4] Surely we should nurture and preserve those we have, even at the expense of progress in the form of superhighways, airports, and similar public "improvements."

3. Fair Housing and Equal Opportunity in Public Accommodations and jobs. The Civil Rights Act of 1964 prohibits discrimination by private employers and owners of places of public accommodation. In 1968 the Congress barred discriminatory practices by lenders, builders, and real estate brokers in the sale and rental of housing. In no area is the gap between public law and effective implementation so stark as in civil rights. Federal and state officials have been reluctant to move affirmatively and some simply do not identify with the objectives. "It is one thing," Harold Laski wrote, "to put through a policy the assumptions of which you accept. It is a very different thing to put through efficiently a policy the very foundations of which you believe to be disastrous."[5] There has been some compliance in connection with public accommodations and a measure of enforcement in the employment of minority workers, but little or no change in discriminatory housing patterns and practices. Moreover, in the absence of deliberate efforts to distribute minority families throughout the urban area, open occupancy all too often means the mass departure of whites from formerly "good neighborhoods." They may remain good if the new families can afford to maintain the properties, but the stable integrated neighborhood is not too common. Fair housing practices alone, it should be added, are helpful only to those with sufficient income to afford good housing. For moderate and lower income families, other social and economic aids are necessary. But resistance to black *and* poor families is especially pronounced.

4. *Equalization of Municipal Service Levels and Fiscal Capacity.* Congressional intent to promote this objective is reflected in the 1965 Education Act, Model Cities aid in 1966, and revenue sharing authorized in 1972. Large disparities in public expenditures per person for education, recreation, transportation and other desired public services widen the gaps in real income between the well-off and poor families. Such service differentials usually reflect the wide disparities from one locality to the next in the value of fixed taxable property. Special federal aids for poverty neighborhoods were started in the mid-sixties, but low levels of funding reflect the limited commitment of the federal government to narrowing disparities. Federal revenue sharing enacted in 1972 recognizes income as one factor in the distribution formula, but will not make much impact because the total allocation is relatively small and there is no priority in law assigned to poor neighborhoods. Court decisions, however, may compel a drastic change in the method of supporting public schools, which could work to the benefit of poorer communities.

5. *Orderly and Efficient Development of Metropolitan Areas. Strengthen General Governments.* Categorical aids for open space (1961), mass transportation (1964), sewer and water grants (1965), and advance land acquisition (1965) were all conditioned on consistency with comprehensively planned development of the area and intended to curb urban sprawl. Legislation passed in 1966 and 1968 require review-and-comment by a regional planning agency of federal-aid projects with regional impact. Revenue shares authorized in 1972 go only to general governments. Orderly development of land and scheduling of public improvements have been frustrated by the existence of many small governments and special authorities and districts empowered to carry out particular functions —education, highways, sewer and water activities, and other functions. Supported by earmarked funds or user charges, many functional authorities have tended to be more responsive to their bondholders than to the people they serve or to the elected officials of general governments in their areas. To induce coordination of public activities that influence the pattern of urban development and to secure potential economies of scale through large-sized plants have been objectives of federal legislation since the early sixties. Congress has insisted upon conformance of federal-aid projects with comprehensive development plans for the entire area, encouraged the formation of councils of local governments within metropolitan areas, and taken other steps to strengthen the role of elected county, city, and township officials vis-à-vis special authorities. The concern of an earlier day to keep politics out of the schools and out of local transportation operations and to allow a free hand to professional administrators has receded before the rising demand for accountability in these sectors to affected residents, the general electorate, and elected officials.

6. *Large Scale Urban and New Community Development.* This was a specified element of the national urban growth policy enacted in 1970. It was encouraged by federal aids passed in 1965, 1966, 1968, and 1970. New towns and large scale development have been late in receiving national support in this country as compared with Western European countries. Opposition to new communities has come from mayors of large cities because of their fear of losing industry, retail trade, and middle class residents; from small home builders who envisioned being displaced by large developers and industrialized house manufacturers; and from suburban officials and residents who sensed being swallowed up by these large undertakings. Johnson administration proposals for federal support of new communities were rejected by the Congress in 1964 and 1965, but FHA insurance of large planned land developments sponsored by private developers was authorized in 1965. The following year this provision was enlarged and extended to new communities that fulfilled certain purposes, including adequate housing for those employed in the community or working nearby. A New Communities Act was passed in 1968 under which the federal government guarantees the bonds issued by private developers to help them finance land acquisition and streets, sewerlines, water facilities, and other improvements required for a new community. If the new community furthers other social objectives, such as providing for a substantial number of housing units for low and moderate income persons, supplementary grants for water and sewer facilities and open space (over and above regular grants for these purposes) are authorized to be made to public bodies serving the new community.

The 1970 law expanded the guarantee program, provided federal loans to cover interest charges on bonds issued by community developers, and enlarged the list of federal aids eligible for supplementary grants. For the first time, *public* development agencies were authorized to participate as new community developers—regional and metropolitan agencies as well as state land development agencies. Four types of new developments were envisioned by the 1970 law: economically balanced new communities within metropolitan areas; additions to smaller cities and towns that have growth potential; new town-in-town developments in central cities; and new cities outside the orbit of metropolitan areas.

7. *Protecting the Natural Environment and Conserving Resources.* These are national objectives under a series of laws: open space grants (1961) and the land and water conservation fund (1964); water pollution control (1956, 1965, and 1972); clean air (1963, 1967, and 1970); environmental policy (1969); urban growth policy (1970); land use policy (passed by the Senate in 1973); resource recovery from solid waste (1970). The earliest form of environmental protection in this country evolved as a reaction to the waste and plundering of the nation's natural resources by timber and mining

interests, hunters, ranchers, and farmers. In the past decade the nation has awakened to the environmental impact of industrial growth, motorization, and urban development. As seen by the Citizens' Advisory Committee on Environmental Quality, there are three challenges:

1. To clean up the mess of dirty water and air, junk and solid waste, and to reduce noise levels;
2. To make better use of land, protect coastal lands and other wetlands against irretrievable damage from improper development, provide breathing and relaxing space for urban populations, and generally use land more sparingly and intensively; and
3. To provide a good social environment for people through adequate housing, health care, recreation, education, and jobs.

For urbanists, the key is balanced growth, recognizing the limits upon development before the land is irreversibly harmed. For example, wetlands must be protected against dredging, draining, or filling because of their vital role as a habitat for wildlife, a source of food to aquatic life, and a natural buffer against shoreline storms and excessive sedimentation. Yet such areas may continue to be enjoyed by men and women as scenic areas and for observing wildlife. In McHarg's eloquent plea, we must design with nature, sewering the plateaus and not the valleys and above all respecting the chain of life.[7]

The urban planner must take a longer view of the use of nature's resources than the average private investor or consumer. In terms of economics, he will discount the future at a lower rate than the private individual. But this does not mean that development must be completely curbed. It means that we—society acting through our governments—must build with care and conserve the man-made environment as well as natural resources. What we are groping toward is a sense of the common good in the way we build and produce things, something the Dutch people have had for centuries. The Dutch have not found it necessary to declare a halt to all growth and development, nor do we.

The Urban Development Process

In the United States urban communities have evolved in response to a myriad of individual decisions—not in the light of publicly debated social goals. Many people have their say in the market place or in the conduct of specific public activites—families, merchants, industrialists, builders, nonprofit groups, and government agencies. For the most part, these disparate actions have not been influenced by a long historic memory, a sense of belonging to a place, or a strong feeling of mutual dependence.

Urban development, nevertheless, is a form of social evolution. For it is a continuous process of building and using space over time, thus linking one generation to the next. We inherit much of our urban capital and add to it decade by decade. Because it is long-lived and fixed in location, the buildings that are put in place today will affect the way people live and work for many years to come. Most importantly, it is the organized authority of society—the state—that protects the private owner or occupant in his rights over property and, indeed, enables him to use it by providing essential facilities and services.

Whether or not we consciously display our goals, we do make choices about our urban environment. Urban development is not an automatic, self-determining phenomenon. "Our communities are what we make them," said President Kennedy in his housing message of 1961. Men decide what to make them. They decide year by year in the course of building 1.5 to 2.5 million new housing units, laying down 15,000 or 20,000 miles of streets and roadways, and opening perhaps 50,000 new classrooms in schools. They decide about their communities also when determining the level of maintenance, repair and reconstruction of existing neighborhoods, public structures, and private homes.

In making these choices, decision makers have generally followed certain rules. Private investors choose these undertakings and locations with prospective returns at least as high as other opportunities of comparable risk. Home buyers want the most amenity they can get for the money —space, schools, status. Public decision makers must select projects that are consistent with their authority, that are technically feasible, and within their budgets and manpower to build and operate.

Who Wants to Be Coordinated?

Only in recent times have we begun to think that private parties and even public agencies should be held accountable for the secondary consequences of their behavior. In 1965 Congress was just beginning to attach planning requirements to some of the new federal aid programs then being initiated. That year the Housing and Home Finance Agency (later HUD) was authorized to make grants to local public bodies for basic water and sewer facilities. Such a grant could be made only if the project was found to be "consistent with a program meeting criteria . . . for a unified or officially coordinated areawide water or sewer facilities system as part of the comprehensively planned development of the area."[8] This was a reasonable requirement in view of the legislative intent "to promote the efficient and orderly growth and development of our communities."

Such facilities had to be tied into treatment plants, which were financed under another program then administered by the Public Health Service in the Department of Health, Education, and Welfare. Moreover, two other federal agencies had just been authorized to make similar grants: the Economic Development Administration in the Department of Commerce and the Farmers Home Administration in the Department of Agriculture. The Bureau of the Budget, as the arm of the President, had the responsibility for seeing that compatible guidelines and operating procedures were established by the several agencies.

The Public Health Service balked at the proposal for common planning requirements. The objective of the Federal Water Pollution Control Act of 1956, which PHS administered, was to reduce water pollution. *Their* law, they argued, did not require that the project receiving federal funds fit into an areawide system that was unified or officially coordinated, let alone a part of the comprehensively planned development of the entire area. Further probing uncovered the fact that most of the grants for waste treatment plants made prior to 1965 by PHS had gone to communities of less than 10,000 population. Congress—or more accurately, the influential committee members who framed the law—probably intended that the money go to smaller localities since the maximum grant for a project serving a single municipality was set at $600,000. This amount would not have made much of a dent in big-city sewage treatment requirements. Moreover, the total budget request for fiscal year 1964 was only $100 million, to be spread among one thousand projects averaging but $100,000.[9] Thus, to impose the areawide requirement would not only make the program more difficult for the Public Health Service to administer, but would adversely affect the clientele group of small localities then being served. The uncooperative stance of the Public Health Service was not unique; most functional bureaus zealously pursue their particular missions and resist efforts to be coordinated.

Federal Support for Planning

Despite such resistance, the idea of planning was taking hold among federal policy makers in the 1960s. Much of the impetus came from the Housing and Home Finance Agency and its successor, the Department of Housing and Urban Development. Federal aid to state and local governments for planning was initiated in 1954. In 1966, at the request of the Johnson administration, Congress provided additional support for planning through Title II of the Demonstration Cities and Metropolitan Development Act. As amended in 1968, the purpose of this title, termed Planned Areawide Development, is to encourage and assist states and localities in making comprehensive areawide planning and programming effective through better coordination of federal programs and through supplementary grants for certain federally aided projects.

"Planning" has always been a nebulous concept. The 1966 and 1968 laws helped to remove some of the fuzziness with a definition:

The term 'comprehensive planning' includes the following:

(A) preparation, as a guide for governmental policies and action, of general plans with respect to (i) the pattern and intensity of land use, (ii) the provision of public facilities (including transportation facilities) and other government services, and (iii) the effective development and utilization of human and natural resources;

(B) long-range physical and fiscal plans for such action;

(C) programming of capital improvements and other major expenditures, based on a determination of relative urgency, together with definite financing plans for such expenditures in the earlier years of the program;

(D) coordination of all related plans and activities of the state and local governments and agencies concerned; and

(E) preparation of regulatory and administrative measures in support of the foregoing.[10]

Planning clearly has to do with physical arrangements on land. Evolving in the United States in close affinity to architecture, landscape architecture and allied professions, planning is still viewed by many people as essentially the physical design of cities and towns. This obviously requires that public infrastructure such as highways, transit lines, and sewer facilities be considered not only as a source of essential community services but as a means of determining the direction, type, and density of new development.

Another consideration, more explicitly stated in the 1965 requirement that troubled the Public Health Service than in the 1968 definition, is that planning is done at several levels. There are wheels within wheels. There are functional plans—as for sewering an area—as well as general or comprehensive plans. A set of facilities like waste treatment works, intercepting and outfall sewers, pumping stations, and other components should be well designed as an internally consistent system. They must also be integrated with housing and transportation layouts and other large elements of area development. They "must" but frequently were not. In one area the sewer commission laid out waste lines without regard for the county's land use plans; in another an airport was expanded too close to federally aided housing; in a third area the urban renewal agency found itself reclaiming a district subsequently designated by the state engineers as the path for a new highway. Such situations were reported in the Washington, D.C. area, Atlanta, Waco, Reno, Seattle, and other places.

So it is not enough to have the big comprehensive development plan into which the functional plans all fit. There have to be governmental arrangements to assure that they will be carried out. In other words, effective planning and financing of public investments and private developments in urban areas call for governments with authority and territorial jurisdiction commensurate with the responsibility.

The Metropolitan Development Act of 1966 envisioned the use of financial incentives to secure compliance with long-range plans. A federal bonus was to be added to regular federal grants for open space, mass transportation, sewer and water facilities, and other types of projects if they were shown to be located and scheduled in consonance with areawide planning and programming. But after the Congress had authorized supplementary grants of this type, the Appropriations Committees declined to provide money for such grants. This is not too common but it can happen when the intended beneficiaries of a new aid program are politically weak (poor people, social researchers) or must be called into being (nonprofit sponsors, metropolitan governmental institutions).

A modest advance in intergovernmental cooperation did take hold. This involves review and comment by an areawide planning body on applications by public agencies from within the area for federal aid for highways, airports, sewerage facilities, and other types of projects. The planning group, which must be composed of or responsible to units of general local government within the area, has sixty days to make comments and recommendations. Such recommendations are not binding upon the federal departments and agencies which administer the particular programs under which aid is sought. But an adverse comment may be influential in blocking or changing a proposed project. For example, in the Philadelphia region several proposed housing developments would have required the rechanneling of streams so that more of the land could be built on. Environmentalists opposed this on grounds that it would choke off aquatic life and contribute to flooding conditions. The Delaware Valley Regional Planning Commission, the review body, concurred in these criticisms and relayed adverse comments to the federal funding agency. This resulted in modifications of the plans by developers to eliminate the environmental hazard and thus qualify the projects for federal support.

Metropolitan planning agencies continue to be limited largely to an advisory role in area development. But the review and comment procedure gives them gums if not teeth. Thus far they have been able to stop some things—a housing project for moderate income families when it posed a threat to the environment. They have been less successful in taking affirmative measures. The regional planning commission, which blocked a subsidized housing development, had before it at the same time a staff study and recommendation for the allocation of some 200,000 new moderate and low income housing units in outlying counties of the Delaware Valley, to be built between 1973 and the year 2000. But on this sticky issue the representatives of local governments which make up the regional planning commission were reluctant to take a stand. The central city had the most to gain from such an agreement, but its mayor said:

I have no objection to the concept of this housing allocation plan so long as the figures are arrived at fairly and properly. But I myself would not thrust on any community anything they don't want and I would not permit this commission to do that either.[11]

Linking Physical and Social Planning

The federal government has also encouraged state and local governments to link planning for physical development with planning for social improvement. At first this was a reaction to the harmful social consequences to some people from federally aided programs such as highway construction and urban renewal. These and other public improvement programs in the early sixties were forcing thousands of families out of their homes and neighborhoods. In the country as a whole, 50,000 to 100,000 households were being displaced each year by public activities. Most of these displaced families were of modest means, some were elderly persons, and many were black people. Such families are not the immediate beneficiaries of public construction activities.

The urban renewal program did provide modest moving expenses to displaced families but hardly enough to compensate for the disruption of their living arrangements. In 1964 the Congress called a halt to wholesale demolition under the urban renewal program by requiring that no residential area could be cleared without a top-level determination by federal officials that a rundown neighborhood could not be restored through rehabilitation. The idea was emerging that neighborhood improvement programs should primarily benefit those already living in the area.

An affirmative link-up between physical and social planning was embodied in the Model Cities legislation of 1966. Under this effort, program planners were encouraged to weave together human resource programs such as education, health services, and manpower training with actions to improve the physical environment such as removal of derelict buildings and provision of neighborhood centers, small parks, and similar facilities. While final responsibility was fixed in city hall, residents of the model neighborhoods were expected to participate in the decisions about their areas. Some neighborhoods received federal money to hire advocate planners to give them technical advice and to help them in negotiations with the downtown experts.

Here we were witnessing the emergence of social planning as a limited if not full partner in the enterprise of planning and the widening of the constituencies with which public planners must deal. These used to be mainly builders and developers, large owners of real estate, downtown merchants and corporate leadership in industry and banking. Now there were residents of poor neighborhoods, legal services groups, churches and nonprofit associations, and veterans of the war against poverty to be reckoned with.

What is planning? Sometimes the philosopher can clarify the work of the practitioner. In the words of Abraham Kaplan, a teacher of philosophy:

Planning is the enterprise of facilitating decisions and making them more realistic and rational. Decisions become more realistic as the values they involve are confronted with facts, and more rational as values are confronted with other values.[12]

Planners are moving away from the 1930 concept of a master plan which pictures some kind of ideal end state. There is no one *big answer*. What is good for some may not be so good for others. The effective planners are coming to view planning as systematic analysis and political adjustment to changing social conditions and the aspirations of diverse elements in the community and the society.

Guiding Growth

In 1960 the influential Committee for Economic Development issued a policy paper on metropolitan growth.[13] In that policy statement CED called for modernizing governmental structures in metropolitan areas so that areawide problems such as transportation and air pollution can be dealt with in an effective way. It recommended periodic study of the local economies and urged businessmen to work with local officials and assume more responsibility for civic affairs. In his 1961 message on housing, President Kennedy struck a similar theme: "The city and its suburbs are interdependent parts of a single community, bound together by the web of transportation and other public facilities and by common economic interests. Bold programs in individual jurisdictions are no longer enough. Increasingly, community development must be a cooperative venture toward the common goals of the metropolitan region as a whole." The world seemed simpler somehow in the early sixties. With some restructuring of government, some economic analysis, and a measure of goodwill, we could solve most of our metropolitan problems.

The years that followed were not without progress. A Kennedy program that started modestly in 1961 offered federal aid to localities for the acquisition of land for public open space. Through 1971 some 350,000 acres of land have been preserved as green areas at an average outlay of $900 an acre by the federal government and about twice this sum including state and local costs. Participating localities ranged in population size from a million or more down to less than one thousand. Another popular and widely used federal program provided grants for water and sewer facilities. Authorized in 1965, more than 1,900 projects were approved under this HUD program through 1971. Federal commitments amounted to $945 million on projects with a total cost of about $3 billion.

Such programs not only helped localities get needed public facilities, they also fostered intermunicipal cooperation and helped structure urban growth in accordance with plans. In adopting such measures, Congress spelled out national objectives for urban development. For the first time localities within the same urban regions were asked to recognize their responsibilities to each other and to work together on common problems. It was a beginning. And if the millenium did not come, at least we seemed to be moving in the right direction.

12 Role of the States in Urban Development

The states have been the sleeping giant in the realm of urban development. They always have had the constitutional power and the legal authority to oversee urban development and to provide public services, but chose to delegate much of the responsibility to local governments. In the 1960s the giant began to stir. Governors and state legislatures found themselves reacting piecemeal to the flood of new federal programs coming out of Washington. At the same time the urbanized states were under increasing pressure to provide more aid to the hard-pressed central cities. One of the first responses in a number of states was to organize themselves to deal better with these new activities and pressures. Indeed, some states, including New York, Massachusetts, and California took important initiatives in advance of federal legislation.

Organizing Themselves

More than thirty states have set up departments of community affairs or similar agencies to coordinate urban programs. Such departments typically provide technical assistance to local governments—especially the smaller towns—on how to make a survey of local housing needs, how to draw up subdivision regulations, or how to finance a sewer plant. These state agencies also serve as a liaison between local governments and other state bureaus and departments. Some departments of community affairs assist in funding local programs such as urban renewal, code enforcement, and recreation. In a number of states, preexisting state planning boards or offices have been incorporated into these new departments. Such planning units not only provide planning services to smaller communities, but typically are charged with coordinating general planning for new development within the state with functional planning for waste disposal systems, stream cleaning, and other areawide activities of government.[1]

These new departments of community affairs have sometimes attracted men of national stature to head them up and such men have, in turn, recruited talented and energetic people to staff the operations. In 1967 Governor Richard Hughes of New Jersey persuaded Paul Ylvisaker to take the helm of the newly-established Department of Community Affairs. Ylvisaker had headed the urban affairs programs of the Ford Foundation.

In the Ford post he had sponsored local experiments that were prototypes of federal efforts to deal with juvenile delinquency, the community action program, and Model Cities.

In the summer of 1967 riots and disturbances broke out in the cities of Newark, Plainfield, Atlantic City, and other localities in New Jersey. As commissioner of community affairs, Ylvisaker played a key role in negotiating an end to the outbreaks and preventing the use of excessive force by state and local police. When the fires died down he told his young staff: "Our job is to be ready by next June. We must not let another year pass without basic work on the causes of riots in black ghettos."[2] Ylvisaker knew that he could not make up in forty weeks for decades of neglect and exploitation. But he was prepared to make a start. Thus did one department of community affairs get under way in the late sixties.

Financing Housing

An increasing number of states have set up housing finance agencies or similar financing institutions. It is not a new idea. In New York the state has been authorized since 1939 to make long-term loans up to 100 percent of the development cost of a housing project at an interest rate equal to the cost of borrowed funds to the state. Similar terms are offered today by housing finance agencies in Illinois, New Jersey, and some other states. The state agencies commonly provide both construction loans and long-term financing and in some cases offer seed money and technical help to church groups, fraternal associations, and other potential nonprofit sponsors of housing. Since the state agency's bonds are exempt from federal income taxation, higher-bracket taxpayers find these bonds attractive at rates somewhat lower than going rates on conventional sources of mortgage funds. The preferential mortgage terms available through state housing finance agencies in 1972 permitted rents to be reduced by 12 to 15 percent. (A two-bedroom apartment requiring a monthly rent of $265 at regular market interest rates might be rented at $225.) Without additional subsidies, this type of aid could help middle income families ($10,000 to $15,000 a year) but not low income people needing housing.

Land Development

A few states have taken pioneering steps in sponsoring land acquisition and development programs. The most dramatic and controversial is the Urban Development Corporation of New York State. Initially, it had the power to acquire land by condemnation and to override local zoning ordinances, powers that had to be used sparingly to avoid a groundswell of local opposition.[a] UDC has the authority to issue tax-exempt bonds and it can act as developer or acquire and sell land to private developers. In its formative years it had vigorous leadership in the person of Edward Logue and the support of Governor Nelson Rockefeller. UDC moved rapidly from plan to production after its creation in 1968, and not surprisingly into some scraps with local jurisdictions. But it was still alive and active five years after it was established and had a number of new communities and large developments under way in various parts of the state. Other states were contemplating the formation of similar corporations.

Industrial Building Codes

At least six states including California and Ohio have adopted industrial building codes. These supersede local building requirements in connection with building components produced in factories if they have been state-approved. Twenty-seven states were reported to have statewide building codes of one type or another at the end of 1972. These laws presage state efforts to move toward modern performance-type building codes, rather than specification codes that minutely detail the types of materials and building methods that may be used and to deal with restrictive labor agreements that prevent the use of more advanced house production techniques.

A companion measure is to improve the skills and information available to local building code enforcement agencies. Local building departments are understandably predisposed to be cautious since they operate in matters of health, safety, and welfare of the community. But some cling to outdated building methods because their personnel are not qualified or equipped to interpret performance codes or to evaluate new building methods. Here the states have a role that they are just beginning to recognize: to promote in-service training and intergovernmental transfers of personnel in this field (among others). Federal and state programs enacted in recent years have authorized such activities. Beyond this, local building departments should be encouraged to recruit engineers and paraprofessionals, as is done in some Western European countries.

---

[a] In 1973 the New York state legislature gave localities the right to reject UDC projects proposed to be built within their boundaries. Localities have thirty days to exercise this veto. This restriction on UDC followed a controversy with a number of Westchester County communities which opposed efforts of UDC to build subsidized housing developments within their jurisdictions.

Equalizing School Expenditures

The states are also under pressure to equalize expenditures by school districts for the education of children. In some states the assumption of larger proportions of education costs by the state government is well under way. The state courts in California (*Serrano* v. *Priest*) and elsewhere have held that some children are denied equality in educational opportunity when school expenditures are dependent upon the amount of taxable wealth in each school district.

A new financing system for education appears to be in the making. In New York a public commission recommended in 1972 that the state assume responsibility for raising and distributing all school funds. A difficult question for a state financing plan—and it has been raised in New York—is whether wealthy districts should be permitted to enrich their local school programs by imposing additional local taxes on themselves. Such additional imposts would of course reflect the high premium that some parents and some communities place upon educating their children. But they could also lead once again to wide disparities in school outlays per child from one district to the next.

In devising new methods of financing school costs, the states must consider how various approaches would affect educational opportunity. They can also influence residential development patterns. Many communities have attempted to exclude moderate and lower income families because such households would require larger local outlays than the local taxes they would pay. The major deficit item for such families is in connection with school costs. A state program that removed the burden of school costs from the locally-collected property tax would eliminate most of the fiscal justification now invoked by suburban localities for excluding lower income residents.

Conditioned State Aid to Localities

Some states have started to condition financial aid to local governments upon a demonstration of local concern for the housing needs of blue-collar workers and lower income families. Pennsylvania's Department of Community Affairs has withheld recreation grants from townships which have land regulations that prevent the construction of housing for moderate and lower income families. The department acted on the basis of a ruling by the State Attorney General that moneys obtained from all taxpayers may not be allocated to a community that wants to remain exclusive. If upheld by the courts, such a policy applied to a wide range of state aids to localities might induce a number of suburban communities to make land available for housing which lower income families could occupy.

The Pennsylvania approach is consistent with a recommendation contained in the President's Second Annual Report on National Housing Goals issued in April 1970. The report urged that federal legislation be adopted which would prohibit state and local public bodies from discriminating against housing subsidized by the federal government, whether through legislative or administrative actions.[3] But there was no follow up by the Nixon administration. Former Secretary of Housing George Romney tried to implement this recommendation but failed to win the support of the White House for his efforts.

Protecting the Natural Environment

In the early seventies many states began to show particular zeal in enforcing policies that limit growth. Measures were adopted to prohibit or restrict construction on seacoasts, along streams and on flood plains, and to protect marshes and wetlands. Maine authorized its Environmental Improvement Commission to halt commercial or industrial investments anywhere in the state. Vermont began to regulate all developments at areas above 2,500 feet elevation and was studying the holding capacity of the state's land and water resources with respect to future development.

We must try to maintain a reasonable balance between protection of the natural environment and the need to accommodate population growth and to provide better living environments for lower income families. Not all states seem to recognize this. Moratoria on new construction have been imposed by state environmental protection agencies in a number of regions, mainly on grounds of inadequate waste disposal systems. Even where blanket prohibitions are not in effect, development on a particular site may be disapproved for other reasons, such as excessive noise due to proximity to highways, airports, or railroads. The National Housing Conference has called for an even-handed evaluation of both environmental concerns and housing needs. Its resolutions for 1973 included the following statement:

NHC believes that we should have a ten-year goal to end air, water and other pollution and create healthy environmental living conditions. However, it is imperative that we should not let our concern for environment replace our priority concern to fulfill our housing goals. We must not be diverted from our commitment to meet the need to provide decent housing for all Americans.[4]

The words of the National Housing Conference have meaning not only for housers but also for environmentalists. For Americans tend to lose interest in causes. One year it is a war on poverty, the next year it is environmental protection, and the following year it may be something else. We have to learn how to enlarge our perspectives and to take a longer view of public needs without impetuously replacing one important goal with another.

Next Steps for the States

Governments at all levels are now grappling with problems of urban development. State governments, only recently awakened to this sector, are weighing strategies and policy choices. Let us sketch out some steps that states may take.

A State Land Policy

A number of states are likely to establish an official land or land use policy within the decade. Proponents argue that localities cannot be expected to concern themselves with problems of a regional or statewide nature; nor do they have the power to do so. In the San Diego region, for example, low density residential developments are encroaching upon the valleys which empty into salt marsh lagoons along the coast. Such areas should be left open, according to Gordon G. Campbell, a young regional planner who has closely studied the San Diego region.[5] The valleys and lagoons should be preserved as wildlife feeding and breeding zones; properly managed, they could also serve nearby residents as places for passive and active recreation. But these coastal lands are controlled by a multiplicity of local jurisdictions, each of which allocates land mainly on the basis of potential property tax returns rather than with concern for environmental quality or regional recreational needs.

Under a bill passed by the United States Senate in 1973, the state governments would be encouraged to designate such zones as "areas of critical environmental concern" and would receive federal aid in developing a program to prevent irreversible damage to natural processes in such areas.[6]

Some people believe that a state land policy is desirable and should be designed to cover not only environmental objectives but other goals as well. Such a policy could also be formulated to promote sound economic development or redevelopment of the state and its regions. Environmental and economic concerns coincide in sections of Appalachia and similar regions where business and job opportunities have dwindled and the depleted fields and hills have been left exhausted and disfigured. A state land policy might also be designed to provide sites in appropriate locations and densities for a wide range of housing, including developments for lower income families.

A State Advance Land Acquisition Program

If a state land policy is to be meaningful, there must be instrumentalities for implementing that policy. The most direct approach would be for the state to authorize and fund a program of acquiring land in advance of need. A state agency would be empowered to take over tracts of land adjoining major public improvements, such as highways, recreational facilities, or other public investments. It could also acquire rights in unimproved land needed to serve a public purpose other than a direct public use. Such purposes justifying land acquisition might include:

1. protection of stream valleys and scenic areas against improper development;
2. promoting economic redevelopment in declining regions;
3. finding suitable sites for balanced residential development including housing for below-market income people; and
4. obtaining and holding acreage for future new communities and large scale developments.

In a state like New Jersey or Massachusetts, a revolving fund of $100 million would be sufficient to initiate the program. While deficits would be incurred in the early years, the program might well show a surplus over time after allowing for interest costs, payments to localities in lieu of taxes, and administrative expenses. This is indicated by the fact that land prices have been rising at 10 to 15 percent a year in some areas, well above the combined costs of interest and taxes foregone on raw land. The state agency administering this program would be encouraged to negotiate land transfers with private owners wherever possible, but should be authorized to exercise the power of eminent domain where necessary. The state agency would have the authority to purchase land directly or to make funds available at reasonable terms to counties and other local governments for advance acquisition of land needed for future public construction or other public purposes.

State Boards to Review Local Land Use Practices

State governments are being urged to supervise the zoning and building code practices of local governments. In some states legislation has been drawn to set up administrative boards which would have the power to review the regulations and decisions of local jurisdictions on new development. As some state courts have found, land use decisions by villages, townships, and other small jurisdictions commonly neglect regional housing needs and reinforce social and racial stratification of the metropolitan population. Moreover, rezoning on a parcel by parcel basis keeps builders in a state of uncertainty and inhibits the aggregating of markets so as to secure economies of scale in house building and in the construction of public facilities. The present system is also wide open to bribery and graft.

A state review board would hold hearings in connection with the local ordinances and regulations as they affect the character of development in the entire urban area. The board would also hear appeals from specific local determinations. The board would have the power to order changes in the ordinances or individual interpretations of zoning and subdivision regulations and building codes upon a finding of injury to the interests of a citizen, another municipality, or the locality itself.

Such administrative rulings could, of course, be appealed to the courts; in such cases, they would expedite and inform the judicial process. Indeed, in the absence of such administrative boards, consumer groups and builders have turned to the state courts for relief from arbitrary local actions. Some landmark decisions have been handed down but local officials have sometimes dragged their feet in complying with the court decisions. A state administrative board could keep the pressure on reluctant local governments and multiply the results of judicial rulings.

State Housing Goals

Once a state government undertakes housing programs, it would seem rational to adopt housing goals for the state. State (and metropolitan) housing targets—x hundred thousand units to be built over the next ten years including a specified portion for lower income families—would be the logical counterparts to the national housing targets laid down by the Congress in 1968. Some states have estimated future housing needs. In Pennsylvania, for example, a housing task force appointed by the governor in 1968 published estimates of housing needs. But these have not been adopted by the governor or legislature as official targets for the commonwealth. Few if any state governments have set numerical goals for housing.

State governments are understandably hesitant about making public commitments of this type. For the factors that largely determine the level of housing production are monetary and fiscal policies, employment and income distribution policies. These are controlled by the federal government, not by the individual states. And the national commitment to subsidized housing is shaky. Subsidized housing programs have long been vulnerable to year-to-year appropriations cuts by the Congress. President Nixon went further and summarily suspended new commitments for subsidized housing by administrative decree in January 1973.

Under such circumstances, it would seem prudent for state governments to issue estimates of needs for housing by different regions and segments of the population rather than to adopt specific targets. For no single state has enough control over relevant determinants to assure that specific housing targets can be met. A good case can be made, moreover, for preparing estimates that are attainable rather than optimal lest the credibility of governments in this sector be further undermined.

State Efforts to Hold Down Housing Costs

The price of housing to the home buyer or renter is affected by initial development costs, transfer or settlement costs, and month to month operating expenses. The number one problem facing builders in many states is the prohibition on construction in areas lacking sewage collection and treatment systems. This means that buildable sites are scarce and expensive and are a major factor in keeping building operations small scale and costly.

The appropriate state response is an enlarged and accelerated sewer construction effort emphasizing regional systems and authorizing the state to install the necessary facilities if localities are unable or unwilling to do so. The states look to Washington for a large part of the funds for these major investments. As with other functions, the degree of state activity in sewage treatment is likely to be closely correlated with the level of federal support called for and released by the White House.

State governments are also being urged by builder groups and consumer organizations to adopt statewide or regional building codes and to help increase the supply of skilled construction workers. For regions with the same ground conditions, climate, and other relevant considerations, uniform building requirements and administrative requirements are indicated. Some progress has been made on this front in recent years. But the shortage of skilled construction workers has, if anything, become more pronounced since the Kaiser Committee identified this as a critical problem in 1968. Some state governments provide modest support for the training of construction workers; few have put real pressure on the building trades to admit more apprentices and trainees to the unions and on the jobs.

Governmental action might yield significant savings to consumers in the area of closing costs. These costs include title search and title insurance, lender's service fees, survey fees, local or state transfer charges, and attorney's fees. The wide variations in these costs from state to state suggest that the charges are excessive in many areas. Moreover, some of the services themselves are questionable, such as the purportedly detailed search of the records back to the Miocene period by title companies every time a property changes hands. This area fairly cries for a Louis D. Brandeis to probe the monopolistic and archaic practices that burden buyers and sellers of homes.

Moving Against Racial Discrimination

Some of the urbanized states have had fair housing laws since the 1950s. In 1968 Congress passed the Civil Rights Act which prohibits discrimination in housing across the land in connection with three-fourths of the nation's housing supply. Yet racial segregation in the largest metropolitan areas seemed to be more pronounced in the early seventies than at the end of the Eisenhower administration. That our legislators enact fair housing laws indicates an ethical commitment to the American creed of fair play and equal opportunity. That so little progress has been made toward integrated neighborhoods and communities reflects the unwillingness of many Americans to break with the past. For throughout our history, black people have been regarded and treated as a caste apart. These caste lines are now cemented by physical barriers and geographic boundaries. In 1970 there were 23 million blacks in the United States; 13 million of them were confined to the central cities of metropolitan areas.

In 1968 the Commission on Civil Disorders called for national policies to bring about the integration of blacks into the larger society outside the ghetto. Congress concurred by approving a broad Civil Rights Act that year. To enlarge opportunities in jobs and housing outside the inner city requires affirmative actions by governments at all levels including state governments.

An affirmative action program must provide incentives to white communities to accept nonwhites as residents and to help blacks make the move to white areas. Such incentives to the white communities might take the form of large sustained grants from the federal and state governments for the enrichment of schools and recreational and cultural services. Participating communities would also receive priorities for aid under regular federal and state aid programs, such as sewer and water facilities and open space. A property value guarantee program might also be devised to insure homeowners against loss of property values attributable to a change in racial composition of the community or neighborhood over a transition period of five to ten years. For nonwhite families who agree to risk the move into all-white areas, there will also be a need for incentives such as low interest rate loans for homes.

These are merely suggestive of what might be tried—if we have the will to try. To undo the social patterns of two centuries and the population trends of the last several decades will not be easy. But a start must be made. Some generation has to be prepared to accept the cost. The upper income families have a special obligation and opportunity to participate. College-trained people, businessmen, and professionals are more inclined to subscribe in principle to equal opportunity in housing and jobs than less well-educated, moderate income whites. The latter families know from experience that "integration" has generally put most of the pressure on their schools and their neighborhoods. It is the well-to-do who can best afford to take the risk of open occupancy living. The upper income families of Bloomfield Hills and the Grosse Pointes in the Detroit area are much more secure than the working class families in Warren or Dearborn. For the well-off, the house does not represent as large a part of the family's life savings as of working class families. Nor need their sense of social status be threatened by the presence of black families as residents in the community. If the affluent accept black families as neighbors, we could in better faith ask the Warrens and Dearborns and all their counterparts in metropolitan areas to open their neighborhoods too. It is in the interest of the affluent to set the pace in integrated living because it means a more stable society over the long run.

Efforts to integrate the metropolitan populations will take a long time. It should be emphasized that such dispersal efforts must not be at the expense of a larger public commitment to the central cities and the ghetto populations. Most nonwhites will continue to live in the central cities for decades to come. Those who remain will need increased employment, income support for people who cannot work, and better schools and housing.

More jobs are critically important if crime and social unrest are to be held within tolerable bounds. Several million hard-core unemployed and underemployed people live in the central cities. Black men between the ages of sixteen and twenty-five make up a critical segment of this surplus labor supply. They are the ones who are most likely to take part in racial disorders and who account for much of the crime in the inner city. Reconciliation between blacks and whites can begin only when there are enough jobs and better economic prospects for young black Americans.

The States Can Do More

Since the middle and late sixties many states have assumed larger responsibilities for urban development. State initiatives have taken the form of public development corporations, laws to facilitate industrial housing, and measures to curb deterioration of the natural environment.

The states can do much more. State governments are particularly well situated to give more direction to the pattern of new development in the outlying parts of urban areas. They can and should move more aggressively against exclusionary zoning. States are in a better fiscal position than localities to narrow the wide disparities in school spending per pupil from one community to the next, thus equalizing educational opportunity and eliminating most of the fiscal basis for excluding lower income families from outlying communities.

The states are latecomers to the shaping of policies for urban development. But this may be turned to advantage. Just as Japan and Sweden could tap the latest technology by reason of industrializing after Britain and the United States, so can the states adopt the most modern institutions and techniques in dealing with urban development. There is a body of knowledge and experience upon which to draw—from the federal government, from some of the larger cities, and from each other. State governments were long maligned, not without reason, for their neglect of urban problems. They can still have a major role in improving the quality of life for their urban and exurban residents—if they choose to.

13 The Government and Urban Change

This book is about housing and urban development. It is also a commentary on America—how we live, what makes us run. We are the children of a heritage that stressed hard work and self-reliance and equated accumulation of wealth with progress. Our forebears were suspicious of government, especially central governments, and devised ways of diffusing governmental power among many centers and conflicting groups. We were taught to believe in democracy—rule by the majority; and also equality or at least equality of opportunity. But we have never been quite sure that equality should be extended to blacks, Puerto Ricans, or Mexican-Americans and in practice tended to treat these groups as inferiors.

American institutions were shaped to allow maximum play to private endeavors and individual initiative. Most nineteenth century economists rationalized such behavior as serving the larger good: the employer provided jobs for workers, the investments of the wealthy increased the productive capacity of the nation, an invisible hand transformed self-seeking into the well-being of the society.

Still, there were obvious and even widening disparities in income and wealth and power between the factory owner and the worker, between the banker and the farmer, between the established burghers and newcomers to cities. The demand for reform grew strong. And the message of the reformers in America came down to one theme: Organize. If you want your share of the pie, get together with others in the same situation. Form unions. Establish associations. Use the political system to protect your interests and advance your group.

Americans did just that. Arthur Bentley, an astute early-twentieth century political writer, suggested that one could understand the entire political and social system by studying pressure groups and interest groups and the way such groups compete or form alliances to achieve their objectives.[1] Each group invoked traditional values—liberty, democracy, progress, self-reliance—as it turned to government to advance its interests. Invariably the interest of the group was equated with the public interest.

We built our cities and towns as we did almost everything else—for economic gain. In the late eighteenth and nineteenth centuries, as in the present era, some people sought to turn population growth into speculative gains. Richard Wade writes: "Men in the East with surplus capital scanned maps looking for likely spots to establish a town . . . They bought up land, laid it out into lots, gave the place a name, and waited for the development of the region to appreciate its value."[2] Many of the towns were patterned after Philadelphia's rectangular grids. No aesthetic image, no notion of public purpose, no historic memory or respect for ancestral place hindered the town developers. And in older cities as well as in raw new towns, builders erected tenements and houses without minimal facilities such as central heating or private bathrooms. The land and the immigrants were there to enable risk-takers and clever operators to make profits.

As people poured into the seaboard cities and as some of the western towns grew into cities, it became necessary to impose more regulations on the development and use of land. Fire was a constant threat in the young cities. Early in their development, Cincinnati, Pittsburgh, and other cities prohibited the construction of wooden structures in their central districts.[3] Municipal regulations were also adopted to protect the health of the community; slaughter houses were restricted to certain sections, land owners were required to drain stagnant ponds, and the building laws began to deal with privies and outhouses. Despite the high premium on private rights, the compactness of life in urban places compelled the extension of public controls.

The municipalities by force of circumstance adopted practices that later came to be explained by the social theory of property. This theory or viewpoint, expounded in the United States by the Wisconsin economist Richard T. Ely, perceives private property as a social trust. A private owner may have exclusive rights in the use of his property, but never an absolute right to do whatever he chooses with it. He may not use it so as to destroy or impair the value or amenity of his neighbor's property. And he is bound to accept certain limitations required to protect the health, safety, and welfare of the larger community.

The municipalities were also called upon to provide services which no individual could provide for himself. Police and firefighting companies were organized, waterworks came to be publicly owned in most cities, public streets were laid out and more or less maintained, and schools were opened.

By the twentieth century the municipalities were responsible for an elaborate and growing bundle of public services. The cities and their environs were enormously productive centers due to increasing specialization in the private sector and large economies of scale. The other side of the coin was rising social costs recognizable as traffic congestion, air and water pollution, crime and social disorder. As urban areas grow in population size and density, social costs climb at an even faster rate.

To deal with these problems, state and local governments have had to hire more and more workers and to absorb an increasing share of the national income. Between 1950 and 1970 state and local employment rose by 141 percent compared with a 49 percent increase in the private nonagricultural sector. The federal government, frequently pictured in cartoons on the editorial page as a bulging bureaucracy, grew in civilian employment by 40 percent in the same period. In 1970 there were 2.7 million federal employees. State and local governments employed almost 10 million people—one out of eight workers in the country.

The federal government has had a considerable, if indirect, influence on urban development from the earliest days. For it was federal land that was turned over to the builders of roads, canals, and railways; the terminals and transfer points of these improvements helped determine the possibilities of town growth. Federal land was also sold cheaply to land companies that hoped to profit from building towns. Not last, it was the Congress that set the liberal immigration policies of the nineteenth and early twentieth centuries, which helped to people the Eastern cities and Western settlements.

But each city and town independently sought population growth and markets, and the folklore of self-help extended to localities as well as to the individual. It was not until the 1930s that the states and cities came to realize that they could not control their own economic destiny. In an earlier day some mining towns and market centers in rural areas had withered and died. When the country fell into the depression of the thirties, even large diversified cities found themselves strapped for funds and unable to cope on their own with their jobless and destitute residents. Without any consistent economic theory or supporting ideology, the federal government under Franklin Roosevelt took strong measures to revive the economy. And Washington began to have large and direct dealings with the cities and towns as well as with mortgage lenders and homeowners.

Federal programs in the thirties were improvised quickly in response to crisis situations. The approach was pragmatic: will it work? Will Congress and the country accept it? Not all programs proved effective and acceptable. Those that did shared two attributes: they were important to a large number of people and they contributed to the recovery of an industry, a region, or the entire national economy.

A high priority in 1933 was to revive the house building industry. Housing starts that year had fallen to below 100,000 units compared with over 900,000 in 1925. In 1932 and again in 1933 a quarter of a million families in cities and towns had lost their properties through foreclosure. A whole new mortgage finance system had to be created. New institutions were set up to salvage the equities of homeowners, to protect the deposits of savers in banks and associations that made loans on real estate, and to insure private lenders against losses on housing mortgages.

One of the successful inventions of this period was the Federal Housing Administration. By guaranteeing savings banks and other institutional lenders against large losses on mortgage loans, FHA helped channel more funds into housing at lower interest costs. In the 1920s a typical house loan was for ten years with a substantial balance remaining to be paid off or renegotiated. Second mortgages at effective interest rates of 10 to 15 percent or more were not uncommon. Under the new FHA system, mortgage loans on new homes could be repaid over twenty years; full amortization of mortgages replaced the big balloon payments that faced many borrowers in the twenties. And lenders were now willing to accept down payments of 20 percent (and later less) compared with the 33 percent or higher requirements of the earlier period. As an example, a 5 percent loan of $10,000 for ten years required monthly payments of $106; but spread over twenty years, only $66. The effect was to bring new housing into the reach of millions of American families. Between 1935 and 1970, 39 million nonfarm housing units were built in the United States. Almost 8 million units came directly through FHA programs, but the financing of all housing built since the thirties has been influenced by FHA.

Federal grants and loans to states and local agencies of government also came into wide use in the 1930s. Federal support for the construction of schools and hospitals, roads, water and sewer facilities was part of the economic strategy of the period. The Public Works Administration, created in 1933, claimed to have made possible four-fifths of all public construction in the United States between 1933 and 1937.[4] The federal grant-in-aid system did not originate in the thirties—it had been in use since 1916 in connection with highway construction. In the depression years federal grants were extended to unemployment relief and to public assistance for dependent children, the aged, and the blind. The low-rent public housing program was also inaugurated during this period with federal commitments to cover the long-term capital costs on bonds issued to build the projects.

The idea of the grant-in-aid is to induce state or local governments to take on or expand an activity which they might otherwise be unable or unwilling to do. The activity is deemed by the Congress to be in the interest of the nation as a whole as well as the particular jurisdiction. In exchange for financial support, the federal government lays down requirements. For example, cities accepting aid from the Public Works Administration had to agree to a schedule of wages and conditions of employment prescribed by the federal authorities and were obliged to permit federal inspection of the activity and a federal audit of the financial accounts. Then as now there was controversy over the degree of federal control that should be exercised versus the amount of discretion to be allowed states and localities in dealing with their particular situations.

While pragmatism guided the extension of federal aids in the thirties, the prolonged depression and high unemployment (there were still eight million out of work in 1940) left a permanent imprint on the nation's psyche. Even as World War II brought everybody who could walk into the factories or the Armed Forces, business leaders and government officials began to prepare for the depression expected to follow the conflict. In 1946 the Congress took the historic step of declaring high employment as a major objective of national policy.

In the 1950s millions of Americans moved to the suburbs, begot many children, tended their gardens, and neglected public problems. During the same decade, more than ten million other people left the farms and rural places and went to the cities. But little was done to prepare them to get good jobs or to live decently in their new surroundings. Thus, one of the major migrations of American history was all but ignored by our national leaders. James Bryant Conant later examined the situation and warned that social dynamite was piling up in the cities.[5] Where were the jobs, he asked, and the schools and community services needed for the growing numbers of blacks living in New York, Chicago, Detroit, and other large cities?

The Eisenhower administration declined to accept larger federal responsibility for these problems. Treasury Secretary George Humphrey warned that increased federal spending and budget deficits would bring about a depression "that would curl your hair." The Republican administration proposed to reduce federal involvement in domestic programs and to turn more of the responsibility over to the states.

But there were exceptions to this belief in federal retrenchment. In 1956 the Eisenhower administration secured enactment of a large new program of federal aid to build a national system of highways. The system was ingeniously financed through a trust fund into which were deposited specified percentages of tax receipts on motor fuel and oil, tires, truck parts, and other items. A network of 42,500 miles was designed at a projected cost of $42 billion. By 1973 the system was largely completed at a cost of well over $50 billion. The federal government paid for 90 percent of these costs, the states only 10 percent.

The mayors clung desperately to one federal program—urban renewal. Enacted in 1949, the urban renewal program enabled some 475 localities to initiate efforts during the fifties to clear blighted areas and to bring private investments into the cities. Federal funds committed to these efforts averaged $135 million a year during the 1950s, a modest level in relation to the size of the problem. (Compare this with federal commitments for highways averaging $2.4 billion a year from 1956 through 1960.) But the urban renewal projects moved slowly and the total cash actually disbursed by the federal government in capital grants from 1950 through 1960 was only $136 million.

The purpose of urban renewal was to restore the attractiveness of older cities and districts to private investors and middle and upper income families. This was expected to shore up the property tax base and help pay for rising municipal costs. While some projects were successful, the program as a whole proved disappointing. By the 1950s families with good incomes had many residential options and most chose the lower density life styles available in the suburbs. And with a motorized labor force, large industrial employers were free to locate in outlying areas. These outward movements of families and firms were generously underwritten, as noted, by federal grants of 50 to 90 percent of cost for the construction of a vast network of urban and interstate highways.

In sum, urban renewal was conceived in the 1930s when many workers still relied on the streetcar and relatively few families could afford the suburbs. When urban renewal came to be tried in the 1950s its underlying assumptions no longer squared with reality. Who wanted to live or shop or spend an evening downtown in Cleveland or St. Louis? The urban renewal program is a striking example of the difficulty of seeking through one public approach to reverse powerful market forces, especially when other public undertakings, such as highway aids, are riding with the tide. And by focusing local energies on the real estate of the community, urban renewal probably delayed governmental efforts to deal directly with underemployment and poverty in the cities.

Then came the 1960s—years of swift change, of active government, and of rising expectations and demands by those at the bottom. Our national leaders promised much: a New Frontier to conquer, a Great Society. Under Kennedy and then Johnson, we began to lay out national goals and to devise all kinds of programs to carry them forward. High hopes were kindled, men in government dared to try new things, and believed that they were making a better society if not a great one.

One cannot recall those years without remembering its leaders. The towering figure was Lyndon B. Johnson, the man who wanted to do something for everybody. In January 1965, flushed with victory at the polls, he told the country:

In the last 4 years . . . the United States has reemerged into the fullness of its self-confidence and purpose. No longer are we called upon to get America moving. We are moving . . . No longer can anyone wonder whether we are in the grip of historical decay. We know that history is ours to make. And if there is great danger, there is now also the excitement of great expectations.[6]

Johnson said that a President collects the vision from the scattered hopes of the American past. Johnson himself was the master collector, piecing everything together, making the parts fit. Johnson the man had to prove himself worthy each day. Johnson the Southerner would get civil rights for the blacks. Johnson the country boy would get a cabinet post for the city folk. Johnson the schoolteacher would see that every kid could learn to read. Johnson the owner of a private spread would have land conserved and recreation opened to the public. Johnson the administrator would watch every detail from burning light bulbs to monthly housing starts. Johnson the moral leader could say: "The Great Society asks not only how much, but how good; not only how to create wealth, but how to use it; not only how fast we are going, but where we are headed.[7]

It was a heady time. The country went along with a war against poverty, with laws extending voting rights and civil rights to blacks, with a new conservation movement to clean the air and the streams and save the land, to revitalize Appalachia, and to build more houses than we had ever built before.

Because the administration was taking on so many challenges, it became necessary to establish national goals and to arrange spending priorities in relation to these goals. In the early sixties the Kennedy administration evaluated legislative proposals and on-going programs in terms of their potential contribution to stimulating a lagging economy—the full employment goal of 1946— as well as their proximate objectives. Other goals that came to be recognized as primary by the Johnson administration and the Congress through policy declarations and a series of laws were:

1. equal opportunity in employment, education, public accommodations, and housing for all individuals regardless of race or creed;
2. eradication of poverty and extension of economic opportunity to some 25 to 35 million people at the bottom of the social order; and
3. protection of the natural environment and natural resources now seriously threatened by the nest-fouling practices of industrial mills, beer drinkers, and local sewage disposal departments.

While these were the larger goals, it would be foolish to believe that the rash of federal programs initiated or enlarged by the Kennedy and Johnson administrations fitted neatly into these categories. The legislative process in America involves a good deal of trading and compromise. Organized clientele groups have more influence than unorganized interests. Powerful committee chairmen in the Congress manage to extract inordinate grants and contracts for their areas and friends. And established bureaus and agencies within the federal government are always working to expand the programs they administer and to enlarge their functional areas. Even Budget officials, men imbued with a passion for anonymity and faithful service to the President, can fall victim to institutional bias and favor programs that appear less costly in next year's budget although they may prove more expensive over the long run. (Example: interest subsidies on private loans for housing at 7 or 8 percent versus direct government loans at the government's borrowing cost of 5 to 6 percent.)

Still many of the new programs were specifically designed to help or to give preference to the poor or near-poor. And as the civil rights acts and the environmental policy acts were adopted, conditions were attached to federal aids to ensure a measure of compliance with congressional intent.

Such requirements or standards were placed upon a growing volume of federal aid. Between 1961 and 1969 the Congress increased federal-aid outlays in urban areas by more than threefold—from $4 to $14 billion; by 1974, such aid was estimated at $31 billion. An inspection of the categories of outlays suggests that roughly half of the total aid was directed toward the poor and the near-poor.[8]

As federal policies for urban areas evolved in the Johnson period, they came to converge on two themes: first, redistribution of income—and to some extent political participation—in the direction of the poor and disadvantaged segments of the population. Second, the promotion of areawide administrative mechanisms—and where possible, political arrangements—for the determination of development patterns in each urban area and the provision of areawide public services.

With regard to income redistribution, there are conceptually two main alternatives: to transfer large sums directly to the poor; or to enable the employable people in the disadvantaged group to work their way into the mainstream and to prepare their children to do the same. The first course appeared too expensive and too un-American; the second was selected as more consonant with traditional values as well as with budget realities. Programs designed in line with the latter strategy included manpower training, the Job Corps, Head Start, aid for primary and secondary education in deprived districts, Model Cities, and the various community action programs.

How was the strategy supposed to work? The training and job programs were clear enough. With training or on-the-job experience, the people would fit into the labor force. Congress was told that "taxeaters" would become taxpayers, just like the rest of us.

The community action programs encouraged deprived groups to stand up for their rights. Group action, even confrontations with local employers or politicians, might be necessary to win concessions from the establishment and to build group pride. The poor, like all influence-seeking groups, needed to organize.

The Model Cities program was a second-generation model, formulated some eighteen months after the Economic Opportunity Act of 1964 was passed. Its designers viewed poverty as a cluster of difficulties that had to be attacked on many fronts. By stimulating innovative approaches from within the poverty group itself and by combining existing programs in creative ways, synergistic effects were expected to appear. Human resource development would be reinforced perhaps by neighborhood rehabilitation projects. Job training not only might qualify some men for jobs with steady pay but also strengthen family life. Perhaps home ownership for the poor family would stimulate self-respect and pride in neighborhood. The possibilities were unlimited if communities and neighborhood groups were sufficiently inventive. On citizen participation Model Cities attempted to walk a fine line. The conflicts between city hall and neighborhood groups financed directly through community action programs were by then a thorny problem for Washington administrators. Under the Model Cities law, residents of the designated model neighborhoods were to have a say in the design of programs; but the final word and administrative responsibility were to be lodged in the office of the mayor or chief elective official.

What were the results of these attempts to redistribute income and power? Obviously there have been some gains for the disadvantaged. In fiscal year 1974 the federal budget provided funds for the urban poor in the form of cash payments or community services that came to something like $1,000 per person in this segment of the population. In 1961 the comparable outlay was about $100 per poor person. But the relative shares of money income received by families at the top and the bottom did not change much between 1960 and 1970: the lowest fifth of all families received the same 4 or 5 percent of total income; the top fifth accounted for two-fifths of the total at the beginning and end of the decade.

The reinforcement effects anticipated in Model Cities did not seem to come off. In practice it proved impossible for Model Cities administrators to draw in large amounts of funds from other agencies. From the outset of Model Cities as well as the community action programs, the old-line service agencies tended to be resentful of these intruders into their areas of responsibility. Despite the high purpose of the War on Poverty, each bureaucracy behaved as bureaucracies are supposed to and fought openly or covertly all attempts by the new agencies to coordinate their activities or to obtain earmarkings of their funds for the poverty sector.

From the standpoint of the mayors, poverty politics proved to be bad politics. How can you channel a stream of new services and aids to the neighborhoods and groups comprising 10 or 20 percent of the population without antagonizing the other 80 or 90 percent? In the early years some mayors got away with it by saying: the federal government requires us to spend it this way. But as rising prices pushed up living costs and as local taxes also rose in the late sixties and early seventies, the resentment of working class people against special treatment of the poor probably deepened. If the districts seeming to get the favors were predominantly black, old prejudices reinforced the opposition.

So long as the administration in Washington was sympathetic to the idea of helping the poor, local opposition could be held within bounds and the programs could go on. During the Johnson period, the federal agencies were sprinkled with advocacy units that dealt with the poor as constituents rather than wards. In the communities, fledgling institutions emerged: community legal services staffed by recent law school graduates; community development corporations formed to advise and help finance neighborhood business enterprises; neighborhood health units and day care centers for children.

In 1973 the outlook for these institutions was less than bright. At the start of his second term, President Nixon announced his intention to phase out programs determined to be inefficient and outmoded. High on the list were programs devised to redistribute income to the poor. To increase efficiency it would be necessary to abolish certain federal agencies. A major unit to be eliminated was the Office of Economic Opportunity, the nerve center of Johnson's late War on Poverty.

What about the second prong of urban policy in the sixties—the attempt to get a handle on areawide development patterns and public services? The arguments for such an approach are mainly to secure efficiency or economies of scale in public services and to conserve on land and other resources of limited supply. Efficiency is highly prized in America, certainly in connection with business affairs and presumably in public affairs. But other values can be raised against this one: for example, the value of citizen participation in local government even if it slows decision making or leads to suboptimum choices.

In any event, federal support in the Kennedy-Johnson period was put behind comprehensive planning for metropolitan areas and areawide arrangements capable of dealing effectively with urban transportation, sewer and water facilities, parks and open space, and the location of housing for the growing population. This federal stance is illustrated by the Urban Mass Transportation Act of 1964. Many highway projects financed under the Federal-Aid Highway Act of 1956 were pushed through without concern for their effects on the central cities or the pattern of development in the areas newly opened to construction. Under the 1964 law, federally-aided mass transportation projects must fit into a unifed or officially coordinated transportation system. This transportation system, in turn, has to contribute to the comprehensively planned development of the entire urban area.

It is not a simple matter to execute such a policy. But the condition of interdependence that is the essence of the modern metropolitan region was recognized in this and subsequent federal aid programs. For more and more of our public concerns are intermunicipal and in some cases interstate. An oil spill in the Schuylkill River at Reading may contaminate the water supply of Philadelphia. The roar of jet planes landing at New York's Kennedy Airport shatters the privacy of homesteaders in Nassau County. The refusal of suburbs to provide building sites for some low income housing keeps the burden of sheltering and servicing the poor on the central city.

The federal laws and requirements of the sixties simply asked the localities to face up to these regional realities. For strictly local solutions are becoming less and less acceptable in the dense conurbations where seven out of ten Americans now live. Federal grants and technical aids were thus developed to induce state and local governments to come to grips with areawide problems on a continuing basis through areawide political agreements and administrative arrangements. In 1973 virtually all metropolitan areas had planning groups which reviewed and commented on the acceptability of projects for which federal funds were sought. This procedure was required by federal laws passed in 1966 and 1968. In some areas, this review and related activities were carried out by councils of local governments. Partly in response, then, to federal inducements, local governments have begun to modernize and to work together on common problems.

The expansion of federal aids in the 1960s was not an unmixed blessing. Jurisdictional rivalries grew more intense among federal agencies and among their counterpart units in state and local governments. Conflicts became more open; coordination was nearly impossible. In addition, the growing number of special-purpose aids added to the difficulties of mayors and governors. These elective officials are supposed to assign priorities in the use of public funds and to carry out broad responsibilities for their residents. Categorical aids, particularly those which go to quasi-independent functional agencies such as highway departments or school districts, tend to lessen the authority of elective officials of general governments.

The need to consolidate many categories of federal aid and to strengthen the hand of elected chief executives became apparent to some people in Washington as early as 1965. In fact, the Model Cities proposal put together by a White House task force in the fall of that year reflected this view. Later presidential study groups and policy advisers in the Johnson administration explored the possibilities of pooling funds, providing block grants for related activities, and allowing more discretion to mayors and general governments in the use of federal money.

By the early seventies there was fairly wide agreement with the idea of consolidating many of the special aids and of allowing more flexibility to local governments in the use of federal funds. But there were sharply conflicting views on the responsibility of the federal government in connection with such assistance. One school, represented by some Democrats in the Congress, wanted to be sure that federal money would continue to be used to advance national purposes as well as to meet local needs. The other, led by President Nixon, proposed that the federal government recede and allow the localities to set priorities in spending money appropriated to them by the Congress.

What happens then to national objectives spelled out by the Congress? In not one but a series of laws, the majority of our senators and representatives have endorsed equal opportunity for racial minorities in jobs and housing, called for participation of the poor in neighborhood improvement efforts, and required areawide approaches in transportation and other public services needed by metropolitan populations.

Can local officials be expected to pursue these objectives if they are locally unpopular or politically dangerous? Would a city council on its own volition give as high a priority to poverty neighborhoods as the Congress did in the Model Cities and community action programs? Would a policeman-turned-mayor allow federal funds under his control to be used for legal services to black kids in trouble with the law? Should suburbs be allowed to use federal money to clear out pockets of slum housing occupied by black families for perhaps three generations or longer, without any obligation to rehouse them decently in the community?

Many of the national goals and laws adopted in the sixties represented a sharp break from earlier American attitudes and practices. A new sense of the common good was beginning to take hold. We seemed more prepared as a nation than as individuals or localities to come to grips with our most challenging problems—poverty, underemployment, racial discrimination, environmental degradation. While many people subscribe to the newer objectives in the abstract, there is a strong propensity to put off the specific actions necessary to carry them out. And local officials are understandably reluctant to take actions that may be unpopular with their influential residents, even when they know that such actions are in the long-term interests of the community as well as the nation.

A national administration persuaded the country to accept responsibilities for the poor, for the disadvantaged, and for the environment of future generations—responsibilities that states and localities were not prepared to assume. It was a tall order. Progress was slow and sometimes painful. But with federal inducements and a measure of prodding, new institutions began to emerge. In one metropolitan area the local governments agreed on a fair-share allocation of housing units for moderate and low income families to be built in their communities. In another, the metropolitan council announced an arrangement to pool a portion of the region's growing tax base and to redistribute the money so as to narrow fiscal inequalities among the local governments. National goals and federal programs created a climate conducive to local innovations of this type. Many more are needed. That is why the federal government must maintain a presence in urban affairs and housing.

Notes

Chapter 1
The Larger View

1. Although most mobile homes are in fact immobile after sale to a family, there is still debate as to how many meet acceptable space and environmental standards. Data from U.S. Department of Commerce, *Housing Starts,* C20-72-10 (November 1972).

2. *Third Annual Report on National Housing Goals,* Message from the President of the United States, House Document No. 92-136 (Washington, D.C.: U.S. Government Printing Office, 1971), p. 24.

3. U.S. Congress, *Defaults on FHA-Insured Home Mortgages –Detroit, Michigan,* Fifteenth Report by the Committee on Government Operations, House Report No. 92-1152 (Washington, D.C.: U.S. Government Printing Office, 1972), pp. 13-14.

4. Richard Hofstadter, *The American Political Tradition* (New York: Vintage Books, 1948), p. vii.

5. Ibid., pp. viii-x.

6. Theodore C. Sorensen, *Decision-Making in the White House* (New York: Columbia University Press, 1963), p. 10.

7. See Pendleton Herring, *The Politics of Democracy* (New York: W.W. Norton & Co., 1940).

Chapter 2
The Housing Problem

1. Herbert A. Simon, *The Shape of Automation for Men and Management* (New York: Harper Torchbooks, 1965), pp. 53-81. Also see: James G. March and Herbert A. Simon, *Organizations* (New York: John Wiley, 1958), pp. 182-190.

2. William G. Grigsby, Louis Rosenburg, Michael Stegman, and James Taylor, *Housing and Poverty* mimeographed (University of Pennsylvania, 1972), chap. IV.

3. Hearings before the National Commission on Urban Problems (Douglas Commission), vol. 2 (Washington, D.C.: U.S. Government Printing Office, 1968), p. 246.

4. This discussion draws heavily upon a presentation by Henry Aaron in January 1971, to a housing study group of the Committee for Economic Development. Also see Henry Aaron, *Shelter and Subsidies: Who Benefits*

From Federal Housing Policies (Washington, D.C.: Brookings Institution, 1972).

5. Stokely Carmichael and Charles V. Hamilton, *Black Power* (New York: Vintage Books, 1967), p. 172.

6. William H. Grier and Price M. Cobbs, *Black Rage* (New York: Bantam Books, 1968), pp. 90-91.

7. C. Wright Mills, *The Sociological Imagination* (New York: Oxford University Press, 1959), pp. 129-130.

Chapter 3
American Values and Community Development

1. For a good discussion of values, read Robert A. Dahl and Charles E. Lindblom, *Politics, Economics, and Welfare* (New York: Harper & Row, 1953; Harper Torchbooks, 1963), pp. 25-54.

2. These comments on welfare and taxes were made by people interviewed in Inglewood, California in late July 1972. Steven V. Roberts, "Voters in Typical Suburb Puzzled over Candidates," *New York Times*, July 30, 1972, p. 28.

3. William D. Bryant, "A Brief Economic History of Kansas City," in Richard P. Coleman and Bernice L. Neugarten, *Social Status in the City* (San Francisco: Jossey-Bass, Inc., 1971), pp. 295-296.

4. See George H. Sabine, *A History of Political Theory* (New York: Henry Holt and Co., 1937), pp. 523 ff.

5. Benjamin Horace Hibbard, *A History of the Public Land Policies* (1924; republished; Madison: University of Wisconsin Press, 1965), chap. XIII.

6. William D. Bryant, "A Brief Economic History of Kansas City" p. 293.

7. Henry James, *Washington Square* (reprint ed., New York: Random House, Modern Library Series, 1950) and cited in Raymond Vernon, *The Changing Economic Function of the Central City*, Committee for Economic Development (New York, 1959), p. 41.

8. Alexis de Tocqueville, *Democracy in America* vol. II (New York: Vintage Books, 1945), p. 144.

9. Dennis W. Brogan, *The American Character (New York: Alfred A. Knopf, 1944), p. 5.*

10. See Herbert J. Gans, *The Levittowners* (New York: Vintage Books, copyright, 1967), pp. 34-36.

11. See Vernon Louis Parrington, *Main Currents in American Thought*

vol. 2 (New York: Harcourt, Brace, and Co., 1927), pp. 145-152; 258-267. Also see Morton and Lucia White, "The Intellectual versus the City," in *Daedalus* (Winter 1961), pp. 166-179.

12. Parrington, *Main Currents* vol. 3, pp. 7-10 and throughout.

13. Henry Adams, *The Education of Henry Adams* (Boston: Houghton Mifflin, 1918), pp. 7-9.

14. Hofstadter, *The American Political Tradition* p. 13.

15. Oscar Handlin, "The Social System," *Daedalus* (Winter 1961).

16. Massachusetts, alone among the North American colonies, had a universal free public education system by the middle of the eighteenth century. But free public schooling was whittled down between 1800 and 1827, while private academies for the sons of the wealthy were subsidized by the state. Free education for the masses was strengthened during the following period; in 1862 the towns of Massachusetts were required to have measures preventing truancy. See George H. Martin, *The Evolution of the Massachusetts Public School System* (New York: D. Appleton, 1894), p. 52 and throughout.

17. Richard P. Coleman and Bernice L. Neugarten, *Social Status in the City* (San Francisco: Jossey-Bass, Inc., 1971), chap. 4.

18. Ibid., p. 66.

19. Homer Hoyt, *One Hundred Years of Land Values in Chicago* (Chicago: University of Chicago Press, 1933), pp. 314-316.

20. Colonial Laws (1660), pp. 184-185.

21. See F. B. Sanborn, *The Public Charities of Massachusetts, 1776-1876* (Boston: Wright and Potter, 1876), pp. clvii ff. for a colorful description of these events and the personages involved.

22. Alvin L. Schorr, "The Duplex Society," *New York Times,* June 4, 1972, p. 15.

23. Vernon L. Parrington, *Main Currents* vol. 2, pp. iii-x.

24. Andrew Jackson's first annual message to the Congress, December 1829, quoted in Hofstadter, op. cit., p. 51.

25. Ibid., p. 170.

26. Roger Burlingame, *The American Conscience* (New York: Alfred A. Knopf, 1957), pp. 328-329.

27. See Committee for Economic Development, *Guiding Metropolitan Growth* (New York, 1960), pp. 42-44. Also: CED's policy statement *Reshaping Government in Metropolitan Areas* (New York, 1970).

28. George, *Life of Henry George,* pp. 216-217, cited in Parrington, op. cit., vol. 3, p. 29.

29. E. A. Ross, *Sin and Society,* cited in Carl N. Degler, *Out of Our Past* (New York: Harper & Row, 1959), p. 363.

30. Joseph P. Lash, *Eleanor and Franklin* (New York: W.W. Norton, 1971), p. 420.

31. William J. Baumol, "Macroeconomics of Unbalanced Growth," *American Economic Review* (June 1967), pp. 415-426.

32. See Robert A. Nisbet, *The Sociological Tradition* (New York: Basic Books, 1966), chap. 4.

Chapter 4
National Goals and Housing

1. Gifford Pinchot, *Breaking New Ground* (New York: Harcourt, Brace and Company, 1947), p. 121.

2. Jacques Ellul, *The Technological Society* (New York: Alfred A. Knopf, 1967), chap. 1.

3. *Goals for Americans,* The Report of the President's Commission on National Goals (Englewood Cliffs, N.J.: Prentice-Hall, 1960), p. 2.

4. See Theodore C. Sorenson, *Decision-Making in the White House,* pp. 18-20.

5. Charles J. Hitch, *Decision-Making for Defense* (Berkeley and Los Angeles: University of California Press, 1965), pp. 28-29.

6. See David Novick, ed. *Program Budgeting* (Rand Corporation, Washington, D.C.: U.S. Government Printing Office, 1965). This gives a good idea of the concept and the state of the art when President Johnson introduced the approach. Chapter 9, "Problems, Limitations, and Risks," by Roland N. McKean and Melvin Anshen is particularly instructive.

7. *The Budget of the United States Government, Fiscal Year 1968* (Washington, D.C.: U.S. Government Printing Office, 1967), p. 36.

8. U.S. Congress, Senate Subcommittee of the Committee on Banking and Currency, *Housing Legislation of 1965,* 89th Cong., first session (1965), pp. 46-48; see chart on p. 97.

9. The story of the Committee for Economic Development is told in Karl Schriftgiesser, *Business Comes of Age* (New York: Harper & Brothers, 1960). CED's role in support of passage of the Employment Act of 1946 is related in Chapter 7. Also see Stephen K. Bailey, *Congress Makes a Law* (New York: Vintage Books, 1964; copyright 1950.)

10. Statement by Marriner S. Eccles before the Joint Committee on the Economic Report, November 25, 1947; reprinted in *Federal Reserve Bulletin* (December 1947).

11. Catherine Bauer, "Redevelopment: A Misfit in the Fifties," in Coleman Woodbury, ed., *The Future of Cities and Urban Redevelopment* (Chicago: University of Chicago Press, 1953).

12. Otto Eckstein, "The Economics of the 1960's—A Backward Look," *The Public Interest*, no. 19 (Spring 1970), pp. 86-97. The entire article is well worth reading.

13. Outdoor Recreation Resources Review Commission, *Outdoor Recreation for America* (Washington, D.C.: U.S. Government Printing Office, 1962), pp. 3-4.

14. Citizens' Advisory Committee on Environmental Quality, *Annual Report to the President and to the Council on Environmental Quality for the Year ending May 1972* (Washington, D.C.: U.S. Government Printing Office, 1972), p. 13.

15. For an extended discussion of this point, see Alan Altshuler, *The City Planning Process* (Ithaca: Cornell University Press, 1965), chap. V.

16. *Goals for Americans*, p. 3.

17. Theodore C. Sorensen, *Kennedy* (New York: Harper & Row, 1965), p. 475.

18. William L. Taylor, *Hanging Together: Equality in an Urban Nation* (New York: Simon and Schuster, 1971), p. 96.

19. Labor Day speech by President Nixon, reported in the *Philadelphia Evening Bulletin*, September 5, 1972, p. 34.

20. Excerpts from Republican party platform, *New York Times*, August 22, 1972, p. 35. The platform also states: "Neither do we favor dispersing large numbers of people away from their homes and neighborhoods against their will." This implies that many blacks live in segregated neighborhoods by preference. In contrast with these positions, the Commission of Population Growth and the American Future, appointed by President Nixon, recommended vigorous steps "to help dissolve the territorial basis of racial polarization" (Report of the Commission, p. 218). The Population Commission also cites a survey conducted for the 1968 Commission on Civil Disorders which found that nearly half of the black respondents preferred to live in a mixed neighborhood, another third did not care, and only 13 percent preferred all black or mostly black neighborhoods.

21. Walter White, *How Far the Promised Land* (New York: The Viking Press, 1955).

22. The Commission on Population Growth and the American Future, *Population and the American Future* (New York: Signet, 1972), pp. 48-49.

23. The National Urban Coalition, *Counterbudget*, Robert S. Benson and Harold Wolman, eds. (New York: Praeger, 1971), pp. 47-58.

24. *Report of the National Advisory Commission on Civil Disorders* (New York: Bantam Books, 1968), p. 467.

25. Ibid., pp. 472-473.

26. Title XVI, Housing and Urban Development Act of 1968, Public Law 90-448.

27. *Second Annual Report on National Housing Goals,* Message from the President of the United States, House Document No. 91-292 (Washington, D.C.: U.S. Government Printing Office, 1970), p. 2.

28. Robert K. Merton, foreword to Jacques Ellul, *The Technological Society,* op. cit., p. vi.

29. *Population and the American Future,* pp. 6-8.

Chapter 5
Government Housing Programs

1. See *Fourth Annual Report on National Housing Goals,* Message from the President of the United States, House Doc. 92-319 (Washington, D.C.: U.S. Government Printing Office, 1972), pp. 47-48. The income figures are adjusted gross income. Only 3.2 percent of taxpayers with adjusted gross incomes of under $3,000 benefited from the deductions for mortgage interest and real estate taxes; their average tax savings was but $30 per return.

2. Ibid., p. 41. This document (p. 40) is also the source of the mortgage loan figures for 1971. The special tax treatment of real estate investment trusts reduced federal revenues by $140 million in 1971.

3. Information for this section was obtained from several sources including the Fourth Annual Goals Report cited above and the *1970 Annual Report* of the Department of Housing and Urban Development (Washington, D.C.: U.S. Government Printing Office, 1971).

4. These figures are from *The Budget of the United States Government Fiscal Year 1973* (Washington, D.C.: U.S. Government Printing Office, 1972), p. 157. They appear to be on the low side as compared with data issued by the Department of Health, Education, and Welfare.

5. Bernard J. Frieden, "Improving Federal Housing Subsidies: Summary Report," in *Papers Submitted to Subcommittee on Housing Panels,* part 2 (cited in Footnote 15), p. 481.

6. *Fourth Annual Report on National Housing Goals,* pp. 44-46. Also see Rural Housing Alliance, *Low-Income Housing Programs for Rural America* (Washington, D.C., 1971).

7. See *1970 Annual Report* of HUD, pp. 48-49.

8. Henry B. Schechter, "Federal Housing Subsidy Programs," U.S. Congress, Joint Economic Committee, *The Economics of Federal Subsidy Programs,* Part 5—Housing Subsidies (Washington, D.C.: U.S. Government Printing Office, October 1972), pp. 614-616.

9. Wylie Greig and Philip Goldberg, "Subsidized Multi-Family Housing in Eastern Pennsylvania," (University of Pennsylvania, unpublished, May 4, 1972). The author appreciates the opportunity to review this study.

10. Message from the President of the United States, "Problems and Future of the Central City and Its Suburbs," March 2, 1965.

11. U.S. Congress, *Housing Legislation of 1965*, pp. 46-48; chart on p. 97.

12. See *1960 Annual Report* of the Housing and Home Finance Agency (Washington, D.C.: U.S. Government Printing Office, 1961), pp. 204-239.

13. The Chicago story is told in Charles Abrams, *Forbidden Neighbors* (New York: Harper & Brothers, 1955), pp. 103-119.

14. These figures are drawn from the *1970 HUD Statistical Yearbook* (Washington, D.C.: U.S. Government Printing Office, 1971), pp. 103-145.

15. Abner D. Silverman, "User Needs and Social Services," U.S. Congress, House Committee on Banking and Currency, *Papers Submitted to Subcommittee on Housing Panels*, Part 2, 92nd Cong., first session (Washington, D.C.: U.S. Government Printing Office, June 1971), pp. 579-606. This is a classic statement on public housing.

16. Ibid., p. 591.

17. Michael Padnos, "The Tenant Movement," *Papers Submitted to Subcommittee on Housing Panels*, Part 2, pp. 662-665; and data from HUD.

18. Silverman, "User Needs and Social Services," pp. 604-605.

19. *Fourth Annual Report on National Housing Goals*, pp. 8-9.

20. *Second Annual Report on National Housing Goals*, p. 4. *Third Annual Report on National Housing Goals*, pp. 11-12.

Chapter 6
Some Alternatives in Housing Policy

1. Irving Fisher, *The Theory of Interest* (New York: Macmillan Company, 1930); and Morton L. Isler, "The Goals of Housing Subsidy Programs," *Papers Submitted to Subcommittee on Housing Panels*, Part 2, pp. 415-436.

2. These views are reflected in the research papers prepared by some analysts associated with the Urban Institute, Washington, D.C., such as Frank de Leeuw, and Ira S. Lowry, New York City Rand Institute. See their statements in *Papers Submitted to Subcommittee on Housing Panels*, cited above. Also see Henry Aaron, *Shelter and Subsidies: Who Benefits Fom Federal Housing Policies.*

3. Welfare economists generally cite these factors as justifying gov-

ernment involvement in the private economy. See William J. Baumol, "Urban Services: Interaction of Public and Private Decisions," in *Public Expenditure Decisions in the Urban Community*, ed. Howard G. Schaller (Washington, D.C.: Resources for the Future, 1963).

4. Clifford R. Bragdon, *Noise Pollution: The Unquiet Crisis* (Philadelphia: University of Pennsylvania Press, 1971).

5. *Fourth Annual Report on National Housing Goals*, p. 29.

6. Donald D. Kummerfeld, "The Housing Subsidy System," in *Papers Submitted to Subcommittee on Housing Panels*, Part 2, op. cit., p. 457.

7. See U.S. Bureau of the Census, *Statistical Abstract of the United States: 1972* (Washington, D.C., 1972), p. 350. Also see Dorothy K. Newman, "Housing the Poor and the Shelter to Income Ratio," in *Papers Submitted to Subcommittee on Housing Panels*, Part 2, op. cit., pp. 555-578.

8. *A Decent Home*, The Report of the President's Committee on Urban Housing (Washington, D.C., 1968), p. 68.

9. Frank de Leeuw, "The Housing Allowance Approach," *Papers Submitted to Subcommittee on Housing Panels*, Part 2, pp. 545-546.

10. Richard U. Ratcliff, *Urban Land Economics* (New York: McGraw-Hill, 1949), pp. 116-119.

11. See Dorothy K. Newman, "Housing the Poor," pp. 569-571.

12. American Public Health Association, *Planning the Home for Occupancy* (Chicago: Public Administration Service, 1950).

13. *Fourth Annual Report on National Housing Goals*, p. 50.

14. Compare with estimates in Frank de Leeuw and Sam H. Leaman, "The Section 23 Leasing Program," *The Economics of Federal Subsidy Programs*, Part 5—Housing Subsidies, pp. 650-655.

15. See Dorothy K. Newman, "Housing the Poor," p. 573.

16. Henry B. Schechter and Marion K. Schlefer, "Housing Needs and National Goals," in *Papers Submitted to Subcommittee on Housing Panels*, Part 1, pp. 37-38. The entire monograph (pp. 1-139) is worth reading.

17. Richard U. Ratcliff, *Urban Land Economics*, pp. 507-512.

18. Ira S. Lowry, "Housing Assistance for Low-Income Urban Families: A Fresh Approach," in *Papers Submitted to Subcommittee on Housing Panels*, Part 2, pp. 489-523, especially pp. 501-503.

19. Frank de Leeuw, "The Housing Allowance Approach," pp. 545-547.

20. *Budget of the United States Government, Fiscal Year 1973*, p. 157.

21. Committee for Economic Development, *Improving the Public Welfare System* (New York, April 1970), p. 13.

22. William G. Grigsby et al., *Housing and Poverty* mimeographed (Philadelphia: Institute for Environmental Studies, University of Pennsylvania, 1972).

23. See Irving H. Welfeld, "Toward a New Federal Housing Policy," *The Public Interest* no. 19 (Spring 1970), pp. 31-43.

24. Henry B. Schechter and Marion K. Schlefer, "Housing Needs and National Goals," p. 38.

25. Prof. Yung Ping Chen of the University of California at Los Angeles tested this idea among elderly homeowners with the indicated results. I am grateful to Henry B. Schechter for calling this to my attention.

26. *Fourth Annual Report on National Housing Goals,* p. 38.

27. Ibid., p. 9.

28. Morton J. Schussheim, study director, *Prospects for Rehabilitation: A Demonstration Study of Housing in Morningside Heights* (Albany: New York State Housing Rent Commission, 1960).

29. See Institute of Public Administration, *Rapid Rehabilitation of Old Law Tenements* (New York, 1968).

30. Letter from Secretary Robert C. Weaver to Senator John Sparkman, July 11, 1967, transmitting "A Report on Rehabilitation Programs by the Department of Housing and Urban Development to the Committee on Banking and Currency, United States Senate," mimeographed.

31. *Meeting the Insurance Crisis of Our Cities,* Report by the President's National Advisory Panel on Insurance in Riot-Affected Areas (Washington, D.C., January 1968), p. 2. Richard J. Hughes, then Governor of New Jersey, was the chairman of this panel.

32. Ibid., p. 30.

33. Ibid., p. 2.

34. *1970 Annual Report of the Department of Housing and Urban Development* (Washington, D.C.: U.S. Government Printing Office, 1971), p. 146.

35. *Defaults on FHA-Insured Home Mortgages—Detroit, Mich.,* p. 4 and throughout.

36. *1970 HUD Statistical Yearbook,* table 184, p. 180. The *Yearbook* is also the source of data on FHA mortgage insurance on new versus existing homes.

37. *Defaults on FHA-Insured Home Mortgages—Detroit, Mich.,* p. 52.

38. Ibid., p. 61.

39. Morton J. Schussheim, study director, *High Rent Housing and Rent Control in New York City* (New York: New York State Housing Rent Commission, 1958), pp. 55-57.

40. Chester Rapkin, *The Real Estate Market in an Urban Renewal Area* (New York City Planning Commission, 1959), p. 61.

41. Housing and Home Finance Agency, *Low-Income Housing Demonstration . . . a Search for Solutions* (Washington, D.C.: U.S. Government Printing Office, 1964), p. 10. The writer, whose office had general responsibility for this and other research and demonstration programs of HHFA from 1961 through 1965, recalls that rents for older houses containing four or more bedrooms and available to low income families in New Haven, Connecticut were mostly $300 a month and higher in 1962-64.

Chapter 7
The Older City and Urban Renewal

1. Louis Wirth, "Urbanism as a Way of Life," *American Journal of Sociology*, XLIV, no. 1 (July 1938).

2. David Riesman, *The Lonely Crowd* (New York: Doubleday Anchor Books, 1953), pp. 87-88.

3. See Jack Rosenthal, "Large Suburbs Overtaking Cities in the Number of Jobs Supplied," *New York Times,* October 15, 1972, pp. 1 and 58. The article is largely based on data from the 1970 Census of Population. These trends have been projected on the basis of earlier data by other analysts. See, for example, Raymond Vernon, *The Changing Economic Function of the Central City* (New York: Committee for Economic Development, 1959).

4. Edward Banfield bases much of his analysis of urban ills on the differences between present-oriented and future-oriented groups of people. He recognizes the existence of some serious urban problems but contends that governmental efforts to deal with them are largely counterproductive. See Edward C. Banfield, *The Unheavenly City* (Boston: Little, Brown and Company, 1968). Daniel P. Moynihan allegedly suggested to President Nixon that the administration consider a policy of "benign neglect" toward disadvantaged population groups. But Moynihan is also credited with designing the Family Assistance Program proposed by the Nixon administration in 1969 as a substitute for other welfare programs. The Family Assistance proposal was turned down by the Congress, and Nixon subsequently abandoned it on grounds of political unacceptability.

5. *Economic Report of the President,* January 1969 (Washington, D.C.: U.S. Government Printing Office, 1969), p. 173.

6. Ibid., pp. 174-175.

7. *Report of the National Advisory Commission on Civil Disorders* (New York: Bantam Books, 1968), pp. 267-269.

8. *Building the American City*, Report of the National Commission on Urban Problems (Washington, D.C.: U.S. Government Printing Office, 1968), p. 6. This commission was headed by former Senator Paul H. Douglas of Illinois.

9. William J. Baumol, "Macroeconomics of Unbalanced Growth," pp. 415-426.

10. *Report of the President's Advisory Committee on Government Housing Policies and Programs*, December 1953 (Washington, D.C.: U.S. Government Printing Office, 1953), p. 186. This committee, appointed by President Eisenhower, was chaired by Albert M. Cole.

11. Hearings on Housing Act of 1954 cited in Charles Abrams, *The City Is the Frontier* (New York: Harper & Row, 1965), p. 86.

12. Housing and Home Finance Agency, *Fourteenth Annual Report for 1960* (Washington, D.C.: U.S. Government Printing Office, 1961), tables VII-1 and VII-2, p. 292.

13. Ibid., pp. 289-290.

14. See *Report of the National Advisory Commission on Civil Disorders*, p. 143.

15. Ibid., pp. 479-480.

16. U.S. Department of Housing and Urban Development, *1969 HUD Statistical Yearbook* (Washington, D.C.: U.S. Government Printing Office, 1970), p. 302.

17. About 40 rental projects insured by FHA under Section 220 and located in 19 different localities had encountered marketing difficulties by the end of 1962, according to a study of the Housing and Home Finance Agency prepared in early 1963. A total of 148 insured mortgages on such rental projects were in force at the end of 1962. See Department of Housing and Urban Development, *Annual Report 1965* (Washington, D.C.: U.S. Government Printing Office, 1966), table 26, p. 74.

18. Robert C. Weaver, *The Urban Complex* (New York: Doubleday, 1964), pp. 112-118. Weaver was the Administrator of the Housing and Home Finance Agency when he wrote this book.

19. *1969 HUD Statistical Yearbook*, pp. 303-304.

20. Department of Housing and Urban Development, *1971 Annual Report* (Washington, D.C.: U.S. Government Printing Office, August 1972), pp. 39-40.

21. Most of this information was derived from the *1970 HUD Statistical Yearbook* and the *1971 Annual Report* of HUD.

22. *Building the American City*, pp. 89-90, 167.

23. Ibid., p. 165.

Chapter 8
Model Cities

1. *Budget of the United States Government, Fiscal Year 1974* (Washington, D.C.: U.S. Government Printing Office, 1973), p. 116.

2. This section on conceptual roots of Model Cities is based upon unpublished materials and discussions with members of the task force who designed the program including Robert C. Wood, the chairman of this group and Under Secretary of the Department of Housing and Urban Development from 1966 to 1968.

3. See Model Cities Service Center, National League of Cities and United States Conference of Mayors, *Model Cities, A Report on Progress,* vol. 2, no. 9 (June 1971), pp. 4-8 and throughout. Also see Judson Lehman James, "Evaluation Report on the Model Cities Program," in *Papers Submitted to Subcommittee on Housing Panels,* Part 2, pp. 839-856.

4. Ibid., p. 845.

5. *Model Cities, A Report on Progress,* p. 41.

6. Sidney Gardner, "Impact on a Federal Agency—HEW," *Model Cities, A Report on Progress,* pp. 14-18.

7. *Model Cities, A Report on Progress,* pp. 61-63.

8. Bjorn Pedersen and Donald Smalley, "Crime and Delinquency," *Model Cities, A Report on Progress,* pp. 44-46.

9. See *CDC's: New Hope for the Inner City* (New York: The Twentieth Century Fund, 1971), including background paper by Geoffrey Faux.

10. *Model Cities: A Step Towards the New Federalism,* The Report of the President's Task Force on Model Cities (Washington, D.C., 1970). Edward C. Banfield was chairman of this task force.

Chapter 9
Revenue Sharing

1. David W. Lyon, "The Financial Future of City and School Government in Philadelphia," *Business Review,* Federal Reserve Bank of Philadelphia (March 1971), pp. 4-5.

2. Calculated from data in *Statistical Abstract of the United States: 1972,* p. 430.

3. David W. Lyon, "The Financial Future," pp. 8-11.

4. Office of Management and Budget, *Special Analyses, Budget of the United States Government, Fiscal Year 1973* (Washington, D.C.: U.S. Government Printing Office, 1972), pp. 239-255. Also see *Special Analyses, Fiscal Year 1970* (same source, published in 1969), pp. 201-219.

5. *Model Cities: A Step Towards the New Federalism*, p. 6.

6. See the article by William Spring, Bennett Harrison, and Thomas Vietorisz, "Crisis of the Underemployed," *The New York Times Magazine* (November 5, 1972), pp. 42 ff.

7. See *Special Analyses, Fiscal Year 1973*, p. 243.

8. *Budget of the United States Government, Fiscal Year 1974*, pp. 13-14.

9. Department of Housing and Urban Development and the Domestic Council, Executive Office of the President, *President Nixon's Plan for Urban Community Development Revenue Sharing* (Washington, D.C.: U.S. Government Printing Office, 1971, 16 pages). Also see Warren E. Farb, "Analysis of the Better Communities Act," Congressional Research Service, Library of Congress (multilith, June 1973).

10. Cited in National Housing Conference Newsletter, July 26, 1971, based on *Housing and Urban Affairs Daily*, ed. Hugh L. Morris (Washington, D.C., 1971).

11. U.S. Congress, House of Representatives, *Report to Accompany H.R. 16704, The Housing and Urban Development Act of 1972*, Report No. 92-1429 (September 21, 1972), p. 59.

Chapter 10
New Development

1. Catherine Bauer, "Social Questions in Housing and Community Planning," *Journal of Social Issues*, vol. VII, nos. 1 & 2 (1951), pp. 1-34. Reprinted in *Urban Housing*, William L.C. Wheaton, Grace Milgram, and Margy Ellin Meyerson, eds. (New York: The Free Press, 1966), pp. 30-52.

2. Committee for Economic Development, *Reshaping Government in Metropolitan Areas* (New York, 1970), p. 39.

3. See Seymour Sacks, "Fiscal Disparities and Metropolitan Development," in *Papers Submitted to Subcommittee on Housing Panels*, Part 2, pp. 809-824.

4. These school expenditure figures appear in *Economic Aspects of Public Education In Pennsylvania, 1969-70* (Philadelphia: Educational Research and Service Bureau, University of Pennsylvania, 1971).

5. See Randall W. Scott, "Exclusionary Land Use Practices," mimeographed (1973), available from American Institute of Planners, Washington, D.C.

6. National Commission on Urban Problems, *Building the American City*, (Washington, D.C.: U.S. Government Printing Office, 1968), pp. 206-207, 215.

7. Brief for Amicus Curiae, Pennsylvania Builders Association and National Association of Home Builders of the United States, in *Commonwealth of Pennsylvania and Bucks County Interfaith Housing Corporation et al.*, vs. *County of Bucks et al.*, p. 27.

8. Ibid., p. 24.

9. Randall Scott, "Exclusionary Land Use Practices," p. 9.

10. See Grace Milgram, *U.S. Land Prices–Directions and Dynamics* (prepared for the National Commission on Urban Problems, 1968), pp. 54-55.

11. *Fourth Annual Report on National Housing Goals*, p. 18; land price data: pp. 104-106.

12. The 1971 Census of Builder Activity sponsored by *Professional Builder* magazine reported that residential builders of 76 or more units accounted for 45 percent of single family units and 72 percent of multifamily units. Another survey of 1969 production credits builders of 101 units and over with 43 percent of single family production but 90 percent of multifamily output. See Michael Sumichrast and Sara A. Frankel, "Profile of the Builder and his Industry," National Association of Home Builders (Washington, D.C., 1970).

13. Data for this section on mobile homes have been obtained from several sources including the Kaiser Committee's report, *A Decent Home*, cited in earlier chapters; and Henry B. Schechter and Marion K. Schlefer, "Housing Needs and National Goals," *Papers Submitted to Subcommittee on Housing Panels*, Part 1, previously cited. Also see "Mobile Homes and the Housing Supply," *Housing Surveys*, Part 2 (Washington, D.C.: U.S. Government Printing Office, 1968) and Census of Housing: 1970, *Mobile Homes*, Final Report HC(7)-6 (Washington, D.C.: U.S. Government Printing Office, 1973).

14. Information for Philadelphia and Pennsylvania used here and elsewhere are drawn from "Residential Development in Pennsylvania: A Report to the Department of Community Affairs," by Morton J. Schussheim, James R. Westkott, Dovie K. Reiff and Julius Levine, mimeographed (December 1971). Copies may be obtained from the Department of Community Affairs, Harrisburg, Pa.

15. *Report of the National Advisory Commission on Civil Disorders*, p. 398.

Chapter 11
Shaping Urban Growth

1. Alan Altshuler, *The City Planning Process* (Ithaca: Cornell University Press, 1966), chap. V.

2. See Herman Kahn and Anthony J. Wiener, *The Year 2000* (New York: The Macmillan Company, 1967), pp. 185 ff; and Robert Murray Haig, *Major Economic Factors in Metropolitan Growth and Arrangement* (New York: The Regional Plan Association, 1927). Haig, a Columbia University economist, pioneered studies of the forces affecting the growth and layout of urban regions. Changes in transportation technology, income distribution, and life styles since the 1920s have rendered his findings obsolete; but his methods of analysis are still valid.

3. Kahn and Wiener, *The Year 2000*, pp. 193 ff. The dilemma of man freed from his historic struggle for subsistence by "science and compound interest" is from John Maynard Keynes, *Essays in Persuasion* (1930; reprinted ed., New York: W. W. Norton, 1963).

4. The comment was made by Stanley Tankel to the writer during a sidewalk tour of New York. Tankel lived in Greenwich Village and was planning director of the Regional Plan Association of New York.

5. Harold J. Laski, *Parliamentary Government in England* (New York: The Viking Press, 1938), p. 267. Cited in Pendleton Herring, *The Politics of Democracy* (New York: W.W. Norton, 1940), p. 372.

6. *Annual Report of the Citizens' Advisory Committee on Environmental Quality*, p. 7-9.

7. Ian L. McHarg, *Design with Nature* (New York: Doubleday/Natural History Press, 1969).

8. Title VII, Housing and Urban Development Act of 1965. Public Law 89-117, 79 Stat. 451, 489; 42 U.S.C. 3101.

9. This illustration is based upon first-hand participation by the writer, who represented the Housing Agency during part of the negotiations. Information on the statute and the appropriations is from *Grants-in-Aid and other Financial Assistance Programs Administered by the U.S. Department of Health, Education and Welfare* (1963) pp. 137-139; and *The Budget of the United States Government for Fiscal Year ending June 30, 1964*, p. 210.

10. Title II, Demonstration Cities and Metropolitan Development Act of 1966. Public Law 89-754, 80 Stat. 1255, 1261.

11. *Philadelphia Inquirer*, December 21, 1972, p. 25.

12. Abraham Kaplan, *The Conduct of Inquiry* (San Francisco: Chandler Publishing Company, 1964), pp. 403-404.

13. Committee for Economic Development, *Guiding Metropolitan Growth* (New York, 1960).

Chapter 12
Role of the States in Urban Development

1. Office of the President, *Report on National Growth 1972* (Washington, D.C.: U.S. Government Printing Office, 1972), pp. 33-54. Also see Norman Beckman and Bruce Langdon, *National Growth Policy* (Washington, D.C.: Urban Land Institute, 1972), pp. 46-57.

2. The writer served as an adviser to Commissioner Ylvisaker during this period and recorded this statement at a staff conference.

3. *Second Annual Report on National Housing Goals,* p. 10.

4. National Housing Conference, Conference Resolutions adopted in March 1973, mimeographed, p. 179.

5. Gordon G. Campbell, "Regional Approach to Resource Management," (University of Pennsylvania, unpublished, June 1972).

6. Senate Bill S. 268, the Land Use Policy and Planning Assistance Act of 1973, was passed by the U.S. Senate in 1973. A companion measure was being considered by the House Interior and Insular Affairs Committee in the fall of 1973.

Chapter 13
The Government and Urban Change

1. Arthur F. Bentley, *The Process of Government* (Bloomington, Indiana: Principia Press, 1908), referred to in Harold Wolman's useful book, *Politics of Federal Housing.*

2. Richard C. Wade, *The Urban Frontier* (Chicago: The University of Chicago Press, 1967, first published 1959 by Harvard University Press), p. 30.

3. Ibid., p. 293.

4. See Harold M. Groves, *Financing Government,* rev. ed. (New York: Henry Holt and Co., 1945), p. 500.

5. James B. Conant, *Slums and Suburbs* (New York: McGraw-Hill, 1961; New York: Signet Books, 1964).

6. State of the Union Message, January 4, 1965, House of Representatives, 89th Cong., Document No. 1, pp. 2-3.

7. Ibid., p. 5.

8. *Special Analyses, Budget of the United States Government Fiscal Year 1974* (Washington, D.C.: U.S. Government Printing Office, 1973), p. 219.

Index

Index

Aaron, Henry, 14, 17-18, 95
Abandoned housing, 19-20, 99
Abrams, Charles, xiv
Absentee landlords, 14, 18n, 19-20
Adams, Henry, 29
Aid to Families with Dependent Children, 38, 60
Air conditioning, 91
Alaska pipeline, 24
Alienation of city life, 29-30, 42, 169
Altshuler, Alan, 167
American Public Health Association, 91
Appalachia, 41, 188, 201
Atlanta, 116, 140, 177
Atlantic City, 184

Baker v. *Carr*, 148
Baltimore, 1, 11, 129; abandoned buildings, 19; rents, 93
Banfield, Edward, 216
Bank of the United States, 28
Barnard, Chester, xiii
Baumol, William, 42, 110-11
Bentley, Arthur, 195
Benton, William, 49
Better Communities Act, 137-38, 139
Blacks, 4, 6, 32, 105, 169, 195, 201; and Black Power, 18-20; and central cities, 107-10, 116-17, 162-63, 192, 193; incomes, 83-84; life expectancy, 110; and open housing, 4, 23, 33, 56, 58, 82; and public housing, 73; in suburbs, 108
Block-busting, 57
Block grants, 120, 137-41; and Model Cities, 131, 138
Boeckh index, 15
Bohn, Ernest, 77
Boise Cascade, 13, 158
Bonds, 14, 21, 74, 79, 92, 156
Boston, 1, 26, 31, 101, 108; and revenue sharing, 140; and urban renewal, 120
Bosworth, Karl, xiii
Brogan, Dennis, 27
Brooke Amendment, 75, 156
Brookings Institution, 14, 95
Brown v. *Board of Education*, 56
Brownlow, Louis, xiii
Brownstein, Philip, xiii
Bryce, James, 39
Bucks County, Pa., 152
Budget Bureau, 46, 51, 72, 96, 176
Buffalo, N.Y., 93, 117
Building codes, 4, 15, 114, 164; enforcement, 17, 18, 189; and industrial building codes, 185; *see also* Housing codes
Building industry, 4, 145-46, 158-60; costs in, 15-16, 164; and labor shortages 50, 82, 191
Building materials, 2, 82, 86, 146
Bunche, Ralph J., 58
Bureau of Labor Statistics, 88, 89-90
Bussing, 58, 106, 125

CED: see Committee for Economic Development
California, 159, 183, 185, 186
Calvinism, 35
Campbell, Gordon G., 188
Capital gains on housing, 2, 54, 147
"Capital Society," 31
Carmichael, Stokely, 18-19
Census Bureau, poverty 60, 81
Central city, 107-21, 162; abandonment, 5, 13, 19-20, 30-31, 94, 99; crime, 110; culture, 24; employment, 108-109, 123; incomes, 108, 123; subsidized housing, 71
Central Pacific Railroad, 39
Charlestown, Mass., 31
Chelsea, Mass., 31
Chicago, 91, 109, 117; rents, 93; riots, 116
Child labor, 29, 38, 45
Church-sponsored housing, 70, 116, 163, 184
Churchill, Winston, 137
Cincinnati, 140, 196
Citizens' Advisory Committee on Environmental Quality, 174
Civil rights, 24-25, 55-58, 201; and revenue sharing, 137; *see also* Discrimination
Civil Rights Act: of 1964, 171; of 1968, 4, 24-25, 57, 171, 192
Civil service, 39, 129
Civilian Conservation Corps, 41, 59
Clark, Joseph, 167
Cleveland, 74, 77, 99, 101; and urban renewal, 117; and riots, 116
Closing costs, 191
Cobbs, Price M., 19
Coleman, Richard P., 31-32
Columbia, Md., 31, 155, 162
Commercial redevelopment, 120
Commission on Civil Disorders, 61, 64, 87, 110, 116-17, 162-63, 192, 211
Commission on Population Growth and the American Future, 211
Committee for Economic Development (CED), 49, 52, 147, 180
Commons, 26

225

Communicable diseases, 40, 41
Community Action Programs, 37, 43, 59, 68, 125, 127, 134, 202, 203, 206
Community development corporation, 130, 203
Community facilities, 2, 6, 11, 17, 113
Conant, James Bryant, 199
Connecticut, 150-51
Conservation, 23, 45, 53; *see also,* Environment
Constitution Plaza (Hartford), 116
Consumer protection, 41; and home builders, 4
Consumption externalities, 43
Coolidge, Calvin, 40
Cooperative housing, 69-72
Corruption, 29, 39, 40; and FHA, 5, 39, 103
Cost-benefit analysis, 7-8
Council of Economic Advisers, 49, 51
Council on Environmental Control, 54
Crocker, Charles, 39
Crime, 22, 30-31, 86; in cities, 110; and housing, 87; prevention, 128, 193
Cultural values, 24, 111

Dallas, 140
Davidoff, Paul, 152
Davis-Bacon Act, 136
Day-care centers, 83, 203
Decision making, 7-8; and political considerations, 8-10
Delaware Valley Regional Planning Commission, 161, 178
Demonstration Cities Act, 171, 176
Depreciation, 112
Depression, 1, 41, 49, 112-13, 197-98
Detroit, 61, 101, 103, 104; employment, 109; open housing, 193; rents, 93; riots, 116
Dickinson, John, 30
Dilworth, Richardson, 167
Discrimination, 4, 14, 18, 24, 33, 105, 171; and federal policy, 56; and state governments, 192-93
Douglas, Paul, 48, 62, 72
Douglas Commission: *see* National Commission on Urban Problems
Dutch, and environment, 174

Earth Week, 53
Eccles, Marriner, 50
Eckstein, Otto, 51-52
Economic Development Administration, 176
Economic Opportunity Act of 1964, 37, 59, 202
Economic Opportunity Council, 59
Economies of scale, 41, 172
Education, 86, 149, 169, 209; costs, 111; expenditures, 186; financing, 6; and government, 41, 135; and Model Cities, 128; and status, 32; *see also* Schools
Education Act (1965), 172
Elderly, 6, 12; in central city, 107, 123; health care, 36, 83, 86; housing, 51, 67, 69, 70, 72, 74, 76, 97-98, 156; political influence, 34; and revenue sharing, 136; segregation of, 163-64
Ellul, Jacques, 45
Ely, Richard T., 196
Emergency Employment Act of 1971, 60
Emergency Housing Act of 1958, 51
Eminent domain, 113, 120, 189
Employment, 1-2, 48-53, 56, 60, 135, 198; decline in cities, 108-9, 161; in cities, 117, 129, 193; and housing, 49, 51-52; riots, 116; and Model Cities, 128, 130
Environment, 4, 48, 53-55, 173-74, 187-88, 201; and energy, 64; and housing, 54-55, 150, 164; and Model Cities, 128
Environmental Protection Agency, 54, 127
Equality of opportunity, 55-58, 192-93, 201
Executive Order 11063 on Equal Housing, 4, 56-57

FAIR (fair access to insurance), 102
FHA: *see* Federal Housing Administration
FHLBS: *see* Federal Home Loan Bank System
FNMA: *see* Federal National Mortgage Association
Fair employment practices, 57
Family Assistance Plan, 95-96, 216
Family counseling, 83
Farmers Home Administration, 66, 67, 68, 69, 79, 176
Federal-Aid Highway Act, 204
Federal Government's role, 41
Federal Home Loan Bank System, 15, 52, 79
Federal Home Loan Mortgage Corp., 15
Federal Housing Administration, 5, 9, 39, 65, 197-98; and equal opportunity, 57; foreclosures, 117; and central cities, 5, 102-5, 114; mortgage insurance, 65, 66, 68-69, 102-3
Federal National Mortgage Association, 15, 51, 52, 79, 114
Federal Reserve Board of Governors, opposition to housing credit, 50, 51, 52
Federal Reserve System, 40
Federal Trade Commission, 109
Federal Water Pollution Control Act, 176
Fefferman, Hilbert, xiii
Filter-down process, 18
Fire, 17, 87, 196; protection, 41, 149
Fisher, Irving, 82

Fisk, Jim, 39
Flanders, Ralph, 49
Flood control, 7, 61, 187; and housing, 48, 54
Folsom, Marion, xiii, 49
Food stamps, 95-96, 135
Franklin Town (Philadelphia), 120
Friedman, Milton, 8
Full employment, 48-49

Gans, Herbert, 28
Garden apartments, 54
Gardner, Sidney, 128
Gaus, John, xiii
Gautreaux decision, 71
General Electric, 13, 158
George, Henry, 39, 42
Ghettos, 10, 109, 184
Gilded Age, 39
Girsh, Joseph, 151
Glazer, Nathan, 14, 17, 18
Gould, Jay, 39
Government Center (Boston), 120
Government National Mortgage Association, 79
Grant administration, 39, 40
Grants: community development, 139; highways, 40; mass transportation, 115, 178; Model Cities, 128, 130, 131-32; for neighborhood facilities, 68; rehabilitation, 67; sewer and water, 66, 138, 178; urban renewal, 112, 113, 114, 138
Gray areas, 12, 99
Great Society, 8, 46-47, 200-1
Grier, William H., 19
Grigsby, William G., xiii, 67n, 96
Gulick, Luther, xiii

HUD: *see* U.S. Department of Housing and Urban Development
Hamilton, Charles, 18-19
Handicapped, 59; and housing, 12, 70; training, 36
Handlin, Oscar, 30
Harding administration, 40
Harrington, Michael, 36
Hartford, Conn., 115, 116
Haussmann, Baron, 26
Hawthorne, Nathaniel, 28
Haymarket affair, 30
Head Start, 59, 202
Health care, 6, 40, 41, 43, 135; for children, 110; for elderly, 21, 36, 83, 86; and Model Cities, 128
Heller, Walter, 111
Herring, Pendleton, 9
High-rise apartments, 54
Highways, 40; and development, 161, 177, 199-200, 204

Hoffman, Paul, xiii, 49
Hofstadter, Richard, 6, 30, 39
Holmes, Oliver Wendell, Jr., 149
Home Builders Association, 52
Home buyer characteristics, 146-47
Home Owners' Loan Corporation, 41
Homesteaders, 25
Hoover, Herbert, 40-41
Hopkins, Mark, 39
Housing Act of 1949, 50, 61, 73, 113, 170
Housing Act of 1961, 51, 115
Housing Act of 1970, 95
Housing allowance, 17-18, 79, 85-86, 90, 93-95; and housing supply, 105
Housing and Home Financing Agency, xiv, 75, 115, 175, 176
Housing and Urban Development Act of 1968, 62, 121
Housing codes, 85; enforcement, 17, 94, 107, 113, 118, 141; *see also* Building codes
Housing costs, 13, 146, 152-58; increases, 50; reductions, 16, 83, 154-57; and technology, 15-16, 83, 155
Housing production, 11, 56-57, 62, 78
How Far the Promised Land (White), 58
Hoyt, Homer, 33
Hudson Institute, 7
Hughes, Richard, 183
Humphrey, George, 199
Huntington, Collis, 39
Hurricane Agnes, 7

Immigrants, 31, 33, 108, 197
Income, 16; and growth, 168-69; and housing, 21, 83-84, 88, 89-90, 95, 97-98; and status, 32
Income maintenance policies, 18, 60-61, 86, 94, 105-6
Income redistribution, 48, 58-61, 106, 202, 203
Income tax, 40; and housing subsidies, 65-66, 92
Indianapolis, 140
Indians, 55, 82
Individualism, 25-26
Inflation, 133-34; and home ownership, 2; and housing credit, 62; and income, 59
Inner city: *see* Central city
Institutional change, 5-7; in housing finance, 52
Institutional lenders, 14, 57, 102; *see also* Savings and loan associations
Insurance, 19, 101-2; of property values, 192
Irish immigrants, 30, 34, 108
Isler, Morton, 82

Jackson, Andrew, 28, 39, 43, 45
James, Henry, 26-27

Japan, 194
Jefferson, Thomas, 25, 28, 38
Job Corps, 59, 202
Job-training, 14, 59, 86, 135, 142; and Model Cities, 128, 202
Johnson, Lyndon B., v, 3, 7, 8, 11, 36-37, 46-47, 52, 134, 165, 167, 173, 200; housing programs, 72-73, 104, 110; and Model Cities, 124, 205; and PPBS, 46-47

Kahn, Herman, 7
Kaiser, Edgar F., 62
Kaiser Committee: *see* President's Committee on Urban Housing
Kansas City, Mo., 24, 26, 31-32, 99
Kaplan, Abraham, 180
Katz, Lawrence, 104
Kennedy, John F., 4, 7, 134, 175; and discrimination, 56-57; and housing, 75, 96, 165; and national goals, 46, 61, 167, 180, 200
Kessler, 26
Key Biscayne, Fla., 4
King Philip's War, 34
Klutznick, Philip, xiii, 77
Kummerfeld, Donald, 87

Labor union-sponsored housing, 116
Lancaster, Penna., 129
Land acquisition, 10, 42, 172, 188-89
Land costs, 15, 113, 151, 155, 157, 161, 189
Land grants, 25, 45
Land use and housing, 11, 61, 117, 173, 174, 189-90; and states, 188, 189
Land values, 10, 33, 119; speculation, 54
Landlords, 18, 91; and civil rights, 57; and maintenance, 99, 111
Laski, Harold, 171
Last Man In phenomenon, 4, 147
Leased housing, 92-93
Lee, Richard, 167
Leisure World, 163
L'Enfant, 26
Levitt and Sons, 158
Levittown, N.J., 28
Lincoln Center (New York), 120
Little Rock, Ark., 56
Local government, 8, 91, 172, 205-6; costs, 42, 110-11, 133-34; and housing allowance program, 105; and poor, 34, 37, 73-74; and revenue sharing, 138; and systems analysis, 8; and taxation, 58; multiplicity, 148
Local housing authority, 73, 74
Local participation: *see* neighborhood participation
Localism, 164; exclusion of poor, 34-36

Location, 91, 99; and interest subsidies, 71; and access to jobs, 99, 108-9
Locke, John, 25, 38
Lockheed Aircraft, 13
Logue, Edward, 121, 185
Lonely Crowd, The (Riesman), 107
Long Beach, Calif., 140
Los Angeles, 116
Low-income housing, 3, 21, 48, 64, 68-79, 114, 117, 206; and Congress, 13, 49, 61, 62, 117-18; subsidies, 67-68, 90-93, 97-98
Lowry, Ira, 94
Lumber, 4, 15, 20, 157

McCabe, Thomas, 49
McNamara, Robert, 7, 46
Madison, James, 30
Madison township, N.J., 152
Maine, 187
Manpower training: *see* Job-training
Manufactured housing units, 158-59; *see also* Rationalization
Marshall, Alfred, 20-21, 81
Mass production: *see* Rationalization
Mass transportation, 115, 172, 178, 204
Massachusetts, 34-35, 38, 148, 183, 189, 209; crime, 31; education, 209; health care, 40; and poor, 35
Medicare and Medicaid, 36
Melville, Herman, 28
Merriam, Charles, xiii
Memphis, Tenn., 140
Merton, Robert K., 64
Metropolitan Development Act, 176, 178
Mexican-Americans, 33, 55, 108, 169, 195
Miami, 140
Middle-income housing: *see* Moderate-income housing
Migrant workers, 59, 60, 82
Migration, 145; farm to city, 2, 29-30, 50, 112; to suburbs, 145-47, 199
Milgram, Grace, 157
Mills, C. Wright, 22
Milwaukee, 104
Mobile homes, 3, 11, 63, 66, 159-60, 207; parks, 66, 159; purchasers, 159
Mobility, 2, 28, 145
Model Cities Administration, 127, 128
Model Cities program, 43, 60, 68, 123-32, 134, 142, 172, 179, 202-3, 205, 206; accomplishments, 128-32; choice of cities, 127-28
Moderate-income housing, 62, 66-67, 68, 79, 96-97, 114, 140
Montesquieu, 38
Montgomery County, Md., 145
Morris, Gouverneur, 30

Mortgages, 27, 86, 91, 153; financing, 2-3, 41; foreclosures, 103; and inflation, 13, 50; and inner city, 5, 19, 114; insurance, 66, 67, 102; rates, 16, 51, 79, 96, 197-98; as savings, 2; subsidies, 65-79
Moses, Robert, 131
Moynihan, Daniel, 216
Multifamily dwellings, 69, 70-71, 117, 158, 161, 220; costs, 152-53; suburbs, 107, 151
Municipal services, 29, 83, 85, 111, 133-34, 148-50; *see also* Community facilities
Murray, James, 49

Nader, Ralph, 4
Naftalin, Arthur, 167
National Association for the Advancement of Colored People, 58, 152
National Association of Building Manufacturers, 159
National Association of Home Builders, 4, 11, 52, 62, 158
National Commission on Urban Problems (Douglas Commission), 17, 62, 110, 119
National Committee Against Discrimination in Housing, 152
National Environmental Policy Act of 1969, 54
National Homes, 158
National Housing Center Council, 62
National Recovery Act, 41
National Urban Coalition, 60, 135
National Welfare Rights Organization, 60, 135
Natural resources, 4, 24, 27; *see also* Environment
Neighborhood participation, 7, 14, 18, 125, 205; and Model Cities, 125, 126-27
Neugarten, Bernice L., 31-32
New Communities Act (1968), 173
New Haven, Conn., 106, 167, 216
New housing, 91-93, 96-97, 105
New Jersey, 23, 152, 183, 189; riots, 184
New towns, 31, 54, 173
New York City, 26, 27, 28, 99, 101, 108, 117, 121; abandoned buildings, 19; employment, 109; housing costs, 91, 156; rents, 93; rent control, 2, 105; revenue sharing, 136; riots, 30, 116
New York City Rand Institute, 94
New York state, 23, 183, 184, 186
Newark, N.J., 99; riots, 61, 116, 184
Nixon, Richard M., 63, 87, 155, 190; and equal opportunity, 58; and income maintenance, 60-61, 94, 95-96, 204; and revenue sharing, 68, 111, 132, 135-39
Norfolk, Va., 93
North City Area Council (Philadelphia), 127

Nursing homes, 83, 163

Office of Economic Opportunity, 48, 54, 59-60, 204
Office of Management and Budget, 96
Ohio, 185
Older housing, 98-106
Omaha, 140
Open housing, 4, 17, 18; *see also* Civil rights, Equality of opportunity
Operating expenses, 90-93, 153-54; subsidies, 97-98
Operation Breakthrough, 4, 101, 155, 157, 159
Opportunities Industrialization Centers, 130
Outdoor Recreation Resources Review Commission, 53

PPBS (planning-programming-budgeting system), 8, 46-47
Paris, 26, 30
Parrington, Vernon, 29, 38
Patman, Wright, 139
Peace Corps, 127
Pechman, Joseph, 111
Pendleton, William, xiii
Penn Center (Philadelphia), 116
Pennsylvania, 152, 190; Department of Community Affairs, 186
Pennsylvania Builders Association, 151
Pennsylvania Railroad, 31
Peter the Great, 26
Philadelphia, 19, 101, 108, 160-61, 162, 167, 178, 196; education costs, 149; government expenses, 133-34; and Model Cities, 127, 131; revenue sharing, 136; riots, 30; suburbs, 31, 161; urban renewal, 116, 120
Phoenix, 140
Pinchot, Gifford, 45
Pittsburgh, 163, 196
Plainfield, N.J., 184
Planned variations program, 131
Planned Areawide Development, 176-77
Planning, 177, 179, 180; federal support for, 172, 176-78; need for, 6
Playgrounds, 6, 11
Poe, Edgar Allan, 28
Police, 30-31, 40, 41, 129, 133-34, 149; and riots, 116
Pollution, 45, 53, 86, 173, 180
Poor, attitudes toward, 34-38; English heritage, 35
Population growth, 45, 64, 82, 112, 168, 169, 197
Portland, Maine, 129
Portland, Ore., 130

Post, Langdon, 77
President's Commission on National Goals, 46, 55-56
President's Commission on Population, 64
President's Committee on Urban Housing, (Kaiser Committee) 62, 88, 191
Principles of Economics (Marshall), 81
Privacy, 2
Private industry, 13; and Central city, 20,
Private property rights, 6, 25-26; as a social trust, 196
Progressive movement, 40, 41
Property maintenance, 75, 95, 98-99
Property tax, 65-66, 97, 149-50, 155, 157, 186, 199
Property valuations, and FHA scandals, 5
Providence, R.I., 129
Pruitt-Igoe project, 77
Public development corporation, 193
Public Health Service, 175-76, 177
Public housing, 7, 48, 61, 65, 73-78; tenant characteristics, 76
Public Housing Administration, 75
Public services: *see* Community facilities
Public Works Administration, 41, 198
Puerto Ricans, 1, 50, 55, 105, 108, 169, 195
Pullman strike, 30

Quakers, 35
Quality of life, 21-22

Racism, 19, 33, 64
Railroads, 25, 197
Rains, Albert, 56, 117
RAND Corporation, 7
Rapkin, Chester, 105
Rationalization of construction, 11, 13, 16, 146, 158-59
Real estate trusts, 66
Recreation, 22, 54, 61, 128, 169, 172, 174
Regional Plan Association, 167
Rehabilitated housing, 17, 66, 82, 98-101, 118, 155, 179; grants, 67, 113, 114, 138
Relocation, 114; costs, 9, 67, 118; and urban renewal, 119
Reno, 177
Rent, 20, 93, 153-55; and income, 89-90; and public housing, 74
Rent control, 95, 105
Rent strikes, 18
Rent supplements, 24, 48, 60, 67, 72-73; and Congress, 106
Republican party platform, 43, 58, 211
Reston, Va., 31
Revenue sharing, 68, 87, 120, 132-43, 172; allocations, 135-36, 138; advantages, 136; special, 137-38

Revolution of 1688, 25
Riesman, David, 107
Riots, 30, 61, 87, 116, 184
Rockefeller, John D., 39
Rockefeller, Laurance S., 53
Rockefeller, Nelson, 185
Romney, George, 4, 11, 13, 16, 121, 155, 187
Roosevelt, Eleanor, 41
Roosevelt, Franklin D., 1, 14, 41, 46, 48-49, 197
Roosevelt, Theodore, 30, 45, 53
Rosenburg, Louis, xiii, 67n
Ross, E.A., 40
Rouse, James, 155
Row houses, 1, 12, 54; costs, 152-53, 156-57
Ruml, Beardsley, xiii, 49
Rural area: housing, 67, 78; migration, 2, 29-30, 50, 145
Rutledge, Edward, 152

St. Louis, 117, 130
Samuelson, Paul, 8
San Diego, 2, 188; rents, 93
San Francisco, 117, 140
Sanitation, 110, 112, 119
Savings and loan associations, 14, 57, 66, 79, 102
Schechter, Henry B., xiii, 98
Schools, 2, 6, 31, 83, 145, 148-49, 186; *see also* Education
Schorr, Alvin, 36
Seattle, 130, 177
Section 115, 67
Section 202, 69, 72
Section 220, 117, 217
Section 221(d)(3), 69, 71, 72, 96, 155
Section 223(e), 67, 103
Section 235, 68, 69, 72, 91, 104, 155
Section 236, 69-72, 73, 77, 89, 91, 93, 96, 155, 157
Section 237, 67
Section 502, 69
Segregation, 23, 56, 61, 162-63; elderly, 163
Senior citizens, *see* Elderly
Serrano v. *Priest*, 186
Sewerage, 4, 41, 48, 146, 150, 164, 173, 177, 180, 191; grants, 66, 138, 172, 175, 178
Shannon decision, 71
Shriver, Sargent, 37
Silverman, Abner, 76-77
Simon, Herbert, 11
Single person housing, 88
Site selection, 71, 91
Skilled labor shortages, 20, 50, 82, 191
Slayton, William L., 115
Slum clearance, 49, 87, 114, 141
Small stick builders, 4, 158

Social security, 36, 43, 76, 142
Sorensen, Theodore, 9, 56
Space Administration, 3
Space: demands for, 145, 146-47, 150,174; standards for housing, 91, 180
Sparkman, John, 56, 139, 141
Spector, Sidney, 98
Spoils system, 39
Stanford, Leland, 39
State and Local Fiscal Assistance Act, 135-36
State governments, 147-48, 183-94; costs, 42; functions, 40, 41; growth, 196-97; and systems analysis, 8; taxation policies, 58; and urban development, 183-94
Status, 2, 107; and housing, 31-33, 193
Subemployment, 109, 129
Subsidies, 43, 65, 88-89, 190; amounts, 90-91; costs, 87; interest, 68-72, 201; new construction, 3, 13, 90-91; shallow, 96-97
Substandard housing, 5, 12, 105
Suburban Action Institute, 152
Suburbs, 1, 31, 107, 145; exodus to, 112, 199; resistance to low-income housing, 72-73, 150-52; and subsidized housing, 71
Sullivan, Leon, 130, 131
Sweden, 141, 194
Systems analysis, 7-8, 46-47, 61

Tampa, Fla., 116, 163
Tankel, Stanley, 171
Taxation, 10, 21, 22, 40, 83; in central city, 108; depreciation, 65-66; exemption, 14, 97; and income redistribution, 58; local, 134, 149-50; base, 119, 120; preferences, 68, 92; regressive, 58
Taylor, William L., 57-58
Technology, 4, 27, 169; and housing costs, 15-16, 83, 155; and planning, 8-10, 46-47
Teenage unemployment, 109, 142
Theory of Interest (Fisher), 82
Tocqueville, Alexis de, 27
Toledo, O., 129
Transportation, 27-28, 41, 86, 146, 172, 197; and central city, 111, 112, 204
Truman, Harry, 49
Trumball Park Homes, 74
Turner, Frederick Jackson, 42
Turnkey housing, 75-76, 158

Unemployment: *see* Employment
Uniform Relocation Assistance and Land Acquisition Policies Act of 1970, 67
University of Chicago, 115, 120
University of Pennsylvania, 115
U.S. Commission on Civil Rights, 56, 58
U.S. Congress, 10, 52; Appropriations committees, 24, 72, 178; and discrimination, 24-25; housing goals, 13, 21, 49, 61-63, 114, 118, 121, 170-74, 181, 201; housing legislation, 11, 24, 28, 49-50, 72, 91, 106, 118, 168, 170, 173; income maintenance, 94; revenue sharing, 135-36, 139-40; *see also* U.S. House of Representatives; U.S. Senate
U.S. Department of Agriculture, 78
U.S. Department of Commerce, 176
U.S. Department of Defense, 7, 37, 46
U.S. Department of Health, Education, and Welfare, 67, 126, 176
U.S. Department of Housing and Urban Development, xiii, 13, 57, 63, 67, 68, 95, 176; and cost reductions, 157; and housing standards, 104; and Model Cities, 127; property insurance, 102; and urban renewal, 117
U.S. Department of Treasury, 51, 96
United States Housing Act of 1937, 49
U.S. House of Representatives: Banking and Currency Committee, 91, 139; Rules Committee, 56, 91, 106, 139; and revenue sharing, 139
U.S. Senate, 101, 188; Appropriations Committee, 75; Banking and Currency Committee, 50
U.S. Supreme Court, 56
Upper-income housing, 21-22; subsidies, 65-66, 68
Urban Development Corporation, 24, 184-85
Urban Institute, 88, 95, 97
Urban Mass Transportation Act of 1964, 204
Urban renewal, 65, 112-21, 142, 199-200; displacement, 76; resistance to, 37, 50, 116-17; performance, 118-21; site selection, 113-14

Vandalism, 5, 101, 102
Vermont, 187
Veterans Administration, 57
Vietnam War, 46, 52
Vinton, Warren Jay, 77

Waco, Tex., 177
Wade, Richard, 195-96
Wagner-Ellender-Taft bill, 50
War on Poverty, 36-38, 47-48, 58-60, 72, 142, 203
Washington, D.C., 99, 109, 117, 129, 177
Washington, George, 30
Water facilities, 4, 41, 138, 146, 173; grants, 66, 138, 175, 178, 180
Watts riots, 61, 102
Wayne State University, 115
Weaver, Robert C., xiii-xiv, 101, 104, 117

Weber, Max, 43
Welfare assistance, 23, 43, 86, 133, 142; and housing, 67, 77-78, 82-83, 105; payments, 38; reform, 7, 60
Welfeld, Irving, 97
Westchester County, N.Y., 24, 185n
Western Addition (San Francisco), 116
Westinghouse Electric, 13
Wetlands, 174
White, E.B., 10
White, Leonard, xiii
White, Walter, 58
Widnall, William B., 118
Wildlife protection, 53, 54, 174, 188
Willingboro, N.J., 28, 147
Winnick, Louis, xiii
Wirth, Louis, 107
Wood, Elizabeth, 74, 77
Workable program, 114, 126
World War II, 1-2, 49, 198
Write-down of capital cost, 155
Wurster, Catherine Bauer, 50, 145

Yale University, 115
Ylvisaker, Paul, xiii, 183-84
Youth, counterculture, 6, 53-54

Zoning, 4, 24, 146, 150-52; and flood control, 7; state governments, 184-85, 189-90, 193

About the Author

Morton J. Schussheim has worked on urban problems and housing in city hall, in state government, and in federal agencies. After receiving the Ph.D. in economics from Harvard University, he returned to his native city of Cleveland to serve for three years as an economist with the City Planning Commission. In 1955 he went to New York and directed research for the State Rent Commission. From 1961 to 1966 he helped shape federal housing and urban policy as assistant administrator for program policy in the Housing and Home Finance Agency. He has been a professor of city planning at the University of Pennsylvania and chairman of the doctoral program in planning. He is senior specialist in urban affairs with the Library of Congress in Washington, D.C. His earlier publications include *Toward a New Housing Policy,* issued by the Committee for Economic Development in 1969.